"As a Patron of Bible*Lands* it is a pleasure to commend Jean Hatton's inspiring book. This story of faith, compassion and courage shows us that God motivates individuals to carry his light into dark places and that he provides the resources to endure hardship and adversity. Even in situations that seem entirely hopeless, the Good News of Jesus Christ can change lives and give healing and hope."

Lord Carey of Clifton
Archbishop of Canterbury 1991-2002

"This book celebrates the people whose energy and dedication contributed to a magnificent story of Christian service. The threads of their lives link together many of the troubled lands of conflict and displacement of the last 150 years – Turkey, Syria, Egypt, Armenia, Bulgaria, Macedonia, Serbia, Israel/Palestine and Lebanon. We are privileged to glimpse not only the resourceful nature of the help that was carried into the regions, but the quality of the lives of those who worked within these lands at enormous cost to themselves. This is a story that links gift and need, joy and pain, life and death, past and present. I wholeheartedly commend it."

Reverend Baroness Kathleen Richardson of Calow OBE
President : Methodist Conference 1992-1993

"*The Light Bearers* is a most inspiring, challenging and enlightening story of adventurous, devout and faithful pioneers. Their ministry of compassion among those whom Christ described as the 'least' – those who are marginalised – the refugees, the blind and the orphans of Palestine, Armenia, Egypt, Jordan and Lebanon – continues to provide hope in what often seems a hopeless situation."

The Rt. Rev. Riah Abu Al-Assal
Anglican Bishop in Jerusalem

"One of the great things about this book is that it tells the story of Bible*Lands* through the lives of the many people involved. This clearly shows that the ministry of Bible*Lands* is not about projects, schools and hospitals, but about people's lives.

"This is what I have experienced through my own partnership with Bible*Lands*. It is always 'the people' that is the focus in every service. Jean Hatton has succeeded in bringing alive the story of the first 150 years of Bible*Lands*.

"We praise the Lord for these 150 years of touching the lives of people and pray that Bible*Lands* will continue to 'Proclaim the Year of the Lord'."

Rev. Dr. Mouneer Hanna Anis
Anglican Bishop of Egypt, North Africa, Ethiopia, Somalia & Eritrea

The
Light
Bearers

The Light Bearers

Carrying healing and hope to the

Middle East battleground

Jean Hatton

MONARCH
BOOKS
Mill Hill, London and Grand Rapids, Michigan

BibleLands

Published by Monarch Books in the UK 2003,
Concorde House, Grenville Place, Mill Hill, London NW7 3SA.

Co-published with Bible*Lands*

Distributed by:
UK: STL, PO Box 300, Kingstown Broadway,
Carlisle, Cumbria CA3 0QS;
USA: Kregel Publications, PO Box 2607,
Grand Rapids, Michigan 49501.

ISBN 1 85424 618 6 (UK)
ISBN 0 8254 6229 0 (USA)

British Library Cataloguing Data
A catalogue record for this book is available
from the British Library.

Cover photos:
Injured child, The Associated Press Ltd;
Armenian woman with child, © Armenian National Institute
(*www.armenian-genocide.org*), photo by Armin T. Wegner,
courtesy of Sybil Stevens.

Book design and production for the publishers by
Gazelle Creative Productions Ltd,
Concorde House, Grenville Place, Mill Hill, London NW7 3SA.

Printed in Great Britain.

Dedication

This book is dedicated to the memory of my father, Frank Hatton, who gave me an insatiable interest in the world; its people, its politics and its ways.

Contents

Preface

During the course of my career as a university professor, I was called to serve as administrator at Haigazian College in Beirut, just prior to the civil war in Lebanon. During those few years, I became aware of the quiet activity of a Christian charity organisation that, without attracting attention to itself, was assisting established welfare and relief agencies to fulfil their mission. I would hear of desperately needed support being made available to orphanages, to institutions for the handicapped and to Sunday School programmes.

Eventually, I learned that this ministry of compassion was carried out by a British-based charitable society called Bible*Lands*. Decades after my academic stint in Lebanon, I am stunned to learn that the Society had been founded a century and a half ago for the very purpose of supporting Christian work in what is now Turkey, the part of the world where Armenians had been established for more than two millennia. As a result, the delegated representatives of the Society were not only positioned to offer support and protection to many Armenians who thus survived the massacres and the ensuing genocide, but they also observed the tragic events and carefully registered their unfolding for the Western media at the time.

Fortunately, the history of this period is neither forgotten nor lost. The Society has produced this fascinating book that recounts the story of its involvements in the events of the time and with the peoples it served. As such, *The Light Bearers* presents a formal record of the massacres that decimated the Armenian people in 1895–96, of the genocide of 1915, of the bloodshed in Cilicia in 1921 and the events at Smyrna in 1922.

The significance of this book for the Armenian community worldwide cannot be overstated. While *The Light Bearers* provides an accurate resource for the understanding of the turmoil that still engulfs this tormented part of the world called the Middle East, it also stands as a witness for a wide readership to events that relate to Armenian history and that the world can ignore or deny only to its own detriment.

Dr Gilbert Bilezikian,
Co-founder, Willow Creek Community Church and
Professor Emeritus of Wheaton College, Illinois, USA
January 2003

Foreword

The *history* of a Christian organisation, in the pages of this book, becomes the *story* of many nations. It is not an executive summary of programmes, budgets, and lists of staff and board members that constitutes the history of a charitable, missionary, or philanthropic organisation, so much as the life story of the recipients, their joy and their pain.

What was initially planned to be a mission of witness to the Gospel of Christ in its simplicity and immediacy, turned BibleLands into a witness to some of the most hideous crimes of history.

The history of BibleLands combines the saving witness of the grace of God with a shocking witness to the ugliness of human sin. It combines stories of goodwill with the tragedies of human ill. The lesson is clear: the true preaching of the Gospel necessarily leads to a solidarity with the victimised innocent and a care for the disadvantaged.

The 150-year-long history of BibleLands is a series of testimonies about dedicated people who not only crossed their borders, but also embraced the lands and causes of the people they had gone to serve or had donated funds to sustain. Thus, almost every page of the history of BibleLands voices an advocacy for people of the Biblical lands who suffered, and continue to suffer, injustice, neglect, migration, and demoralisation. In each instance, BibleLands has responded by graceful and unconditional giving.

History becomes a cause for pain when it shows that the story of the suffering people has not been well told or acknowledged. Books of history show that not all issues are solved in time. The Armenian Genocide, the pain of which the missionaries and donors of BibleLands shared, remains to this day only partly addressed by the world. And the same mistake is repeated all over the globe. Stronger than all the pain, however, is the reminder that God is, and will be, actively pastoring the people through agents of care and peace.

I humbly write these lines on behalf of all those massacred Armenians for whom Bible*Lands* was a manifestation of that which is sacred. I write on behalf of the ones who survived evil, or survived in part, or survived in pain. I write on behalf of all those, be they Armenian or Greek, Bulgarian or Palestinian, Lebanese or Sudanese, Egyptian or Assyrian, who, in these 150 years of ministry, met the just hand of God, the sacrificial empathy of Christ, and the sustaining mystery of God's Spirit in and through the service of Bible*Lands*.

Rev. Paul Haidostian, Ph.D.,
President, Haigazian University, Beirut
January 2003

Introduction and Acknowledgements

When I began this book I was looking for something else. Some years ago, the promotional literature of Bible*Lands* claimed the origins of the charity were associated with Florence Nightingale's work in the Crimea, and as part of a project for an Open University history degree, I began searching the first minutes books of what was originally the Turkish Missions Aid Society, for references to the Lady with the Lamp. My disappointment, when I failed to find her there was intense. I had already begun to feel I had a claim staked to Florence and had imagined the small stir that might arise if some new information were to be presented about such a well-known figure.

Although one result of my research was that Bible*Lands* removed the name of Florence Nightingale from its literature, (the error had resulted from a misreading of an American missionary's autobiography many years ago), the uncovering of the Society's real history proved to be far more exciting than anything I could previously have imagined. It was certainly more exciting, and, I hope, more useful, than any small additions to Florence Nightingale's already copious history could possibly be. It not only led me to areas that I personally knew very little about, but also to some major events in the history of the world that have been forgotten or neglected. In the case of the Armenian Genocide there are some people who would argue that it has been deliberately overlooked.

Perhaps one of the most enjoyable aspects of my researches into Bible*Lands'* archives, was my encounters with the people who have been part of the Society's long history. Some of them are well-known figures, most notably Lord Shaftesbury and the two Lord Kinnairds, whereas others have been less well known, making an occasional appearance in the archives of other organisations or in specialist histories, while some appear only in the Society's own documents. It has been a particular pleasure for me to bring these more forgotten people to life again and to allow them to speak once more to the world. Indeed there were times when I felt that they were leaning over my shoulder as I read their own words and were taking a keen interest in the work. In order to give the characters as much reality as possible, I tried to use their Christian names whenever I could. In some cases, particularly those who date back to the Society's earliest years, when language and manners were very formal, tracking down Christian names was not easy. However, in every instance I was successful, except for one, and in the case of Mrs Bowen Thomson, I myself christened her Fanny. It seemed suitably Victorian, eminently suited to a woman of evident courage and ingenuity, and I hope the lady herself would approve.

There have been times when writing the book has been quite disturbing and there were occasions when I cried. The effects of historical material on an individual are quite personal of course, but among those groups and individuals who touched my own heart most keenly were the Macedonian refugees of 1903 who told of "fearful things", Robert Vaughan, killed at the battle of Arras in 1917, Marian and Azniv and their fellow workers at the Rescue Home in Aleppo, the Palestinian farmer at Zerqa who remembered his olive trees with such tenderness, and the two women, one Jewish, one Arab, who died of cancer at Nazareth Hospital. To me their experiences seemed to speak with great eloquence about the terrible brutality of which we all seem capable, the extraordinary heroism of which we are also all capable, the workings of individual destiny and of the fragile humanity which we all share and which unites us more than it divides us.

Although it has taken over two years to complete, this book represents only a small part of the story of Bible*Lands*. I was confronted by an enormous amount of material, most of it not archived, and as a writer whose particular passions are people and history, I chose those people and events that most appealed to my own sense of the dynamics of history in general while at the same time doing my best to bring 150 years of Bible*Lands*' own narrative to life. This meant that in order to tell a story which I hope is readable and exciting, I selected a few people and a few Christian projects from an enormous range of possibilities. Over its 150-year history, the Society has supported and partnered hundreds of Christian projects in the lands of the Bible, as well as hundreds of individuals who each have a story to tell. Only a few of the many possibilities appear in this book, and hopefully, one day, someone else will find themselves as intrigued as I have been, and will tell some of the stories that are still to be told.

Finally, this book could not have been produced without the co-operation, encouragement, comments and advice of a number of people. My thanks go to Maggie Stothart, my Open University tutor on Course A425: Women, Evangelicals and Community, who first suggested I write the history of Bible*Lands*. Also to Ara Sarafian of the Gomidas Institute for bringing to my attention James Bryce and Arnold Toynbee's compilation of eyewitness accounts of the Armenian Genocide. I would also like to thank Tony Collins and Rodney Shepherd at Monarch Books for their very encouraging comments as the manuscript progressed and for overseeing the progress of the book almost from its conception to its birth. I am also indebted to a number of other authors whose books are listed in the bibliography. Whilst I have only quoted from Bible*Lands'* own archive material, the background information gained from additional reading has been invaluable.

There have been many people among the past and present staff and Trustees of Bible*Lands* who have followed the progress of this book with great interest. Several of them have dipped into their own memories to provide recollections and information that have added to my own insights and understanding and thanks go especially to Kathleen Young, Ralph Wilkins, Tony Crowe and John Stilwell. I would like to especially acknowledge the help of Maureen Lampard, who worked for Bible*Lands* as sponsorship secretary in Israel/Palestine between 1960 and 1973 and then as Deputy Chief Executive of the Society between 1985 and 1998. Maureen's careful reading of the text and her comments, especially those derived from her long years of experience in the Middle East, have been of great benefit. Maureen also prepared the index, a complex task and an invaluable asset. I would also like to thank her for sharing with me her memory of "Blind Krikor" Demerjian.

I would also like to give special thanks to Hugh Boulter, Vice-Chairman of Bible*Lands*, for his continuing interest in the project, for the great deal of time he devoted to reading the drafts and for his wise and helpful comments. Finally, I would especially like to thank Hugh, Cyril Young, Bible*Lands* Chairman, Ken Mills, its Treasurer, and Andy Jong, Chief Executive from 1993 to 2002, for sharing my belief that the story of Bible*Lands* needed to be told and providing me with a very generous amount of time to tell it. I would also like to thank Andy's successor, Nigel Edward-Few, for maintaining the agreement. I hope, that like me, they will all feel a pride not only in the book itself, but in the inspiring story it tells of the work that has united Christian people in Britain and in the lands of the Bible for 150 years.

Jean Hatton,
Chesham,
Buckinghamshire, UK
January 2003

Key People

Reverend Cuthbert Young   Passionate evangelist, dying slowly of consumption. Founder of the Turkish Missions Aid Society

Reverend Cyrus Hamlin   American missionary. Introduces Cuthbert Young to the Armenian people

Lord Shaftesbury: Anthony Ashley Cooper   Victorian Britain's most well-known Evangelical Christian and a leading social reformer. First President of the Turkish Missions Aid Society

Sir Culling Eardley   President of the Evangelical Alliance and first Chairman of the Turkish Missions Aid Society

The Hon. Arthur [10th Lord] Kinnaird, MP   Treasurer of the Turkish Missions Aid Society: 1856–1887

Mrs Fanny Bowen Thomson   Widow of the Crimea. Founder of "English ragged, industrial and evening schools in Syria". (The British Syrian Mission)

Reverend Henry Jones   Secretary of the Turkish Missions Aid Society 1856 (approx)–1882

Gregory and Emma Baghdassarian   Founders of Broussa Orphanage near Constantinople. The first orphanage to be supported by the Turkish Missions Aid Society

Dr Hogg   Founder of a school in a donkey stable at Assiout in southern Egypt that becomes Assiout College

Maria West	Founder of the Strangers' Rest, Smyrna. "The coffee house plan for reaching strangers"
Gerasim Kyrias	Albanian evangelist kidnapped by brigands. Founder of the Kyrias School at Kortcha, eastern Albania
Dr John House	American missionary. Director of Samokov Institute, Bulgaria and founder of the Salonica Farm School
The Hon. Arthur Fitzgerald [11th Lord] Kinnaird	Treasurer of the Turkish Missions Aid Society: 1887–1923
Reverend William Essery	The "beloved W.A. Essery". Secretary of the Bible Lands Missions Aid Society 1892–1904
Dr Mary Pierson Eddy	American physician and evangelist. Founder of a clinic near Junieh, Lebanon. (Later the Hamlin Memorial Hospital)
Reverend Samuel Gentle-Cackett	The "indefatigable" Secretary of the Bible Lands Missions Aid Society: 1904–1943
Alderman Harry Fear	Businessman and Treasurer of the Bible Lands Missions Aid Society: 1923–1949
Reverend Dimiter Furnajieff	Bulgarian pastor: President of the Bulgarian Evangelical Society and Principal of the Bulgarian Bible School
Dr Robert Vaughan	Hero of the Great War. Leader of the Bible Lands Medical Unit: 1915–1916
Darinka Gruitch	Heroine of the Great War. Leads Serbian orphans to safety ahead of an invading Austrian Army
Pastor Dikran Antreassian	Armenian Protestant pastor. Led 4,000 Armenians in a heroic resistance against Turkish forces at Musa Dagh: 1915

Mary Jane Lovell	Founder of the Mission to the Blind in Bible Lands. Translated and produced the 31 volume Arabic Braille Bible
Martha Frearson	"One of the great servants of God". Heroine of the Aintab Orphanage and founder of the Armenian Widows Home at Shemlan in Lebanon.
Krikor Demerjian	"Blind Krikor". Armenian pastor and a pilgrim heading for the Celestial City
Dr Ruth Parmalee	"The brave, tired woman". Founder of the American Women's Hospital in Salonica
Karen Jeppe	Danish schoolteacher. Founder of the Rescue Home in Aleppo. Honorary Commissioner of the League of Nations
Sir Leon Levison	Vice-President of the BLMAS during the 1930s. Also President of the Hebrew–Christian Alliance
Mary and Elizabeth Webb	Founders of the Lighthouse Mission in Beirut. Elizabeth also helped found the Armenian Social Centre at Trad in Beirut
Adele Dafesh	Mary Lovell's blind pupil and founder of the Lovell Home for the Blind in Bethlehem
Siranoush Ketchejian	Mary Lovell's blind pupil and founder of the Lovell Home for the Blind in Jerusalem
Bob Clothier	Entrepreneur and Secretary of the Bible Lands Missions Aid Society from 1952 until 1985
Dr Helen Keller	Among the twentieth century's most famous and successful campaigners on behalf of the blind

Sister Johanna Larsen	German Moravian nursing sister among leprosy patients in the Holy Land. Began the Star Mountain Leper Home near Ramallah
Father Andy Andeweg	Founder of the Deaf Club in Beirut and Schools for Deaf in Lebanon and Jordan
Nadeem Shwayri	"We are all disabled in some way". Founder of Al Kafaat, centre for the disabled in Lebanon
George Markou	Founder of School for the Deaf in Cyprus as well as one of the first co-operative industrial enterprises for the disabled
Reverend Audeh Rantisi	Minister of the Arab Evangelical Church and founder of the Evangelical Home for Boys, Ramallah
David Izzett	Trustee of the Bible Lands Society from 1953 and its President from 1998 to 1999
Reverend Mouneer Hanna Anis	The doctor who revived Menouf Hospital, Egypt. Later Anglican Bishop of Egypt, North Africa, Ethiopia, Somalia & Eritrea
Bishara Awad	Principal of Bethlehem Bible College
Suad Younan	Principal of Helen Keller School, Jerusalem
Andy Jong	Chief Executive of Bible*Lands*: 1993–2002
Nigel Edward-Few	Director of Bible*Lands*: 2002–

Key Dates

1853	Cuthbert Young reaches Constantinople
1854–1856	Crimean War
1854	July 3: Foundation of Turkish Missions Aid Society in London
1854	American Protestant Mission in Egypt founded
1856	American Bulgarian Mission founded
1860	Civil War in Lebanon: Massacre of Christians
	Fanny Bowen Thomson founds the British Syrian Mission
1865	Dr Hogg begins educational work in Egypt
	Earthquake in northern Syria
1871–1872	Famine in Persia
1874	Famine in Asia Minor
1874	Gregory and Emma Baghdassarian found the Broussa Orphanage
1876	Bulgarian Atrocities
1877	War between Turkey and Russia
1878	Maria West founds the "Rest" at Smyrna
1880	Famine in Persia
1883	*Star in the East* begins publication
1885	Gerasim Kyrias captured by brigands in Albania.
1888	"Trouble at Erzroum"
1892	William Essery becomes Secretary of the TMAS
1893	TMAS becomes the Bible Lands Missions Aid Society
1895	Mary Lovell arrives in Jerusalem
1895–1896	Massacres of Armenians in Turkey: 300,000 murdered
	Armenian Massacre Relief Fund. Founding of Armenian orphanages
1903	Uprising and massacres in Macedonia
	Founding of Essery Orphanage at Monastir
	Founding of Salonica Farm
1904	Death of William Essery
	Samuel Gentle-Cackett becomes Secretary of the BLMAS
1908	The Committee of Union and Progress (the "Young Turks") takes power in Turkey. Constitution revived
1909	Massacres of Armenians in Cilicia: 30,000 murdered: 35,000 refugees
1912	First Balkan War

1913	Second Balkan War
1912–1913	Siege of Adrianople
1914–1918	First World (Great) War
1915	Serbian Civilian Relief Fund
1915	Armenian Genocide
1917	November: Balfour Declaration
1917	December: British Army captures Jerusalem
1918	Samuel Gentle-Cackett founds the Bedfont Orphanage
1919	Samuel Gentle-Cackett represents British Government on American Commission for Relief in the Near East investigation into Armenian Genocide
1921	Massacres of Armenians and Greeks in Cilicia
1922	"Smyrna Catastrophe"
1923	Great Population Exchange
1929	BLMAS purchases Bulgarian Bible School at Samokov
1936–1939	Palestinian Revolt
1939	France cedes the Sanjak of Alexandretta to Turkey
1939	Palestine Orphans' Fund
1939–1945	Second World War
1943	Death of Samuel Gentle-Cackett
1943	Bob Clothier meets Adele Dafesh and the blind children at Bethlehem
1948	April: Palestinian villagers massacred at Deir Yassin
1948	May: State of Israel declared
1948	Bob Clothier joins committee of BLMAS
1949	Bob Clothier becomes Chairman of BLMAS
1952	Bob Clothier becomes Secretary of BLMAS
1954	BLMAS Centenary Appeal: Vocational Training Centre for Blind in Jerusalem
1954	First Bethlehem Carol Sheet
1956	Suez Crisis
1959	Palestine Liberation Movement founded
1964	Helen Keller School, Jerusalem: foundation stone laid
1967	June: Six-Day War: Israel occupies West Bank and Gaza
1967	Bob Clothier meets Nadeem Shwayri, founder of Al Kafaat, Beirut
1970	Black September
1974	Turkish invasion of Cyprus
1975	Lebanon: Beginning of Civil War
1977	Israel invades South Lebanon
1982	Israel invades Lebanon: siege of Beirut
1987	Palestine: First *Intifada*
1990	Death of Bob Clothier
1991	Lebanon: End of Civil War

1994	Oslo Agreement: Palestinian Authority established
2000	*Al-Aqsa Intifada* follows Ariel Sharon's visit to *al-Haram al-Sharif*
2001	September 11: Al Qaeda attack World Trade Center
2002	December: preparations mount for war on Iraq

Secretaries since 1854

The Turkish Missions Aid Society
The Bible*Lands* Society

Revd Cuthbert Young	1854–1856
Revd George Royds Birch	1856–1866?
Revd Henry Jones	1856?–1882
Revd Thomas Brown	1882–1892
Revd William Essery	1892–1904
Revd Samuel Gentle-Cackett	1904–1943
Revd Harold Gardiner	1943–1950
Revd Leslie Farmer	1950–1952
Mr C. Bob Clothier	1952–1985
Mr Peter Emmerson	1985–1993
Mr Andy Jong	1993–2002
Mr Nigel Edward-Few	2002–

It is not clear in the Society's minutes as to when Henry Jones became Secretary. He was originally employed, together with several other men, on an expenses only basis, as a travelling secretary with a remit to maintain contact with the Society's auxiliary groups throughout the UK (including Ireland). George Royds Birch resigned the office at some point between 1856 and 1866 during which time Henry became office-based secretary of the Society.

Chapter 1

A Passion
for Armenia
The Beginning

In 1854 the eyes of the world were on Turkey. The Great Powers were at war in the Crimea and people in Britain followed the campaigns on maps they bought at city stationers and railway station bookstalls. For the first time in history, "our own correspondent" was at the seat of war, and despatches reaching *The Times* in a record two to three weeks described much more than soldiers and their battles. Readers at British breakfast tables could picture in their mind's eye the great city of Constantinople, with its bazaars and bathhouses and pleasure gardens. They could almost hear the muezzins who called the Muslim faithful to prayer from a hundred minarets, and they could imagine themselves mingling among the many races who flocked to cosmopolitan Constantinople from every part of the vast Ottoman Empire. From the European Balkans, the Empire straddled the Bosphorus and then stretched away eastward over the vast interior of Anatolia to the south-western borders of Russia. To the south, it curved through Asia Minor and Syria, and the birthplace of Christianity in Palestine. Finally it reached the Nile River, the great waterway that flows out of Central Africa, through Sudan and through Egypt, until finally it empties itself into the Mediterranean Sea.

Since the eighth century, when the Turkish tribes began the westward journey from Central Asia that ended with the conquest of Anatolia and the Balkans, and the lands of the eastern Mediterranean, many races had been overrun and subjected to Turkish rule. But, it was the Armenian people, whose ancient homeland lay at the foot of Mount Ararat, who most captured the imaginations of British Christians. Armenia was the oldest Christian nation in the world, Christian since its conversion by

Gregory the Illuminator less than 300 years after the death of Jesus, and the Armenian people had upheld their faith in the face of many invaders. Despite persecutions by Roman, Persian and Arab conquerors, Armenia clung resolutely to its faith and to its nationhood. It continued to uphold faith and nationhood under Turkish subjugation. When Lord Shaftesbury rose in the House of Lords, in March 1854, to "assure the nation that the war will not be indifferent to the just desires and future welfare of the Christian populations of the Ottoman Empire", many in Britain hoped the Armenians were uppermost in his thoughts.

The Truth as it is in Jesus

One man whose passion for the Armenian people would become the foundation of a great enterprise, was Cuthbert Young, a young English clergyman and earnest evangelist. "The truth as it is in Jesus" was the motivating force of Cuthbert's life and his greatest desire was to take the good news of salvation to every person still untouched by the Gospel and to win souls for his Saviour. When Cuthbert's doctors told him the progress of the consumption that was gradually devouring his lungs might be slowed by a journey through the warm lands of the Bible, Cuthbert believed that God had called him and that a mission lay ahead of him. In the early 1850s he travelled through Egypt and Syria, fascinated by the ruins of past civilisations but disturbed by the Eastern Christians who seemed more concerned with ritual than with what Cuthbert believed to be the real treasure at the heart of Christianity, the words of the Bible.

When he stood in the great Crusader Church of the Holy Sepulchre in Jerusalem, gazing at the banks of candles that flickered in the darkness of cavernous chapels, and watching the elaborately robed priests who reverently kissed the icons and Bibles they carried in stately processions, Cuthbert felt himself almost overwhelmed with sorrow. "They kiss these Bibles," he thought, "but the truth they contain goes unheard." How could it have happened, he wondered, that in the lands where Jesus first preached his message, his precious words had become buried in archaic languages and lost in a mass of ritual? "These churches are most grossly in error," he wrote later. And was there anything he could do, he wondered, to restore the Gospel to its rightful place at the centre of Christian life? Was Evangelical reformation of the Eastern churches the true reason for his journey to the lands of the Bible?

Vision for the future

In the summer of 1853 Cuthbert Young reached Constantinople. The city that was once the capital of Christian Byzantium had fallen to the Turks exactly 400 years earlier, but its strategic position on the frontier between Europe and Asia, between West and East, made it a hub for Christian missionary work in the Ottoman Empire. It was during his stay in Constantinople that Cuthbert Young had a vision, and realised why God had called him to the East. It was a vision that would begin 150 years of devoted Christian service to the people who live in the ancient lands of the Bible.

All the major Christian nations and churches had representatives in Constantinople, but perhaps the most enterprising and vigorous of them all were the missionaries of the American Board of Commissioners for Foreign Missions. The Board's pioneers in Turkey had set sail from Boston in 1819, with the intention of founding a mission to Islam, but when Pliny Fiske and Levi Parsons landed at Smyrna nearly one year later, to discover that Asia Minor was home not only to Muslim Turks but to Armenian and Greek Christians whose ancestors had a far longer history in Turkey, the American Board reconsidered its plan.

Just as Cuthbert wondered later about the church in Jerusalem, in 1820 Pliny and Levi wondered about the history of Asia Minor. Surely the churches there were founded by the Apostles and by Saint Paul, and they had given Paul's letters to the world. Moreover, they were the inheritors of the Seven Churches of Asia who had received the message of the Revelation. How had they lost the pure Gospel? What had caused them to succumb to idolatry and superstition?

As Pliny and Levi continued their way through the lands of the Bible, the American Board, at its Boston headquarters, discussed their reports, and prayed earnestly for guidance. Most of its members had been touched by the Great Awakenings, the Evangelical Revivals that had swept America since the 1700s, and as they discussed what they believed to be the doctrinal errors of the Armenian and Greek churches of Turkey, they came to the conclusion that the American Board was meant to rekindle the fires of Asia Minor's ancient churches. They also saw a way to fulfil their original plan. Although the Armenians were a subject race, considered inferior by Muslims, forbidden to bear arms and subject to arbitrary taxation and sporadic outbursts of Turkish violence, they were also intelligent, hardworking and eager for education, and the American evangelists decided to concentrate their efforts upon them. The Gospel and liberty, education, hard work and self-sufficiency, all the great Protestant virtues, would lead the Armenian Christians of Turkey, not only to salvation but to future political leadership of a modern state, and "pure religion", devoid of idolatry and ritual, would enable them to become the future missionaries to Islam.

Prote! Prote!

Most Armenians in the 1800s belonged to the Armenian Apostolic Church, often called Gregorian after the Illuminator himself. For the Armenian people it meant more than most Westerners could imagine. Their ancient church was the focus of Armenian nationhood, their refuge through long years of servitude to Turkey, and the people loved it. The American Protestant newcomers were viewed with suspicion and their evangelists were chased from Armenian villages, sometimes dragged sleeping from their beds, by crowds of cursing and stone-throwing women who yelled, *"Prote! Prote!"* at the backs of retreating missionaries. But the Americans believed in their mission and they persisted, and as the years passed some Armenians began attending Evangelical meetings where the Bible was read in their own modern language, and the preachers proclaimed that each individual was called to a personal relationship with a risen Lord.

By the 1840s, Armenian Protestantism had gained strength, and although the intention of the first converts was to reform the Gregorian church, and to make the Bible in modern Armenian available to the people, persecution and anathemas eventually led them to found an independent community. They were aided in their enterprise by Sir Stratford de Redcliffe, Britain's Ambassador to Turkey. Years later, one American remembered Sir Stratford as, "a man who would befriend the persecuted of whatever faith or race". The first Armenian Evangelical Church was founded in Constantinople in 1846, and it was, according to the American missionary, William Goodell, "neither a Presbyterian, Congregational, Lutheran, Methodist, nor Episcopal Church, but a New Testament Church, a truly Apostolic church". In 1850, the Sultan of Turkey, Abdul Medjid, granted formal recognition to an Armenian Protestant *millet*, or independent religious grouping.

By 1853, the year that Cuthbert Young arrived in Constantinople, an influential and expanding network of Evangelical missions was established across Turkey. All of them were Bible based and most of them, even in the smallest village, provided schools for children and education for adults. In major metropolitan centres, education on Western lines was available, from elementary grades to high school, as well as an emerging system of higher education. Armenian Protestant pastors, teachers and evangelists, trained at local mission schools and were sometimes sent on scholarships to American universities, subsequently taking leading roles in their communities in Turkey.

Cuthbert meets a kindred spirit

Many of the Armenian evangelists received their early training at Bebek Seminary in Constantinople, and it was there that Cuthbert Young found a kindred spirit. Cyrus Hamlin, the seminary's founder, who began the enterprise with just two students, was an enterprising and outgoing missionary from Massachusetts and together with his wife, Henrietta, they welcomed Cuthbert into their home. "He often used to take tea with us," Cyrus wrote later in his autobiography, and in the Hamlin family drawing room and at Cyrus' study at Bebek, the two men discussed their shared passion, the restoration of the churches of the East to their apostolic foundations. With Cyrus as his guide to Constantinople and the work of the American Board, Cuthbert learned more about missionary enterprise in Turkey. At the Mission Press, in the heart of Stamboul, the Turkish quarter of the city, he saw Christian books printed in 25 languages and scores of Armenians, Greeks, and even Muslim Turks queuing to buy. *"The Pilgrim's Progress,"* Cuthbert noted, "John Bunyan's inimitable allegory", was very popular with Armenian readers. "More books," Cyrus told Cuthbert, "more books, more training for evangelists and more churches, are all needed for our Armenian friends in Turkey."

Cuthbert was already an eager supporter of the Evangelical Alliance, founded only seven years earlier in London with the aim of uniting Evangelical Protestants across the world. In the spirit of the Alliance, Cuthbert resolved to foster unity between British, American and Armenian Christians, and after his discussions with Cyrus he became an equally eager supporter of the American Board. His best plan, he thought, was to stay in Constantinople and he began teaching a theology class at Bebek and studying the Armenian language. But as the months passed, something began to change Cuthbert's mind. Even as he made plans for his wife, Hannah, to join him in Constantinople, Cuthbert found himself thinking about all he had seen in the lands of the Bible, especially the people who crowded their churches but lacked the one thing necessary for their salvation, the Gospel. More books, Cyrus had said, more books, more evangelists and more churches. One more teacher at Bebek could never answer that great need, Cuthbert thought, but maybe there was something that could. A British society to aid the American Board, not with men but with money.

Cuthbert broached the idea to Cyrus early one morning as the two men gazed from the Bebek study window across the shining Bosphorus towards the East. Cyrus was enthusiastic. He knew the American Board would welcome the help of British Christians. It would be a testimony to the world, he said, "of the true catholicity of Evangelical missions". As they discussed the new society, Cyrus saw the project taking shape in his friend's mind, but even so, he was not prepared for the sudden speed of Cuthbert's departure. "The idea had taken full possession of him and swallowed him up," he said later. As the two friends said goodbye, they agreed that Cyrus would visit London as soon as he could to canvas support for Cuthbert's new society, and just as he boarded the ship for home, Cuthbert made Cyrus a promise. "I shall work with you to the end of life," he said.

Openings for the Gospel in Turkey!

Back in Britain, Cuthbert lost no time. He had already sent articles from Constantinople to *Evangelical Christendom*, the monthly journal of the Evangelical Alliance, and he continued to highlight the Armenian cause in its pages. He wrote a pamphlet, "Openings for the Gospel in Turkey", and he began to canvass Britain's most influential Christians.

In April 1854, Britain allied herself with Turkey and declared war on Russia. The Sultan's Christian subjects, the status of Christianity in Turkey, and questions of religious liberty in Islamic lands, all became matters of concern to Western Christians. Cuthbert wrote to *Evangelical Christendom* saying, "There seems to be a pretty general feeling that something should at once be done for Turkey." Other men shared his opinion, and on a bright morning in May they joined Cuthbert at a breakfast meeting at Robert Street, Adelphi, just off the Strand and one of London's most fashionable addresses. The minutes of that meeting record the names of the 63 men from many Protestant denominations who were present. Most were members of the Evangelical Alliance. Sir Culling Eardley, its president, was there, with Edward Steane, editor of *Evangelical Christendom*. The Honourable Arthur Kinnaird MP, aristocrat and close friend of Lord Shaftesbury was there, as was John Angell James, one of Victorian Britain's most popular religious authors. Dr Holt-Yates, traveller to the East and founder of missions at Suediah in Syria joined the company too. Many of those present were clergymen, while others belonged to the army or navy or held office in municipalities across the country. Between them they represented every area of Britain's establishment; the church, the armed services and the civil administration. When Cuthbert proposed the formation of a Turkish Missions Aid Society, the meeting endorsed him unanimously.

Cuthbert's vision becomes reality

Just two months later, on 3 July, Lord Shaftesbury, the new society's president, took the chair at Exeter Hall, London's great Evangelical meeting house in the Strand, and Cuthbert Young saw his vision become reality. When he stood up to read his paper, "Evangelical Missions in the Turkish Empire", and gazed at the audience of earnest British faces, it was as if he saw throngs of Armenians too, all eager for the new churches, the teachers and evangelists, and the modern Armenian Bibles, their friends in Britain would help to provide. "Due to American efforts," said Cuthbert, "the Bible is becoming the great statute book in the East, and, while formerly the cover was reverently kissed as holy, now the truth itself is prized."

Alongside the enthusiasm however, there was a note of caution. The meeting was well aware that Britain was engaged in a war to safeguard her interests and Lord Shaftesbury spoke about his recent meetings at the Foreign Office. The opinion of Sir Stratford in Constantinople, he said, was that Britain's imperial interests could compromise British Christian missions in the Ottoman Empire and the Ambassador's advice was to support the Americans, who were not subject to the "international jealousies" aroused by Britain. With Shaftesbury's advice in mind, the newly formed Turkish Missions Aid Society began its life with a highly original decision. It agreed, that rather than send workers of its own, its funds would support existing Evangelical missions in Turkey, especially the American. It also agreed to give special emphasis to "the native agency", that is, to local Christians in the lands of the Bible.

A host of Christian missions

Cuthbert Young became Secretary of the Turkish Missions Aid Society, and in the minute book he records himself as saying, "I will gladly devote my whole time and strength to the promotion of an object which is second to none in importance." He was as good as his word and within days of the Society's foundation he had rented an attic office from the Evangelical Alliance, at their headquarters in Adam Street, Adelphi, furnished it with a desk, an armchair, several rugs and a set of fire irons, and with funds raised from the inaugural meeting at Exeter Hall, he despatched the Society's first grant. Cyrus Hamlin, in Constantinople, received the sum of £65, worth approximately £2,650 or $3,975 today,[1] for the education of Armenian evangelists and students and the expenses of Bebek Seminary.

As the Society constituted its managing, corresponding and

---

1 Refers to approximate purchasing equivalent at December 2002 throughout. The figures are derived from the Retail Price Index, based at January 1987 = 100.

honorary committees, and began to raise funds for American enterprises in Turkey, unsolicited requests for aid began arriving at Adam Street. The audience at Exeter Hall in July had included supporters of many other Evangelical organisations, and with members of the new Society's managing committee represented on many of their boards, within weeks of its formation, news of the Society's novel constitution had spread. The requests came as something of a shock. Although the Society's founders had agreed to support "existing Evangelical missions in Turkey, especially the American", they had not really considered the implications. What should they do? The new requests spoke of a host of Christian missions in the Ottoman Empire, many of them founded by British men and women, and all needing help. The Society's managing committee convened at Adam Street, they discussed the issue at length and they consulted with Lord Shaftesbury. Eventually, after weighing up how the assessments should be made, the Society's chairman, Sir Culling Eardley, announced very cautiously that if requests came from a recognised organisation, then funds might be forthcoming.

One of the first recognised organisations to receive a grant was the Society for the Promotion of Female Education in the East. In both Britain and America, thousands of Christians, both men and women, were confirmed supporters of the pioneering women who defied convention to tread the sometimes dangerous path of the missionary teacher. As well as admiring the courage and adventurous spirit of the women pioneers, their followers supported their emphasis on Western family life, on woman's role as partner, or "helpmeet for man", and their view that the early marriage, polygamy and easy divorce prevalent throughout the East, were evils to be combated and overcome.

Perhaps not much thought had been given to fund-raising when the Society began its work, when Cuthbert wrote, rather optimistically, in the minutes, "Much time will be devoted, especially during the first year, to canvassing for subscriptions and diffusing information." It soon became clear however, that Cuthbert's original plan was far too limited, and that canvassing for subscriptions was an almost full-time operation, and as more requests for aid arrived from the American Board, from the Society for the Promotion of Female Education in the East and from a growing number of other organisations, Cuthbert began to plan a new strategy. First of all, he distributed another 1,000 copies of "Openings for the Gospel in Turkey", then he arranged to take a regular eight pages in *Evangelical Christendom* for the Society's news, and finally, despite his increasingly bad health, he set off to Scotland to publicise the cause and raise money.

"A Turkish missions aid society in himself"

In his autobiography, Cyrus wrote that Cuthbert was "a Turkish missions aid society in himself", and by the time its Second Annual Report appeared in 1856, its enthusiastic Secretary had built the Society into a nation-wide organisation and raised over £4,000, something in the region of £160,500 or $240,780 today. Braving London smogs, draughty railway stations and damp lodging houses, he travelled and spoke constantly. Branch associations sprang up from Exeter to Dundee and from Islington to Belfast. Ladies Associations, "to which your Committee attaches special importance", said the Second Annual Report, were formed in London, Cheltenham, Clifton, Manchester, Liverpool and Dublin. Public meetings were held across the country, and drawing rooms were opened nationwide for private gatherings of neighbours and friends. In March 1856, when peace was declared in the Crimea, the TMAS was so well known that a substantial percentage of the national thanksgiving collection from Britain's churches, was donated to Turkish missions. The peace brought other good news from Turkey too, that caused the Society to rejoice. As part of the peace process the Sultan signed the *Hatt-i Hümayun*, another episode in the *Tanzimat-i Hayriye*, the Auspicious Reorderings that began in 1839 when Turkey's government, under pressure from the West, was encouraged to modernise, weed out corruption, and limit the special privileges of the Muslim *millet*. To Cuthbert Young, it seemed that a new era was dawning in Turkey. He felt certain that the bright future for the Armenian people, envisioned by Cyrus and the American Board, was within reach. More efforts from the Society he had brought into being, he believed, would bring that future even closer.

With peace and prosperity apparently in store for Turkey, Cyrus Hamlin set out from Constantinople. Cuthbert had written to him about the influential men who made up the Turkish

Missions Aid Society and Cyrus was eager to meet them. He was eager to meet Cuthbert again too and as his ship made its way into British waters, he imagined their joint fund-raising tour and how they would speak from the same platforms, Cyrus giving the latest news of missions in Turkey, and his friend suggesting how the British public could support the Armenian cause. But when Cyrus arrived in London he was met with a note, "written in a trembling hand", urging him, "Come as soon as you can." A second note, from Hannah Young, accompanied the first. Her husband was too ill, she said, to see anyone beyond his own family. Cuthbert Young died of tuberculosis in June 1856; he was 32 years old. "Your husband's name," wrote Sir Culling Eardley to Hannah, "will be ever associated in the minds of multitudes with the cause of the Gospel in the lands of the Bible." And Cyrus Hamlin said of his friend, "The Turkish Missions Aid Society is his memorial."

The most excellent Christians of England

Cyrus spent the 40 days after Cuthbert's funeral on the speaking tour they had planned together. But instead of Cuthbert, it was the Reverend Dr Blackwood, who as Military Chaplain to the British Hospital at Scutari had brought the terrible condition of the wounded men there to public attention, who accompanied Cyrus. Years later Cyrus wrote about that visit to Britain and although he recalled that the late night suppers of the English upper classes upset his digestion for months afterwards, he remembered it as one of the best times of his life. "I cherish the memory," he said, "of persons and scenes that I shall not behold again. I had the privilege of meeting some of the most excellent Christian men and women of England, I may say of the world." One of those men was Lord Shaftesbury who spent a private evening at his London home with Cyrus where they discussed the potential for Evangelical work in Bulgaria, a country whose people were struggling against Turkish rule and were close to Lord Shaftesbury's heart. On the advice of Shaftesbury and Cyrus Hamlin, and with the promise of financial support from the Society, the American Board began a mission in Bulgaria. It was the beginning of an association that would have far-reaching consequences for the Society and for Bulgaria in future years.

The sky parlour

By the late 1850s, British seaports, with their access to huge coal stocks, had become favourite coaling stops for American transatlantic steamships. For American travellers, the stops meant an opportunity to relax in friendly surroundings and the attic office in Adam Street became the most well-known venue in London for American missionaries passing through Britain. One American lady missionary always referred to that cosy room, at the summit of so many flights of stairs, as "the sky parlour".

It was from the sky parlour that the Society arranged public meetings all across Britain where visiting Americans spoke on behalf of their work that was supported by British funds. Wherever they went, people thronged to hear them. Although British missionaries worked in the same regions as the Board – India, the Middle East and the South Seas – the English audiences loved to hear tales of America, especially of the revivals that drew huge crowds all over the country, from church halls in Chicago to tents in Tennessee, where thousands of people made renewed pledges to Jesus. By 1866, so many Americans were passing through London and speaking for the Society that a special apartment, the Missionary Home, was provided for the Board's workers and their families, "whose numbers", read a comment in the Society's minutes, "frequently rendered their reception into private families impracticable".

Slaughter and smoking ruins

During its first years the Society largely followed the advice given by the American Board, that the main part of its funds should go towards erecting new churches, to support for Bebek seminary, for "native preachers, native colporteurs" (i.e. itinerant booksellers), or to assist the publication of Christian books. But, in 1860, something happened that changed the Society's ministry for ever. When the public in Britain read in their morning newspapers the graphic details of a civil war in Lebanon, then part of Syria, between the Islamic Druze and Maronite Christians, the reports caused horror and distress. After stories told of villages left as smoking ruins, of the wholesale slaughter of their male populations, and of refugee columns of women and children fleeing to Beirut, the Society joined others in Britain, Germany and America, to donate funds to Syrian Protestant Relief on behalf of 20,000 largely Christian refugees.

One woman deeply affected by the newspaper reports was Fanny Bowen Thomson, a widow whose husband had died in the Crimea. "As a widow caring for the widow," she said, shortly after arriving in Beirut, "I felt specially called to try and alleviate their distress, and make known to them the only balm for a broken heart – the love of Jesus." Fanny planned to open a small industrial refuge in Beirut, based on a British model, where, after being trained in useful crafts, refugee women could then sell their work to support themselves and their children. Then, she reasoned, she would leave the workshop in safe hands and return home to Britain. But by the end of the first week, after 30 women and 16 children had become 200, Fanny abandoned her plans to leave Beirut, and by 1861 she had established a network of "English industrial, ragged, and evening schools in Syria". Her friends in England included Lord Shaftesbury, President of the TMAS, and on his advice, Fanny's projects became the first educational and training schemes for refugees to receive funds from the Society. The British Syrian Mission, as it became known, eventually embraced people of all faiths in Lebanon and made special provision for the blind and disabled. In May 1862, when the Prince of Wales, later King Edward VII, visited Fanny's projects, he was so impressed that he contacted the Ottoman Government to ensure that official recognition and support was forthcoming.

The gift of Christian charity

When Syrian Protestant Relief, the main aid agency for the refugees of the 1860 conflict, closed its accounts, the Committee of the TMAS faced a dilemma. They knew that many people in Lebanon remained homeless and destitute and they saw in Fanny Bowen Thomson's work a way of continuing to be of service. How would people in Britain respond, wondered Sir Culling Eardley, if they were asked to give further aid to the orphans and widows of Syria? Would those who gave so regularly and so generously to the cause of the Gospel, to the salvation of human souls, also give towards the salvation of human bodies? The committee were uncertain as they met together in the sky parlour. Did they have the right, they asked themselves, to ask the British public to contribute towards a cause that did not seem to directly further the cause of the Gospel?

After another long discussion, and much soul-searching and prayer, the TMAS finally agreed that it might sometimes provide aid for refugees. Fanny Bowen Thomson had provided a model, the Committee believed, where innocent victims of conflict, especially orphans and widows, could recover dignity and hope by becoming self-supporting. Although they prayed that there would not be many more conflicts like that of 1860, where innocent people were massacred and driven from their homes, should such horrors occur again, they agreed, the Turkish Missions Aid Society would be ready to support the victims with the gift of Christian charity.

Chapter 2

Light and Dark in the Ottoman Empire

The 1870s

"The fields are white for the harvest," came the call from Turkey, "where are the workers?"

The only thing, said the missionaries of the American Board, that prevented the further evangelisation of Turkey was a lack of money and a shortage of trained men and women. Where missionaries were once chased from Armenian villages by angry crowds, by the 1870s emissaries arrived from those same communities begging for help. Children needed teachers. Young men wanted higher education. New congregations were asking for advice on church government. Schools were crying out for books. Some missionaries reported themselves exhausted by their endeavours, as they travelled the country on horseback, supporting existing congregations, founding new congregations, exhorting the pastors, preaching at services and teaching in schools.

Fortunately, said the missionaries, despite their own continual shortage of funds, the fruits of their earlier labours had laid a sound foundation for future Armenian success. The Evangelical community was growing, 23,000 in 1870, and a report for the Ottoman Government compiled by a member of the Armenian community had claimed that following conversion to Protestantism, Armenian family life and the status of women improved, and sobriety, hard work, philanthropy and self-improvement flourished. Forty per cent of Protestant adults could read, said the report, and one of every 60 had travelled to Europe or America at their own expense to improve their employment prospects.

Moreover, said the missionaries, in the Armenian Protestant community, a generation of earnest young men was emerging, with many of them sensing a call to serve their own people as pastors. In its annual reports, the Society reprinted the enthusiastic comments of its American colleagues. During college vacations, said the Americans, young Armenian ordinands set out in bands to remote villages, often the first Protestants to pass that way, and in spite of opposition from Gregorian priests, they gathered the people to open air meetings, read the scriptures to them in their modern Armenian language and preached the good news of the Kingdom. After ordination, the same young men threw themselves into their pastoral work, adding to their congregations, raising churches and schoolhouses and encouraging their people to greater efforts for themselves and their communities.

Through hard work and self-sacrifice many of the communities became self-sufficient and the Society pointed out in several of its annual reports that the zeal for tithing exhibited by the poor Armenians of Turkey might prove a useful example for their wealthier co-religionists in the West. The Society's grants to the American missions assisted those Armenian communities unable to raise the total salaries of their pastors and teachers, and they provided scholarships that enabled the most gifted young men to take further degrees in Britain and America. It also took particular pleasure in fulfilling one of its founding objectives, to provide places of worship, and among the many new churches funded by the Society, in 1871, its most generous supporter, the wealthy Mr W.C. Jones of Warrington, paid for several new Armenian churches with one single donation.

The Mr Joneses of Warrington, however, were rare, and most of the Society's funds were raised by the hard work of its second Secretary, Reverend Henry Jones, and by various members of its managing committee. They placed advertisements constantly in the Christian press and sent out appeals by hand and by post, but just as Cuthbert Young had discovered, support tended to drop away without frequent reminders to the Society's subscribers of the urgency of the work and the success that resulted from their continued efforts. In order to keep the Society at the forefront of its supporters' minds, Henry and his colleagues made regular visits to its auxiliaries, the regional groups whose subscriptions were collected by local secretaries. They were also regular preachers in friendly pulpits where they inspired the congregations with tales of missionary endeavour in the lands of the Bible.

Stories of success

The auxiliaries and congregations loved to hear stories of how their collections were used by the missionary teachers and evangelists they admired, and Henry did his best to convey to them all the information he could gather from the letters and reports he received at Adam Street. He spoke about the successes of the American Board, the new colleges it was raising in Turkey and how part of their endowments were stored safely in British banks. He spoke about the scholarships that sent Armenian youths to Harvard and to medical schools in Scotland. And with the Society supporting work all over the Ottoman Empire in the 1870s, he also spoke about children in mission schools in Egypt and Syria, the subjects they learned and the books they read, how parents heard the Gospel from their children's lips, and how the Gospel itself was taken to remote regions and to followers of other religions.

In Syria, with the Society as its major supporter, Fanny Bowen Thomson's mission flourished. Henry told his audiences how the original industrial refuge had become a network of schools and training schemes where children and young people from every background, the wealthiest merchant groups to the poorest refugees, made up a student body 2,000 strong. There were 26 day schools, he said, in Beirut, Damascus and Tyre, where all religions and all denominations sat side by side, Druze, Muslim, Christian and Jew. In fact, Henry told his eager listeners, a local Muslim governor, visiting a Beirut school, had remarked that, "The English woman's achievement would render another massacre impossible!"

Henry also told his British audiences about the sponsorship of students at the Syrian Mission's teacher training college at Beirut where local Christian girls trained for employment in the British Syrian Schools themselves. And should anyone in the audience wish to join the Society's sponsorship scheme for the college, they could support a promising student teacher at a cost of just £12 a year, £529.68 or $794.62 today. There were also training courses for harem visitors and Bible women, Henry said, quiet workers who were welcomed into the enclosed worlds of Muslim wives and Orthodox Christian families, and who were often the only witnesses to women's secret hopes and fears.

Perhaps the most exciting British Syrian project, said Henry, was a school for blind men, the first of its kind in the Near East, where Moon's system of raised type was taught. Some of its graduates had already become itinerant Scripture readers, and drew crowds of fascinated onlookers who listened in awe as the holy words were repeated by blind men who traced them first with sensitive fingers.

Hearts and minds

Beirut, where the British Syrian Schools were based, said Henry, was also home to the East's largest mission press, "the battleground", he called it, for the hearts and minds of the people of the Bible lands. All the text books for the region's Christian schools were printed there, he said, "primers, Bibles, testaments, Anxious Inquirers, and Saints' Rests", that were all loaded onto mules by the Bible colporteurs funded by the Society, who then trekked across mountain and desert to sell the books in distant towns and remote villages. "Cheap books, Holy books", was a cry well known in the streets and bazaars of the Near East.

Henry Jones was enthusiastic about the new Arabic Bible. A tremendous achievement! A completely new edition, translated by the American Arabic scholars, Drs Smith and Van Dyck, and printed finally at the Beirut press in 1867 using moveable type, an extraordinary technical feat! And hundreds of copies, Henry said, were sent out from Beirut to mission stations wherever Arabic was spoken. Henry had received a letter about the Arabic Bible from Sir Bartle Frere, an enthusiastic supporter of the Society well known to the British public from his Indian Civil Service days when he acted as British Government negotiator in the suppression of the African slave trade. He had seen the Bibles coveted and admired, Sir Bartle had written, by Arabic scholars as far as the Comoro Islands and Madagascar.

Sir Bartle had also spoken highly of the Society's support for American work in Egypt. It was a connection that dated back to 1854, the year the Society was founded, when Reverend Ridley Herschell, a founder member, and father to a Lord Chancellor of England, had preached at the first public service of the first American Protestant mission to Egypt. He himself, had first been in Egypt in 1834, Sir Bartle wrote, when very few of the ordinary people could read, but on a recent visit he had seen great changes.

"I see your Society supports Miss Whately's schools in Cairo," Sir Bartle went on, referring to the daughter of a former Anglican Archbishop of Dublin, whose schools were a popular choice for children of Cairo's Muslim and Christian elite. "They are a noble example of what can be achieved by one devoted lady," he concluded. Miss Whately herself was proud of her high standards and she wrote regularly to Henry Jones with news of her progress. Like all her missionary teacher colleagues, she said, the Bible was her principle textbook and there were few subjects to which it did not provide entry or allusion. But she was also careful to ensure that her pupils knew modern languages, as well as domestic virtues and healthy recreations for the body and mind. "I aim," she said, "for them to be a credit to their school and to their families, and that they should contribute to the flowering of Egyptian womanhood." Although it was always her intention that the Gospel should be carried into the homes of her pupils, even Miss Whately confessed herself surprised when one Muslim mother entertained her with a chorus of Christian hymns. "She told me," Miss Whately explained, "that her girl was singing them all day long, and that she herself had learned a great deal of Scripture from the same source." The girl, said Miss Whately, "is also teaching her father to read".

Miss Whately's educational work in Cairo was echoed by Miss Arnott at Tabeetha School in Jaffa, Miss Rose and Miss Hobbs at Nazareth, Mrs Watson and Miss Hicks at Shemlan in Lebanon and Miss Taylor at Beirut, all of them recipients of the Society's funds. Henry liked to reassure his hearers, particularly the women, that all the Western female teachers were eager to raise the status of women in the East, and like Henry himself and the Society's managing committee, they saw it as essential to any long-term social change. But, at the same time, he said, Miss Whately and her colleagues were realistic, and they recognised they were sometimes called to fight small battles in great campaigns. They loved their faith and preached the Gospel whenever they could and prayed the Evangelical seeds they planted would take root and flourish in Muslim and Orthodox hearts. They also recognised that schooldays for most of their female pupils would end in a very early marriage, but they took pleasure in the weddings, and sometimes wrote to Henry about the customs involved. They also believed that if polygamy and divorce could be prevented by a young bride having a sense of individual value, interesting conversation, and an aptitude for needlework and thrift, then another victory had been won.

Henry liked to read excerpts from the reports he received from the schools to his British audiences. "Care is taken," said one from a British Syrian School, "to teach female and domestic work, and to elevate these young Syrian girls to be indeed the helpmeet for man." Another report spoke of the evident pride felt by a young husband who said, "My wife can sew my shirts." The same school also reported that of more than 40 Muslim pupils who were married, not one was divorced, nor had the husband taken a second wife. There were other successes too. Although some girls broke with tradition entirely and followed their teachers into the schoolroom, even among those who married young, contact with their teachers was often maintained for a lifetime and their own daughters were sent to mother's old school. A satisfactory conclusion to the progress of the Society funds, Henry thought, and he hoped that his audiences agreed.

The *Apology of Al-Kindi*

Henry was enthusiastic about another of the Society's projects too, one he had personally helped bring into being when he introduced a young clergy friend, Anton Tien, to the Society's leading men. Anton was an Arabic scholar of considerable merit and a authority on Islam, and he had already founded a mission in London that reached out with the Gospel to Muslims visiting the capital for business or pleasure.

Although the American Board had abandoned direct confrontation with Islam in Turkey in order to focus its work on the Armenians it hoped would one day become successful missionaries to Muslims, the Society, conscious of the large Muslim population of Britain's own empire, believed challenges should be mounted. Its leading men also felt the British Government should do more to support Christian missionaries in India. When Anton requested support for another of his projects, the Society saw how it could be of service, both to the workers it supported in the Ottoman Empire and to their British colleagues working among Muslims in India. After Henry and the Society's committee had read Anton's précis of a controversial ninth century text, the *Apology of Al-Kindi*, a defence of Christianity against Islam by Abd al-Masih al-Kindi, a minor member of a famous academic family, they recommended that the Society fund and publish a complete translation. Two Arabic scholars, Dr Cornelius Van Dyck, translator of the Arabic Bible, based at Beirut, and Sir William Muir, Chancellor of Edinburgh University, authenticated Anton's translation and the completed work was published by the Society at the Beirut Press.

Can anything be done in England?

As Henry Jones and his colleagues encouraged the Society's supporters with tales of missionary advances and the successes of projects such as *Al-Kindi*, as the 1870s advanced reports in Western newspapers alerted the public to a series of natural and economic disasters, national uprisings and ethnic conflicts that took place across the Ottoman Empire and the Eastern lands beyond. Christian workers in the lands of the Bible, witnesses to events that were generally distressing and sometimes shocking, appealed to Britain and America for help. Their messages spoke of thousands of people dying of famine and made homeless by earthquakes, and the news stirred the souls of people who lived in more fertile and stable lands.

Sometimes the very first news of Eastern disasters to reach Britain came from supporters of the Society who were members of the diplomatic service. They used their access to military telegraphs to send news and requests for aid directly to the Foreign Office, where kind friends walked messages around the corner to Henry Jones near the Strand. "Distress among the poor at Mosul and vicinity now reaching crisis," said one, "children sold or abandoned... No effective steps taken by local Government to afford relief. Can anything be done in England?"

Somehow, something was always done in Britain, and the Society raised the necessary funds and sent them to those in need. Sometimes members of the Society's committee found themselves involved more intimately in the disasters. When Dr Holt-Yates, a founder member of the Society, and his wife, arrived home from Syria after installing new teachers at the school they founded at Suediah in the 1840s, they were greeted by a telegram and the news that an earthquake had destroyed the school and years of their work. It had also killed thousands of people in Suediah and Antioch and left thousands more homeless. The doctor and his wife threw themselves into the fund-raising effort, speaking at meetings in London and around the country, and helping to raise the relief to feed the hungry and repair the damage.

In the same year, a devastating famine in Persia caused by years of poor rainfall and plagues of insects, caused starvation among tens of thousands of people, and with the Society's Honorary Treasurer, Lord Kinnaird, leading the campaign in Britain, a total of £20,000 was collected in Britain and America for Persian Famine Relief. As missionaries, colporteurs, and Bible women distributed the aid in Persia, to people who had never before received such help from overseas, just as the massacre victims of Lebanon caused the Society to reflect in 1860, questions were raised once more. Famine relief was a new enterprise, Henry Jones told the Society's managing committee, news of such disasters had never reached Western newspapers before, but it did seem that when the public learned of the misery in Persia, many people wanted to help. Perhaps it was another area where the Society could be of service? Some members were doubtful. Was famine relief a proper destination for the funds of a missions aid society? Would the public respond in the same way a second time? How would it help the cause of the Gospel? Another long debate took place at Adam Street, with the managing committee seeking God's guidance as it deliberated. Finally, when a conclusion was reached, the Society made another decision that shifted its direction and outlook. "It was decided," Henry wrote in the minutes, "that the Turkish Missions Aid Society would contribute to famine relief when it could, as such donations would aid the cause of the Gospel by opening men's hearts to receive its blessed message of love at the hands of their Christian benefactors."

Gregory and Emma: the Broussa orphanage

In 1874, Anatolia and Asia Minor were hit by famine and economic disaster at the same time. It followed a financial crisis when European banking houses had refused more credit to the deeply indebted and extravagant government of the Sultan. When Turkey's response to the refusal of European loans was to demand that its own regional authorities increase their tax gathering efforts, the poor paid the price. Especially the Armenian poor. At the bottom of Turkey's rigid system of hierarchies, and with no redress in the Muslim courts, the Armenian peasants had no means of refusing additional demands for taxes that were traditionally taken as crops and cattle. They were already suffering the effects of summer drought and a winter of devastating floods, and when their remaining means of sustenance were taken, they began to starve. As bread prices rocketed after merchants sought to recoup losses, the famine even overwhelmed Constantinople itself where hundreds of dead bodies eventually lay in the streets.

As the people of Asia Minor starved and hungry orphans roamed the towns and villages, Christian hearts were moved to action. One of those hearts belonged to Gregory Baghdassarian, an Armenian teacher and graduate of Bebek Seminary and the Basle Missionary College, who worked in Constantinople for the Basle Missionary Society. One cold night, during the famine year, as Gregory made his way home, two hungry orphan children ran in front of his carriage and pleaded with him for bread. Gregory was shocked by the condition of the emaciated children, and as he peered into their pale faces and listened to their hoarse voices, something told him to take them home. He had no qualms about the reactions of his wife and when he handed the two ragged children to Emma, just as Gregory had anticipated, she fed them, bathed them, and tucked them safely into warm beds. Irish-born Emma worked with Jewish orphans in Constantinople, and when the children lay sleeping, she debated with Gregory what God meant them to do. They both reached the same conclusion. The children had been sent for a purpose, they decided. The Baghdassarians were to found an orphanage where young victims of famine could be sheltered, educated and trained for useful careers.

As the Baghdassarians began their new venture of faith, they found themselves opposed by Armenian priests and Muslim imams. The priests accused Gregory and Emma of using the orphanage scheme as a ploy for the conversion of Gregorian children to Protestantism, and they did their best to ensure no premises were forthcoming. When the Baghdassarians used funds from their own friends to rent a dilapidated house at Broussa, a silk manufacturing town south of Constantinople, the imams, claiming that no Christian should look out upon Muslim houses, forced them to shutter their windows and use only the back entrance of their home. Despite the opposition, Gregory and Emma and their growing band of orphan children, moved from one tumbledown house to another, each one a little better than the last, until in 1876, Emma applied to the Society for a grant and the Baghdassarian orphanage enterprise moved to a larger and more comfortable home.

To celebrate the new house, and difficulties overcome, the orphanage held its first public examinations in 1876. Emma and Gregory invited the whole town, including their fiercest opponents. In a hall prettily decorated with laurels, flags, and Scripture texts, the children in their clean shirts and pinafores lined up to greet their guests, including their guests of honour, the British vice-consul to Turkey and his family. They also prepared to display their accomplishments and the results of their hard work. To the delight of the townsfolk, and the surprise of their former opponents, Gregory and Emma's proud orphans were examined in a range of subjects, scripture, Biblical history, geography, grammar, hygiene and singing as well as English, Armenian and Turkish. Emma told her guests that needlework and cooking also featured on the school's curriculum, together with daily Bible lessons from Gregory. As soon as they saw how nicely the children were cared for, Emma wrote to Henry Jones, the hostility of the priests and the imams immediately ceased. In fact, she said, "Those who persecuted us in former times are the first to help us now."

Famine, massacre and war

While famine raged in Asia Minor, in Bulgaria, on the European edge of the Empire, there was a crisis of a different kind. The struggle of the Bulgarian people for freedom from Turkish domination erupted into ethnic conflict in 1876, and in April that year an uprising by Bulgarian Christians was brutally put down by thousands of *Basi-Bözöks*, Ottoman irregular soldiers determined to extract revenge for the reported massacres of Muslims. What became known as the Bulgarian Atrocities caused horror and outrage in Britain as newspapers carried graphic reports of the massacre of thousands of Christians. The American missionaries estimated 15,000 dead. Despite its earlier hopes and prayers that massacres on the scale of 1860 would never be seen again, the Society found itself raising funds for more innocent victims of ethnic conflict. As it sent financial aid and bundles of clothing to the Bulgarian mission stations, the Society told its supporters, "It was impossible for the Committee to abstain from the sympathy and exertions called for by the occasion."

Famine, drought and massacre were followed in 1877 by war between Turkey and Russia, and when another economic crisis, this time provoked by the conflict, produced another round of brutal consequences for the Armenian population, the Society began to realise what the inferior status of Turkey's Christian population really meant. It also realised that the promised reforms it had greeted with such optimism in 1856 had never materialised. As well as the taxes levied on them by the Ottoman Government, the Armenians, forbidden by law to carry weapons, were also at the mercy of their well-armed Kurdish and Turkish neighbours. As the Kurds and Turks bought tax farming options from absentee landlords, or claimed traditional rights to quarter themselves in Armenian homes, they also used their privileged position to steal. The helpless Armenians could do nothing but watch as their crops, their livestock, and often their daughters, were carried away. Letters from American missionaries in Turkey, describing the misery in Armenian communities, were received by a distressed Henry Jones in London, and as he sent grants for Armenian relief, he prayed that as the war reached its end, so too the suffering of the Armenian people would also become a thing of the past.

Visitors from the East

As well as immediate public reactions to natural disaster and violence, the Society's fund-raising efforts had always been boosted by the personal appearances of American visitors. But while the Americans spoke on behalf of their missions, when Emma Baghdassarian arrived in London in 1879, as guest speaker at the Society's annual meeting, she pleaded the cause of her own Broussa orphans. The novelty drew a big crowd, eager to hear Emma tell the story of how Gregory brought the first two children home, how persecution was overcome, and how the children were now flourishing and needed a much larger home. "We are trusting the Lord," Emma told the audience as she opened the Broussa Appeal, "to move hearts in Britain for the orphans of Turkey." As Emma went on to speak about individual children and to suggest that supporters of the Society might like to sponsor a little Armenian girl or boy, the appeal fund began to swell, and when Henry Jones deposited the sum next day at the Society's bank in Pall Mall, he assured Emma that the new orphanage would soon become a reality.

The Persian Famine Relief Fund was boosted too in 1880, when Pastor Yacob David from Oroomiah, with his wife Moressa, visited Britain at the expense of the Society, to petition Queen Victoria for British government aid. As nationals of Persia, the Davids excited as much interest among the Society's supporters as Emma Baghdassarian. Moressa in particular, "truly a helpmeet to the pastor", and a gifted speaker of exotic appearance, drew large crowds at meetings around the British Isles. The public were fascinated to meet a foreign Christian couple, engaged in Christian work for their own people, who had braved the long journey, overland and by sea, to meet the Queen and speak to British audiences. Stimulated by their meetings with Emma and Moressa, supporters of the Society began to request much more news. Had a new home been found yet for the Broussa Orphanage? Was there any news of individual children? Had Moressa returned safely to Oroomiah? Was the famine at an end? In its turn, the Society began to see an opportunity.

The *Star*

The idea of a publication produced by the Society had been considered with varying degrees of enthusiasm ever since 1854, and a variety of experiments had been tried. However, in 1882, the subject of a periodical was raised again. The discussion was provoked by the Reverend Thomas Brown of Newcastle, who had become Secretary of the Society after Henry Jones resigned due to failing health. Like Cuthbert Young, Henry was worn out by the constant travelling required to keep the Society in the public eye and at the forefront of its supporters' notice. Mr Brown had found himself in a similar situation. Despite setting out enthusiastically on his first fund-raising trip as secretary, he returned from the north of England, tired, depressed and discouraged by the failure of British Christians to live up to his expectations. He had been shocked, he told the managing committee, to discover how few people knew of the Society's existence, and then, after his spending considerable time furnishing them with all necessary information, of their reluctance to add it to the other missionary societies they supported. Mr Brown wondered if the time had not come to begin publication of an attractive quarterly periodical filled with news of overseas work and appeals for funds.

The managing committee agreed with Mr Brown, and the new secretary, hugely encouraged, wrote to the missionaries and local workers in the lands of the Bible, with requests for regular reports of their work. They would be published, he said, together with general information about the Society and lists of contributions received, in a new journal to be called the *Turkish Missions Intelligencer*. Within a year, the name was changed to the *Star in the East*, after a Christian newspaper of the same name, funded by the Society and published by the Greek Evangelical Church in Athens.

Almost the first feature to appear in the *Star* was the story of the new orphanage at Broussa. Emma and Gregory's faith was rewarded, British hearts had opened and enough money was raised for a new building. When the widow of the Italian consul in Constantinople rejected all higher offers and sold her spacious home in Broussa to the Baghdassarians at an extraordinarily low price, Gregory and Emma knew God had opened his heart to them too. The widow's fine house was in the best part of town, on the healthy slopes of Asiatic Mount Olympus, and Mr Thomson, American missionary at Constantinople, and author of the feature in the *Star*, described two ranges of sturdy buildings that sat behind strong walls and a separate building called a kiosk that would make a fine hospital. There were also spacious gardens and good walks. Mr Thomson went on to describe the spacious, light and clean schoolroom where the walls were decorated with coloured illustrations of Bible stories and natural history donated by the Religious Tract Society, and he wrote in glowing terms about the children's grasp of languages, history and geography.

With the house secured, further funds were needed to maintain the work. "Who will count it a privilege to provide what is required?" asked the *Star*, and to stimulate their appetite, readers were encouraged to visit the displays of Broussa work held regularly in London. Emma sent it to Britain in the charge of Mr Gilbertson, the British Consul, whenever he went home on furlough. The Society's supporters responded with great generosity and in May 1883, when the Baghdassarians received the deeds of ownership to the widow's house, and the Society pledged regular support for the orphans, Gregory raised the Union Jack over the orphanage and Emma led the children in a chorus of "God Save the Queen".

Chapter 3

The Star in the East
The 1880s

The *Star in the East* brought the Bible lands to life. People and places, previously just names to the Society's supporters, took on substance in its pages. Emma and Gregory Baghdassarian and the orphans of Broussa entered British drawing rooms. Moressa David and her family became a topic of conversation in village halls. The desperate plight of the Armenian nation was a matter for concern at parish meetings. Constantinople, Cairo, Beirut and Aleppo seemed almost within reach, as their sun-baked streets, their shady courtyards, and their groves of towering palms, hovered in the minds of readers who devoured the news written by their heroes and heroines, the Evangelical Protestant missionaries in the Bible lands.

So much Christian work in the region had previously gone unreported that even Mr Brown, the Society's Secretary, when he toured the mission stations in the mid-1880s, exclaimed with delight, "I am free to say that my anticipations were more than fulfilled. The half had not been told me."

The half that had not been told Mr Brown, appeared in the pages of the *Star*, and as the Society's supporters became more aware of the enormous efforts spent for the cause of the Gospel, the labour of missionaries and the thousands of pounds donated in British churches, they had every reason to feel proud and satisfied. Although there were areas of unrest, especially in Turkey and the Balkans, there was no reason to suppose that they were any more than passing local difficulties. Although there were earthquakes and famines, the generosity of Western Christians and swift responses from missionary agencies could lighten the burden of suffering, feed the hungry and rebuild fallen cities. More effort, more money, and more prayer, would surely hasten the day that British Christians longed for and sang about so earnestly, when every nation on earth was finally gathered to the Gospel of Jesus Christ.

The school in the stable

The British Army occupied Egypt in 1883, the year the *Star* began publication, and the country immediately became a source of fascination to the British public. The pyramids, the sphinx and the mummified bodies emerging from the sands intrigued everyone, and every schoolchild learned about the River Nile whose yearly floods watered the land and made it fertile. Readers of the *Star* liked to wander in their imagination with Dr Lansing, who travelled with his waterborne dispensary among the isolated villages of the Nile Delta. They imagined him welcomed by leaders of the Protestant churches that had spread over Egypt since 1854, treating his patients in mudbrick houses and sitting among white-clad congregations beneath the palm-fringed roofs of tiny village churches.

One man responsible for some of those Protestant churches was Dr Hogg, an evangelist and teacher who began work in 1865 at Assiout, in southern Egypt, 400 miles south of Cairo. In those days, he told readers of the *Star*, "All was dark, from Cairo to Khartoum and even to Gondar." There were no schools in the region and no Christian teaching but as Dr Hogg watched the barefoot boys running in the streets he felt that God was encouraging him to open a school in Assiout. He searched the town for a suitable house, but found nothing; every door was closed to him, except one. "My donkey stable," a merchant who traded in oil and grain told him, "you may use." The man had smiled as he spoke. He thought it unlikely the school would last very long.

At first, Dr Hogg told readers of the *Star*, there were boys at one end of the stable and donkeys at the other. "I began with six boys," he said, "who sat in the straw to learn their lessons and who listened as I read the Scriptures to them." Eventually, he continued, the six had become ten and then 50 boys. "And now they are hundreds," he said, "and our school trains Christian teachers, pastors and colporteurs for work all over Egypt, everyone of them an upright and moral young man." The new school was built with funds from England and Scotland, and prided itself on its combination of "personal Christian salvation and the highest attainable learning". He liked to think, said Dr Hogg, that it followed the ancient Christian traditions of Egypt, from long before the Islamic conquest, when Origen and Clement taught at Alexandria.

Some of Dr Hogg's older boys, the students who one day would be Egypt's Protestant teachers and evangelists, sometimes travelled with him on his mission boat, the *Ibis*. In one dusty riverside village after another, the boys learned their profession, teaching the small, serious Evangelical congregations, and preaching the Gospel to the crowds drawn to the water's edge whenever the sound of Dr Hogg's harmonium drifted over the flat fields and through the sandy village streets.

When they read how Dr Hogg's harmonium had attracted soldiers of Sir Herbert Stewart's Guards battalion on their way to relieve General Gordon at Khartoum, the readers of the *Star* felt immensely comforted. They had all prayed for Gordon and for those brave men who attempted his rescue. The Guards were bivouacked close to the river and some of them had spent a long evening on the *Ibis*, intrigued by Dr Hogg's work and happy to join the Egyptian students in fellowship and prayer. Before they went on their way, the soldiers took a collection for the mission and donated all the books they carried with them to the boys.

Independent spirits and adventurers

Guaranteed to interest the *Star*'s female readers were tales of the adventurous women who felt God's call to become pioneers in new ventures. Their independent spirits and the trust they had in God, as they left their homelands to brave violent climates and the threat of disease, made them the inspiration for women in churches all over Britain who were encouraged to offer their talents and their lives in the service of others.

In the 1880s, medical work among women was almost unknown in the East. Local women revealed little of themselves to any man beyond the most intimate members of their own families and their anxieties and their illnesses generally went unrelieved. They suffered and they died, untreated and often in pain. When the first female medical practitioners made their appearance, the numbers who flocked to their clinics, willing to wait sometimes for days, amazed the regular missionaries. "The number of patients who have applied to her for relief, coming from villages far and near, has quite astonished us," wrote Miss Watson, a teacher at Shemlan in Lebanon, after her medical friend, Miss Perston-Taylor, joined her mission. "She is a blessing hugely esteemed by the suffering women here, who would sooner die in many cases than be examined by a medical man."

When Bible women sat among the throngs of sick and anxious women who waited to see the female doctors, waiting rooms were transformed. The sound of their comfortable voices reading the Scriptures calmed the atmosphere, and the holy words brought reassurance to women who were sometimes in great fear. When the Bible women invited the sufferers to unburden their hearts to them, then sometimes the sharing of troubles was the first step on the road to healing.

People unburdened their hearts to Maria West too, mother and counsellor to huge numbers of British sailors and one of the *Star*'s most popular and prolific correspondents. For 30 years she had been a successful missionary in Turkey, ministering to women in poor Armenian villages, arranging Bible classes and fellowship groups, mothers' meetings and Sabbath Schools. In every village and town Maria had been successful, until she reached Smyrna. "That God-forsaken city of the Seven Churches," she called the huge international seaport on Turkey's Aegean coast, as she described her frustrated efforts to reach its cosmopolitan population.

It was as if the whole city was in league with the devil, Maria thought, wealthy, worldly and oblivious to the fate that waited for its population in the life to come. She had no idea what to do. Every missionary enterprise failed. When she set out for England in 1878 she wondered if perhaps God was closing a door to her in Turkey. In England, as Maria renewed acquaintance with old friends, she called on Annie McPherson, Superintendent of the Strangers' Rest, a mission to seamen in the docklands of London's East End. How like Smyrna it was. Ships from every country and sailors from every nation, and a local population who catered for their needs, drinking, gambling and whoring. And none of them thinking about anything but the pleasures of today. Except those who found their way to Annie at the Rest.

The Bible! In a coffee house!

Maria returned to Smyrna inspired. But her more conservative colleagues were shocked. "The Bible! In a coffee house!" The place for the Bible, they said, is in churches not among sinners in coffee houses! But Maria was not the sort of woman to be discouraged and she persisted with the "coffee house plan for reaching strangers". Before long, with the help of Maud Grimston who had answered her advertisement in an English newspaper, Maria rented a house on the Smyrna quayside, right among the city's worst drinking dens, and opened the Smyrna Rest. Very soon Maria told readers of the *Star*, the local people, her Armenian and Greek neighbours, were calling the Rest, "the holy idea" and "the house of Christ".

Maria's estimation of Smyrna's absence of godly citizens was echoed by Reverend J. More from Cheltenham, when he visited the city in 1884 and wrote about it for the *Star*. He described the quayside, broad and magnificent, that stretched two or three miles along the seafront and was lined with cafes. Each profession or trade had one of its own, he said, all with wine and spirits in abundance, and "to represent our English drinking dens and ruin our English sailors there among the rest is the Liverpool cafe". Mr More painted a vivid picture of Smyrna's cafe nightlife, the quayside packed with men of every nation, every colour and race, who jostled and laughed and swore together as they debated the attractions of half-naked dancing girls while the night resonated to the music of travelling German bands. But, shining in the midst of the iniquity, said Mr More, was Maria's Rest, "cosy and clean and homelike exceedingly!"

The Rest was homelike, its sitting room was filled with little tables and comfortable chairs, a newspaper stand displayed familiar magazines from home, and Scripture texts adorned the walls. One corner of the room was curtained off for private prayer. Many of the sailors who found their way to the Smyrna Rest were very young, often lonely and frequently drunk. Sometimes they were in tears. "I am alone and going astray," said one, "will you pray with me?" Maria was able to reassure readers of the *Star* about that young man. She had received a letter months later posted in Trieste, assuring her his conversion was real and that he was now "a Christian brother". Some of Maria's sailors kept in touch for years, while of others, "we lose sight and can only pray and commit them to the great King".

Kidnapped!

Despite the successes, the doctors, the teachers and the souls saved, missionary work could be fraught with danger, especially for workers who left the safety of well-trodden pathways. In 1885, readers of the *Star* were distressed to learn that a young Albanian missionary, Gerasim Kyrias, had been captured on a lonely road by bandits. The young man, a graduate of the American mission at Samokov in Bulgaria, and only recently employed by the British and Foreign Bible Society, had been carrying the first translations of the Scriptures in Albanian dialects into his homeland when he was waylaid. He had known it was unwise to travel without a large company, but he was in a hurry and all he was carrying were cases of books.

Gerasim and his guide were stopped in a desolate mountain pass as they neared their destination, Kortcha in eastern Albania. Armed men, who had been lying in wait, stepped out from among the rocks that lined the narrow road and as Gerasim was led away into the mountains, the guide, after a brutal beating, was handed a ransom note. Five hundred Turkish pounds were demanded for the release of the young preacher. "The brigand business must be very dull if they can find no-one but penniless Bible colporteurs to deal in," one of Gerasim's colleagues at Monastir in Macedonia observed.

The bandit leader, so said the rumour that began to spread through Albania, was a bosom friend of the Orthodox Archbishop of Kortcha. And furthermore, it went on, Gerasim's capture was part of a plot to damage the Protestant cause. While Gerasim remained in captivity, his friends at Monastir and Constantinople were desperate to obtain his release. The mountain winter was approaching and everyone knew that few people survived in that harsh climate unless they were well sheltered and well fed. Eventually, Western diplomats were rallied to Gerasim's cause and a troop of Albanian government soldiers was despatched to search the rugged terrain. They found Gerasim, eventually, after the ransom was paid, blindfolded and with his hands tied, lying at the roadside.

"His captivity was no matter of light romance," said the *Star*, whose readers contributed generously to Gerasim's ransom, "but aggravated sufferings at the hands of wicked and lawless men." Gerasim, released and back among family and friends, was soon back at work. His preaching packed halls in Kortcha and his translations of Ira Sankey's *Sacred Songs and Solos* were favourites in Albania's Evangelical churches. He founded a Christian school in Kortcha that became one of the most successful in the Balkans. But the injuries he received at the hands of the bandits, according to a contemporary biography, led to Gerasim's early death just nine years later.

Samokov: small beginnings, great ends

The American Board's Samokov Institute, where Gerasim studied theology and linguistics, was one of the most popular Evangelical colleges in the Balkans. Its students were drawn from every surrounding nation, and there were so many applications from poor students, said Dr John House, the Director, that he planned to open small workshops for printing and carpentry where they could work to offset their fees. Samokov was Dr House's vision, and it was his hard work that had built its success. Over the years he had bought land in small lots until the mission site had eventually become a huge acreage, he had overseen the erection of scholastic and domestic buildings, and then laboured hard for the academic achievements of the Institute. He was a great believer in small beginnings that led to great ends, and he favoured self-help projects that encouraged self-reliance and self-worth. The skills the students learned at carpentry and printing would supplement their future income, he thought, and teach them to be industrious and not to despise manual labour.

Could the Turkish Missions Aid Society help? Dr House asked. The Society's supporters responded generously when an appeal was made in the *Star*, and machinery and tools were provided for the carpenters and presses and cases of type for the printers.

Dr House chose the books that were translated into Bulgarian and printed at the Samokov press and they reflected his own independent spirit. Samuel Smiles, Scottish political reformer, moralist and author was high on the list with *Self-Help, Character,*

Duty and *Thrift*. And, just as in Turkey, the *Pilgrim's Progress* was popular in Bulgaria too, and Bulgarian editions were printed at Samokov.

Christian books a threat

But, even as Dr House was supervising the translations of Samuel Smiles and John Bunyan, literature and textbooks were no longer safe in the Ottoman Empire. Christian books that had once travelled freely through Ottoman lands were becoming a threat. For nearly 200 years the Turkish Government had found its enormous empire almost impossible to administer, but by the 1880s, as subject nations began to clamour for independence, a network of censors and secret policemen began to read the mail and check books for subversion.

In 1884 Christian schools became subject to inspection and preachers at religious meetings were sometimes uncomfortably aware that their most attentive listeners had not come to hear the message of the Gospel.

The following year, Dr House wrote from Monastir that the mission there no longer received the *Star in the East*. "Like other religious papers that mention Turkey without a thick coating of flattery," he said, "it doesn't pass the local censors of the mail."

In 1887, after new regulations in Syria demanded that every fresh edition from the Beirut press be sent to Damascus for approval, the volumes loaded into the panniers of colporteurs' mules, awarded as Sunday School prizes or stocked in mission libraries across the Empire, were all to be marked with the censors' official stamp. How to proceed with the current edition of Anton Tien's *Al-Kindi*, with its criticisms of Islam, was a problem. It was unlikely to be received in Damascus with anything other than hostility. Eventually, at the end of one of the Society's more unusual debates, the managing committee decided to become smugglers. *Al-Kindi*'s pages should still be printed in Beirut, they agreed, but then they would be carried secretly to England by British and American missionaries. In London the pages would be collated at Adam Street and then taken to a friendly printer for binding between blank book covers, ready for other missionaries to smuggle the finished volumes back into the lands of Islam.

Saving the Broussa Orphanage

As fear drove the Ottoman Government to more rigorous censorship, famine and economic depression caused hunger and unemployment among the people of Asia Minor. One man who was hit harder than most was Gregory Baghdassarian. Emma had died in 1884, of a mysterious wasting illness whose cause no doctor could discover and three years later, as recession closed the Broussa silk factories and famine drove hungry orphans to his door, Gregory seemed ready to collapse under the strain. Emma had not only been his wife but the orphanage's major fund-raiser and the increasingly desperate Gregory petitioned the Society for more funds. The *Star* publicised the sad state of the Broussa orphanage and encouraged readers to visit sales of work held at London's YWCA.

Broussa Orphanage became a problem. For the first time, the Society was uncertain whether it could trust Gregory; his accounting was erratic and sometimes he failed to acknowledge receipt of his grants. What should the managing committee do? They were reluctant to abandon Broussa, it was one of the Society's most popular missions, some of the children had individual benefactors in Britain, and readers of the *Star* were constantly demanding more stories. Eventually, Miss Good was sent, a reliable British matron who took charge of the orphanage and took charge of Gregory. In a flush of optimism the Society also provided a covered gymnasium, a new kitchen and a laundry.

Miss Good was the spur that Gregory needed and by 1890 he had rallied completely, found new donors in Switzerland and Germany and married the Swiss matron that succeeded Miss Good. In the same year, he wrote with enormous pride for the *Star* about treasured visits from his very first orphans. "Some have taken degrees," he wrote, "and have become professional men. Others work in post offices and telegraph stations, while some are military officers in uniform, and with swords." I hardly knew them, he said, they were so grown-up and so fine.

Cruel and outrageous wrongs

It was not only Broussa that suffered during the economic recession of 1887. Maria West left Smyrna that year on an extended visit to old friends at Erzroum in eastern Anatolia. She wrote about her experiences there for the *Star*. Once again, she said, the Armenian people were paying the price for the bankruptcy of the Ottoman Government. "The crushing degradation, the cruel and outrageous wrongs, that are inflicted on the people by Turkish officials, are terrible to behold." She described one scene she had witnessed herself, where she had stood by, desperate to intervene but powerless to do so, as a tax gatherer drove away the cow whose milk sustained an Armenian family of ten children. "The mother's desperate pleas went unheeded," said Maria, "as she begged for her children's lives."

In another article in the *Star*, the Reverend H. Grattan Guinness wrote of the Armenians, "Their sufferings are dreadful; wrongs, direct and indirect, multiplied and varied, press upon them from the cradle to the grave," and in another, the American missionary, Mr W. Chambers, described what happened if Armenian villagers refused to hand over the taxes demanded. "The Kurds, often acting as irregular militias, are accustomed to visit the threshing-floors to collect wheat and barley," he wrote, "but if a poor villager refuses their demands, he is marked for vengeance, his haystack is burned, his oxen are stolen, or possibly he is forced to fly for his life."

"Trouble in Erzroum" was another article by Mr Chambers that appeared in the *Star* in 1888. The news it conveyed was ominous. It suggested that a sustained campaign, something more than excessive taxation and local violence, was being directed by the Turkish authorities against the Armenian people. Unusual atrocities, said Mr Chambers, were being seen in eastern Turkey. Hundreds of Armenian Christians had been imprisoned and schoolteachers and priests stood accused of rousing the Armenian national spirit. He had seen nothing himself, he went on, to suggest the allegations had much substance, but one of his most promising students at Erzroum, a boy of only 17, had recently been seized and imprisoned. It seemed a trivial thing, said Mr Chambers, just a song that Sumpad wrote in his school-book, accusing the Turks of oppressing his people, the sort of thing idealistic boys liked to do, but someone had informed and the boy and his teacher had been jailed. Almost before we could act, said Mr Chambers, before he had time to muster support from Western diplomats, Sumpad was dead, from the injuries he received in the Turkish prison. I have a great fear, said Mr Chambers, that these events herald the onset of further tragedy. "We must pray for Armenia."

"The Armenian Question", an article that appeared in the *Star* one year after the death of Sumpad, marked a significant change in the attitude of the Turkish Missions Aid Society that had once viewed the Gregorian Church with suspicion and hostility. "The Gregorian Armenian Christians," said the article, "are our co-religionists, and we cannot be indifferent to their wrongs." The article went on to outline the history of Gregorian Christianity. In very positive language it explained how the Armenian people were justifiably proud of the church that had upheld their nation through centuries of oppression. Idolatry and superstition, issues that had first brought the Armenian Christians to the attention of the American Board and the Society, no longer roused Evangelical passions in quite the same way, and the article emphasised co-operation rather than conflict. The fruits of co-operation were celebrated in the *Star* in the early 1890s, when Gevout Shishmanian, the Gregorian Bishop of Erzroum, thanked the Society for its contribution to famine relief in the city. "We have learned with joy," wrote the Bishop, "that you are comforting by substantial material aid, without partiality, all who are needy, of whom the largest part are Armenians."

Waves of blessings

There was more reason for joy in the early part of the new decade, when it seemed as if heavy clouds had parted and bright rays of light poured down on the Christians of the Ottoman Empire. Missionaries who had become dispirited were uplifted and local pastors were filled with hope as a series of great revivals swept through the Armenian Protestant churches and colleges of Turkey. There were hundreds of new converts, reported Dr Shepherd from Aintab, and so many special meetings the missionaries were quite exhausted. In the city's Armenian district, he said, many family altars had been erected, and he described early morning streets alive with the sounds of prayer and hymns. The Gospel is preached with renewed fervour, said the missionaries in Harpoot, "not only among Protestants but among the Gregorian priests too!" Churches were praying for each other, they said, and revival followed. From Erzroum, came reports of confessions and reconciliations between old enemies and renewed pledges to Jesus.

"Wave after wave of blessing seems to have broken upon us," wrote Maria from the Smyrna Rest. Mrs Constantine, the one-time Maud Grimston, who had married a Greek preacher with a reputation for fiery oratory, and who now ran a branch of the Greek Evangelical Union with him at the Rest, said, "Many souls were saved, and some entire families converted to God. Men, women and children were filled with the Spirit and with joy."

Jews and Christians on the move

For some people in other lands there was little in the way of joy. Just as the Armenians suffered persecution in Turkey, in the 1880s, the Jewish communities of Russia became victims to anti-Semitic attacks more vicious and violent than in previous years, that drove thousands of Jews to seek refuge in safer lands. "Many of them," said the Reverend James Neil of the London Jews Society Mission in Palestine, "are thronging back to Palestine." James was vicar of Christ Church in Jerusalem, and as guest speaker at the Society's annual meeting in 1890, he spoke warmly of the Society's grants to Christian missions in the Holy Land. With 70,000 Jews already settled in Palestine, James said, as he called for more funds, "The hands of our faithful missionaries must be strengthened that the Gospel can be preached to the returning exiles."

As Jews flocked to Palestine, Dr H.H. Jessup warned about the emigration of Christians from the Near East. Despite opposition from the Ottoman Government, he said, thousands of Christians were leaving their homelands, for the United States, for Brazil, for Argentina, and for Australia. Poverty and oppression drove them, he said, and the urge to find opportunities for their children, peace for themselves, and the right to think and act as they chose. In one ward of Chicago alone, he said, there were 500 Syrian Christians, whose books and texts in Arabic were printed and shipped from the Mission Press in Beirut and whose Sunday School teachers were formerly missionaries in Syria. Many of Turkey's Armenians joined the exodus of Christians. "Taxation is reducing previously wealthy people to beggary," wrote American missionary, Mrs Flora Barton, and although the Ottoman government makes it hard for Armenians to obtain passports, "any that can leave go, mostly to America".

Armenians who lacked the means to go to America or to anywhere outside Turkey, faced an uncertain future. In the European Balkans, subject nations were becoming more vociferous in demanding freedom from Ottoman rule, underground revolutionary groups waged campaigns of violence and nationalist speakers encouraged the people to call for liberty. As the Sultan's vast spy network became increasingly watchful, increasingly inclined to see threats, the Christian Armenians were seen as more unreliable than in previous years, more subversive, and co-conspirators perhaps with their fellow Christians in the Balkans.

William Essery looks forward

It was in the situation of growing crisis for the Christian people of the Bible lands, that the Society advertised for a new secretary to replace the ageing and infirm Mr Brown. The successful candidate was the Reverend William A. Essery, an eager and forward-thinking clergyman who was resolved, he said, to increase the Society's fortunes and carry it forward towards a new century.

His first step, said William, as he took up his new post, was to change the Society's name. Turkish Missions seemed rather out of date, he thought, and was not a name to attract new supporters who had little idea or interest in the motivations of the men of 1854. And besides, William told readers of the *Star*, he foresaw a coming battle, not between Christians of differing sects and denominations, but against Islam, and the victory of that battle would be won when the Bible, "with all its hallowed power, was restored to those very Bible lands whence it had come to us". The great weapon in the coming fight, he said, would be the power of Evangelical truth! "Is that not an aim to fire the imagination, and to kindle a flame in the heart of every loyal disciple of Jesus?" he asked.

In order to highlight the Society's new focus, in 1893 the Turkish Missions Aid Society became the Bible Lands Missions Aid Society, and in the same year, William's modern ideas refashioned the *Star in the East*. "Crisp Notes" replaced long theological editorials, and framed blocks and a combination of typefaces replaced pages of tiny print. Photographs appeared too. One of the first was of William himself, a pleasant, comfortable-looking man, with a round plump face, a gold watchchain, and a high Victorian black frock coat.

William had modern ideas about marketing too. Free copies of the *Star* were sent for one year to selected London clergymen, and a follow-up letter or visit from William encouraged them to add the Society to the list of organisations supported by their congregations. A series of advertisements appeared in *The Christian*, one of Britain's most popular religious newspapers. And 5,000 information sheets and contribution forms, at the rate of 400 a month, were sent to carefully selected potential new subscribers.

William's advanced methods were rewarded and donations doubled during his first year in office, hundreds of new supporters were registered, and several overseas missions, to their great delight, received twice their usual grant. Bolstered by the success, William went on to plan a "new thing in our Society's history! A pictorial pamphlet!" Illustrations of cities where missions were supported would be featured, he said, as well as photographs of the mission schools, the churches, the preachers and the schoolchildren. Would readers help by distributing the pamphlet to their family and friends, William asked eagerly in the *Star*. Yes, they would, and thousands of pamphlets were sent out at the end of 1894. "Shall we form a prayer circle?" William asked readers too. "Shall it soon include all our subscribers?"

Chapter 4

Massacre
The 1890s

"The smoke from rifles, and from houses burning in the Armenian districts, surrounded the town. On all sides cries began to be heard; one was crying, 'Oh! My brother,' another, 'Oh! My father.' Many fell in our sight like partridges," said the letter from an anonymous missionary at Marash. From Aintab, came another, dated 23 November 1895, "We have suffered a baptism of fire and now we sit in grief among ruins."

William Essery was horrified. He had never imagined, when he became Secretary of the Society, that he would be confronted with atrocities on the scale the letters described. He knew, of course, that the Armenians of Turkey suffered cruel and unjust treatment. He knew, that as Christians they were regarded as inferior to Muslims and had no redress in the Ottoman courts. And he also knew, and this distressed him most of all, that Kurdish tribesmen regarded it as sport, to steal and use Armenian girls for their own brutal pleasure. There had been an account in the *Star* in 1891 that had particularly upset him. The report, from Erzroum, had described how an Armenian bride dragged from her wedding procession was saved only by the intervention of her brothers and husband-to-be who were almost killed in the process.

But the reports that arrived at Adam Street in 1895 spoke of something worse than the traditional violence. They spoke of the wholesale murder of Armenian communities.

Angry young men

Most Western eyewitnesses in Turkey agreed with the estimate of Mr Chambers, author of "Trouble in Erzroum" in 1888. They saw little to suggest that the Armenian population was a threat to the Ottoman Empire. But, as the nineteenth century drew towards its close, there were some voices, even among the traditionally passive Armenians, that were calling for justice and for liberty. They belonged to impatient young men in two Armenian revolutionary organisations, the Dashnaks and the Hunchaks.

In 1894, after Sultan Abdul Hamid formed the *Hamidiye*, armed Kurdish regiments that were encouraged to attack Armenian villages, the Hunchaks attempted to instigate an uprising at Sasun in Turkish Armenia. It was put down by the Ottoman Army with enormous brutality. An international outcry followed and the Ottoman Government promised reforms. But the hostile reaction from world opinion, and a violent demonstration in Constantinople organised by the Hunchaks, opened a floodgate of violence. All across the country, but especially in eastern Anatolia and Armenia, Turks and Kurds turned on their Armenian neighbours in an orgy of killing. Western eyewitnesses to the events were quite certain that the Ottoman authorities, from the Sultan to lowly army officers, were implicated in the atrocities.

"No-one can imagine the extent and the degree of the desolation wrought all about us," wrote an American missionary at Harpoot to William Essery, "even we ourselves cannot take it in. It is too vast for the human mind to comprehend."

A tide of destruction

William wondered how he should go forward. Already the Society's supporters, alerted by reports in their daily newspapers, were contacting him, anxious for information about the Armenian communities they supported in Turkey. Were the reports true, they asked, had murder on such a scale really taken place? Was it possible that the communities who had featured for so many years in the *Star*, whose best men had spoken at meetings in Britain, and whose churches and schools were built with willing donations from British churches, may have all disappeared in a tide of destruction?

William knew it was true and he wanted to convey the urgency and the horror. He wanted his readers to feel as he did, as if they too had been personally violated.

"Telegrams are flashed," wrote William, spelling out how the terrible news was communicated to the outside world, "there is panic in the city, more victims, more victims are dead!" Then, under the heading, Sorrowful Asia Minor, he highlighted the names of massacre locations in bold, black capitals. **TREBIZOND, MARSOVAN, ERZROUM, BITLIS, HARPOOT, AINTAB, MARASH, CESAREA, GEMERAK.** All of them cities that had witnessed revival and outpourings of the Spirit only a few years earlier but were now filled with anguish.

In the *Star* of January 1896, William included a Special Supplement, headed Armenian Massacre Relief. He spared no sensibilities and readers were brought face to face with the ugly realities of massacres described by American missionaries, the horrified eyewitnesses to events in Turkey. "Murder, plunder, arson; murder, plunder, arson," began a letter from Trebizond, and similar expressions of dismay were echoed in nearly every other account.

"Thousands of soldiers came," wrote a missionary from Marash, "they were killing the Christians they met, pillaging the shops and committing all kinds of wickedness." From Aintab, once a city of family altars and streets alive with hymns, came reports of a different kind of music. "What we heard," said the missionary writer, "was the indescribable roar of the mob, pierced by the sharp report of pistols and guns, with now and then shrieks of agony or fear and shouts of defiance and command, and over all, and most horrible of all, the loud shrill *Zullghat*, the wedding cry, raised by Turkish women crowded on their roofs and cheering on their men to the attack."

Many battles took place in the streets, as Armenians, forbidden by law to carry weapons, attempted to defend themselves with kitchen knives, hammers, and home-made swords. For long hours, sometimes for days, some Armenian communities sheltered behind the massive wooden gates that protected their streets. But when continual battering finally shook the gates loose, and the endless bombardment of flaming brands set Armenian districts ablaze, then the defenders fell beneath the fury of the mobs that streamed into their streets and into their homes. Houses were looted of all possessions. Men were killed outright and nearly every woman was repeatedly raped.

Martyred!

For some Armenians death did not come quickly. Armenian Christianity and the Armenian Churches, Gregorian, Protestant and Catholic, were singled out for special treatment. "If you embrace Islam," priests and teachers were told, as they were dragged from crowds and stood before their terrified students and congregations, "then your life will be spared." Many did embrace Islam. The thought of the cruel death that waited for those who refused, and the loss of beloved wives and children, was too much, and to their bitter shame they renounced their faith. Those who refused to convert were tortured before they were killed. Some were given no option.

At Kutterbul, just across the Tigris from Diarbekir, the Armenian populations of three villages took refuge with all their household goods in an old stone church. After bullets fired through the windows failed to dislodge the crowd, the attackers shot flaming brands through the broken roof and poured kerosene on the blaze. A hail of bullets met the panic-stricken people who finally smashed their way out. Jurjis Khudhersa Anteshlian was among those who escaped the burning church. He was well known in the whole region as a Protestant evangelist who travelled all over the Near East, he was highly respected in the Armenian community, and he was just the sort of victim the Turkish mob were hungering for. After they clubbed Jurjis to the ground and beat him and kicked him, one of his tormentors stuffed pages from a Bible into the evangelist's bloody mouth and called on him to preach. Tiring of that sport eventually, the mob burned Jurjis alive.

At Marash, Dr Avedis, an old pupil of Cyrus Hamlin, was burned alive too, in his own house together with his wife and eldest son. Elsewhere in the same city, the wife of an Armenian teacher at the Mission Academy was forced to watch as her husband was flayed alive and then cut into pieces. "Thousands of houses were robbed of every fragment," wrote a missionary from Marash, "and nothing but starvation and cold is before an uncounted number of bereaved and stricken families. While I am writing I hear the groans of the widows and starving men who throng our door. The devastation is indescribable."

Turkish sins: Armenian sorrows

William Essery did his best to describe the indescribable. And in doing so he changed the way the *Star* reported its news and the way its readers responded. The use of bold, black capitals to highlight the worst massacre sites meant the names of those cities and their horrific events lodged in the imagination. The Special Supplements, headed Armenian Massacre Relief, that contained eyewitness accounts of atrocities, had a reality that was hard to avoid.

The list that appeared on the back of the *Star*, dated April 1896, lodged in readers' imaginations too. It put the Armenian tragedy into stark, simple language, reduced it to bare bones, and in doing so was a more powerful statement of human barbarity and its consequences than any amount of descriptive paragraphs. And, it marked the end of William Essery's previously rather flowery language, sentences that seemed more designed to cater for delicate sensibilities than to confront painful realities. In January 1896, he had described Turkish cities as surprised and troubled, lifting up their voices, and that massacre held a feast in their streets. "Rumour publishes it," he said. By April, as rumour became the terrible reality that 300,000 Armenians had been murdered, William listed statistics. Turkish Sins: Armenian Sorrows, said his headline on the April back cover, above a record of violence in Harpoot. Killings, rapes, miscarriages, suicides, martyrdoms and forced conversions were precisely detailed together with the amount of property destroyed, the churches burned, and the thousands of people desperate for relief.

It was impossible for any reader of the *Star* to be mistaken about the events in Turkey and not to be painfully aware that they were called upon to help. The facts spoke for themselves.

William himself was a changed man. His kind heart grew increasingly resolute and his gentle manner more determined as he tried to make sure that no one who read the *Star* should forget who was responsible for the carnage in Turkey. He also wanted to make sure that the Armenian survivors could always count on the Bible Lands Missions Aid Society for help.

Armenian massacre relief

To ensure that help was forthcoming, William opened the Society's Armenian Massacre Relief Appeal and a specialist advertising agent was engaged to advise on maximum impact and maximum response. William personally wrote 4,000 appeal letters and sent each one with a reprint of the *Star*'s Special Massacre Supplement. Newspaper appeals, signed by the Society's Honorary Treasurer, Lord Kinnaird, the second Lord Kinnaird to hold the post, appeared in the Christian press. Armenian pastors, accompanied by William and members of the Society's managing committee, spoke at packed public meetings all over the country. From a snow-covered Scotland, "despite the boisterous weather", William and Pastor Yardumian reported full churches, drawing rooms and public halls, and articles in all the Scottish morning papers. "Everywhere," said William, "the story of Armenia's sorrows touched the heart."

The appeal reached a wider audience in 1897 after *The Times* carried reports of the Society's Annual Meeting, where Mrs Isabella Bishop, "the greatest English lady traveller of the day", was the keynote speaker. Isabella had been travelling in Turkey during the massacre months, accompanied by a Turkish Army escort. She described to the horrified London audience how she watched helplessly as Armenian flocks were stolen by Kurdish tribesmen while her indifferent escort stood by. On the plain of Moosh, Isabella said, she had seen 60 Christian men with their arms tied behind them, their scanty clothing stiffened with blood from wounds made by bayonets... "for no other reason than that they were Christian and that false charges had been made against them". Isabella went on to describe her stay at a tiny, isolated mountain village where the people had shown her their precious icons of Christ and told her, "We do not know much, but we love the Lord Jesus well enough to die for him." There was an Armenian bishop in that village, Isabella told her audience, who had been tortured and left for dead at a desolate roadside after refusing to deny his Christian faith. "How many of us would do the same?" asked Isabella.

Britain was shocked by the massacres; the death toll far exceeded the Bulgarian Atrocities 20 years earlier and people were troubled to think, that at the end of the nineteenth century, whose watchword was civilisation and progress, that just beyond the edges of Europe, hundreds of thousands of people could be slaughtered in their own land. By the end of 1897 over £10,000 had been donated to the Society's Relief Fund and the flood of bank notes and cheques showed no signs of diminishing. Churches and Sunday Schools made regular collections and the Society's supporters raised money at sales of work and afternoon teas. Contributions came from people of all walks of life and from all over the world, from New Zealand and Australia, from India, Palestine, and across Europe. In one or two cases, William learned that extracts from the *Star* had appeared in foreign newspapers after editors had taken it upon themselves to raise money for Armenia. "The individual donations commence with half-a-dozen lowly penny notes bearing the royal image," William told his readers, describing one day's post, "ascending by divers magnitudes to 50 guineas, and once reaching £100; they include a cameo brooch, once a pleasant ornament of the giver in far-back days of youth and means; and also a young lady's golden chain bearing a label of just one word, 'Armenia'."

The wards of Christendom

Before the massacres, the Armenians of Turkey had little need of orphanages. Their extended families were large, their communities were close-knit, and churches, Gregorian and Protestant, ensured that widows and orphans were cared for. Broussa and a few similar institutions answered isolated pockets of need. After the massacres the situation was desperately changed.

With 300,000 Armenians dead, mostly adult males, all the existing institutions were overwhelmed. Estimates from the Red Cross suggested 50,000 children whose fathers had been murdered and 15,000 more with no relative left at all. When the Ottoman Government insisted that no orphan could leave Turkey, and revealed its plan to convert them and bring them up as Muslim men and women, the American missionaries were horrified. It would be a terrible thing, they said, if the children of parents massacred for their Christian faith, were themselves to be denied its saving grace.

The missionaries named the orphans "the wards of Christendom" and if the children could not be sheltered in

Christian countries, they said, then Christendom must provide shelters for them in Turkey. Desperately concerned for the children's welfare himself, William became an enthusiastic supporter of the solution proposed and under the heading, A New Open Door in Asia Minor, he encouraged readers of the *Star* to support it too. "The martyrs' orphans have touched the conscience of the Protestant world," he said, "and these children will not be abandoned by us but will be brought up in new orphanages, converted mission schools, where they will be educated, taught handicrafts, and led to become disciples of Jesus Christ."

The work was already underway, William told readers, "quietly, without trumpet blowing, and in dependence on our own Lord alone". The Americans were leading the work, with orphanages already opened at Van, Oorfa, Malatia and Marash, while German and Swiss Protestants were quickly establishing foundations too. There will be difficulties, said William, but none that cannot be overcome. The total cost, he said, about £100,000 each year, nearly six million pounds or nine million dollars today, is less than the Christian nations pay for one ironclad battleship! "Shall we go forward at once into this new open door?" William asked.

The Society's supporters responded enthusiastically and the Massacre Orphans Fund joined the Massacre Relief Fund. For their part, the missionaries, who were now devoted to the education and well-being of the orphans, supplied a steady stream of news to their foreign supporters. At first it was full of pain. Stories were told of destitute children arriving at the new orphanages, filthy and starving after wandering the countryside alone and scavenging from rubbish heaps. Some children, often no more than nine or ten years old, had struggled to keep the remnants of their families together, caring for little brothers and sisters who longed for their parents.

The Turks have killed my father

All the children were traumatised. They had witnessed brutal scenes of butchery and rape and many had seen their own parents and other relatives killed. Wacharshag and his brother Mushesh had watched as the corpses of their murdered grandfather, cousin and uncle were stuffed by their killers into a well.

Little Sourpouhie's father was beheaded and cut to pieces. "The Turks have killed my father," was all some children could say. Some arrived at the orphanages injured and sick, while others had escaped or been rescued from enforced labour in Turkish homes. Many suffered nightmares and woke throughout the night in paroxysms of fear, believing that Kurdish tribesmen were hammering at the doors. While some children were difficult to control, others were withdrawn. Some repeated the violence they had seen, some spent all day in silence. Our work requires much love and patience, said the missionaries, and although they loved to describe newly arrived children happy to be bathed, fed and dressed in clean clothes, they also confessed that some of their charges were "scarred or maimed for life". Some orphanages reported children whose lives could not be saved, despite devoted medical care, whose wounds, hunger and torment had sapped the strength needed to fight injury and disease.

At Broussa, where for a twelve-month period during 1895 and 96 the terror of massacre was so great that the orphans did not dare to go out for exercise and air, Gregory doubled the number of orphans. "The Lord will provide," he said. Among his new inmates were the very distressed children of Protestant pastors who had been martyred. The surviving children of Pastor Avedis, Cyrus Hamlin's old pupil, who had been burned at Marash, were sheltered at Broussa, together with the orphans of Pastor Hagop who once studied with Gregory at the Mission College in Basle.

The distant ones in Great Britain

Almost since its beginning the Society had operated various sponsorship programmes, for trainee teachers at the British Syrian Schools and for children at Broussa, but after the massacres of 1895, William Essery made the schemes a regular part of the Society's work. It was one more addition to his resolution that the orphans of Armenia would have a constant friend in the Bible Lands Missions Aid Society.

William loved children dearly, although he had none of his own, and it became one of the most pleasurable aspects of his role as Secretary to receive the bundles of children's letters, the school reports and photographs, that came from the Armenian orphanages, and to pass them on to the generous-hearted people in

Britain whose regular donations of "£5 and multiples thereof", supported the orphans. It gave the Society a human face, he felt, rather as if it were one large family where uncles and aunts in Britain waited eagerly for letters from adopted children in Turkey. William liked to imagine those children, safe in the warm and comfortable surroundings the Society helped to provide for them. He liked to picture them, pencils in hand, perhaps asking for a word or a phrase from their American and European carers, before bending their heads once more to the pleasant task of imagining their own benefactors far away in Britain. "We the children of the orphanage," wrote a little boy in Van in 1897, "entreat that you accept the appreciative gratitude of us all. We send it with our salutations, on paper wings, across the mountains and beyond the seas to our many friends, the distant ones in Great Britain."

The distant ones in Great Britain liked to read tales from the orphanages. They wanted to know all about the children they helped to support, and as time passed and the horror retreated a little, the stories in the *Star* became happier. In 1897, under the heading Christmas with the Orphans at Van, the Society's supporters, who had made the festive celebration possible, were able to share in a small way the children's pleasure. On Orthodox Christmas Eve, they read, the Van schoolroom was decorated with bunting and pictures, and a large, lighted Christmas tree took centre stage. Brightly coloured pocket-handkerchiefs, tied and filled with nuts and raisins, were strung on ropes around a room where the orphans, in fancy-dress, entertained their teachers. One teacher described the Armenian folk dances and songs where the children "joined hands and moved slowly around in a circle, to weird, plaintive music, in the sad minor key which ages of oppression have made the natural expression of even their most joyous feelings".

Other stories described how well many children eventually responded to their new lives and how the missionaries were careful to respect the traditions of the Gregorian church, "the faith of the orphans' fathers", and the faith their fathers had died for. Cyrus Hamlin's daughter, Mrs Clara Lee, working at the Marash Orphanage that had five houses and 185 children in the city, told William, "These orphans have become so dear to me but for fear of wearying you, I should go on like a fond mother and describe each one." Care, education, training and love, were gradually transforming children who had arrived "in filth and misery" into bright-faced, healthy youngsters who were eager for life. We aim for the girls to be good needlewomen, Clara said, while all the boys over ten years of age go daily to the city's most reliable craftsmen to learn trades. "How we pray they will grow up to be a blessing and a light to their nation," she said.

A dangerous and uneasy land

While Clara and her colleagues planned for the future of the orphans and hoped there would be no repetition of the massacres, the adult survivors of 1895 were desperate for relief. Many of them were utterly destitute. Where homes were not destroyed by fire, some had been stolen in their entirety, even rafters and window frames looted and carried away. Craftsmen had been robbed of tools and farmers of stock. Thousands of widows were entirely without support.

The Society entrusted its Massacre Relief Fund to the American missionaries it had supported for so many years. "They have the best sources of knowledge," said William, "and use their best judgement in utilising the funds entrusted to them." However, even the Americans, with their years of experience, found it necessary to be cautious. Turkey had become a dangerous and uneasy land, spies were everywhere, and as the outside world poured criticism on the Ottoman Government, and as unrest continued to grow among the subject nations, hostility and retribution towards foreigners was never far away. "We must withhold names," said William, when he began publishing reports of relief distribution, "for fear of reprisals."

The absence of names in the reports, of missionaries and the towns where they worked, emphasised the precarious situation in Turkey and brought the danger to life.

"_____ has suffered so terribly, that we thought best to put 21£Turkish to that village," said one report. "To the _____ and _____ Pastors who lost everything we voted 5£T." said another. Other reports described payments made to widows. "Three widows, all church members, from one family in _____ whose husbands were all killed, their houses looted and burned." And "_____ , a massacre widow whose husband was a Christian physician, and her sister (now insane)."

Some of the unnamed missionaries described the conditions in which the destitute people lived. "It is a wintry day," wrote one at _____, "and the snow is falling, and one would wish to stay indoors; but this is the very weather to drive them to us for a comforter to cover them at night, or for a few pence of money with which to buy a pan of coal, or a loaf of bread." As well as distributing money and supplies, some missionaries transformed their own homes into cottage industries employing local people to manufacture the goods that were so desperately needed. "Our house," wrote one, "is now turned into a coverlet or quilt factory. Four persons are constantly beating up cotton, two are cutting out covers and sewing up on two machines, and a dozen or so women and girls are putting together and quilting, while dozens of city people are waiting for the finished articles."

Thanks to William Essery

As the missionaries and the Armenian survivors worked to restore broken lives and shattered communities, old divisions became less bitter and were sometimes overlooked altogether. The *Star* reported Protestant and Gregorian Armenians joining together for Christian work and worship. Under one heading "Gregorians and Protestants Unite", readers learned that a Gregorian boys' school in Trebizond was to become a joint venture with Protestants and that a Union Sunday School was also planned. A missionary at Oorfa wrote, "our most pleasant relations with the Gregs. [sic] continue", and said the Armenian Bishop had arranged that water from his aqueduct should water the Protestant churchyard. Another town planned a joint kindergarten. In Aintab, joint services proved so popular that four were held each week. It was a pattern repeated throughout the Armenian communities and most Christians rejoiced to see it. In 1897, the Gregorian Archbishop Migerditch of Aintab, on a visit to London, called at Adam Street to thank William Essery personally for the Society's aid and support.

Most of that aid and support had been raised, maintained and directed, almost single-handed, except for the occasional help of the elderly Reverend J.B. French, by William Essery. "If you only knew the half of what Mr Essery has done!" Lord Kinnaird told the audience at the Annual Meeting of 1898. It was to the secretary's credit, he said, that news of the massacres, the care and instruction of massacre orphans, and all the Society's wide-ranging medical, educational and evangelistic work, was kept before the public. Sometimes, said His Lordship, it was Mr Essery alone, who had been the office contingent when the Society's prayer circle that William had created in 1893, came together at midday each Monday to lift the Armenian people to the Lord. "And also alone, Mr Essery prayed for the whole of the Bible lands," said Lord Kinnaird.

Lord Kinnaird also told the audience about the Essery Cabinet Shop at the Boys' High School at Sivas. It all began, he said, after the unruly behaviour of little Armenag Moomjian led to his exclusion from school, and the Sivas Principal, Mr Perry, who felt sorry for the little charity pupil, offered Armenag an opportunity to learn cabinet work in the school's vocational training centre. Undersized and underfed, poor Armenag could not manage the plane and saw but he wove chair backs so well that he was soon teaching the skill to other boys. "Eight months of wholesome toil made a man of the little fellow," said Lord Kinnaird, who went on to say that following Armenag's success, Mr Essery personally donated tools and materials for other boys with no interest in book learning to be trained in the cabinet shop during school lunch breaks. "By all accounts," his Lordship said, "the Essery Shop is like a beehive during the noon hour."

William himself, who disliked any publicity about his personal donations, was nevertheless extremely proud of advances made under his leadership and as a forward-thinking man he wanted the Society to enter the twentieth century as a modern and up-to-date organisation, utilising all the latest methods to draw the attention of the British public to the needs of the Bible lands. At the end of 1899, under William's direction, the *Star* became a "fully illustrated periodical", and the first of the new series contained a portrait photograph of Gregory Baghdassarian, another of the Armenian pastor, Garbet Sarkisyan, in his national costume, pictures of the orphans at Van and a photograph of their orphanage grounds where 15,000 Armenians had sheltered during the massacres. More general pictures that gave additional insights into life in the Near East included Arab gleaners "amid the date gardens of Arabia", a group of Greek boys, and the mud-brick home of a Palestine missionary.

Several thousand copies of the *Star* were printed and posted each quarter, and William acknowledged their immense value to the Society and how they passed from hand to hand, in Britain, throughout the British Empire, and in America and Europe. But he also knew that keeping supporters and attracting new ones required a sustained effort and new ideas. By 1899 the Society was supporting over 50 different missions in the Near East, all of them requiring funds not only to maintain the existing work but also to expand it, and just as he had modernised the *Star*, William wanted to modernise other areas of the Society's publicity and fund-raising programmes. At the end of 1899, with the full agreement of Lord Kinnaird, he advertised in the Christian press for an additional member of staff. The new man, the advertisement said, must be familiar with modern technology, he must know how to use a magic lantern to its best advantage, and he should also be able to speak at public meetings in a manner to "touch the heart and kindle a burning enthusiasm". The successful candidate, the Society's new Deputation Secretary and William Essery's assistant, was a young clergyman and missionary, the Reverend Samuel William Gentle-Cackett.

Chapter 5

William's Grand Tour
Into the Twentieth Century

"Fellow labourers with us for Christ's work in Bible lands," said William Essery in January 1901 to readers of the *Star*, "as we pass beneath the majestic archway of the twentieth century, we greet you all with hearty hope for the future."

What does it hold for us, he asked, this twentieth century? The old nineteenth, he said, carried away with it the record of the greatest missionary successes of all the Christian centuries. What wonders, mysteries, hopes and demands now lay ahead?

William was about to see some of the hopes and demands for himself. Since becoming secretary in 1892 he had worked hard to transform the Society into an up-to-date organisation and the *Star* into a modern journal and he had been very successful. But success had taken a toll, and there were times, he admitted to the missionaries who passed through Adam Street, when there were so many requests for aid he could hardly bear to make a decision. Sometimes he could not sleep at nights for thinking about the Armenian orphans and who would care for them if the Society lost its supporters. And for the first time since becoming secretary, he was unable to write his usual letters. Ever since 1893, William had personally acknowledged every donation of half-a-crown and upwards, a grand total of over 12,000 letters, but now, "his right hand had lost its cunning", he said, and young Samuel had taken on the task instead.

Lord Kinnaird had raised the matter with the Society's managing committee. Mr Essery was clearly unwell, he told them, and he recommended a long sea-voyage and tour of the mission stations to restore their secretary to perfect health.

William had needed little urging. For eight years he had worked almost without a break, devoting himself to Christian missions in the Bible lands, and now, in the opening months of the new century, he was about to see them for himself. He packed several fresh notebooks and his new Kodak camera and prepared to record his journey for the *Star*.

Off to Bible lands

William left England on 4 January 1901 on board the Orient liner, *Oruba*, bound for New Zealand. "At exactly one o'clock," William recorded later in his journal, "we began to lose sight of our friends bidding us farewell from the Tilbury wharf as our great steamer headed slowly out into the Thames." Then, later that day, he said, in the late afternoon, as the *Oruba* slid through the darkening waters of the English Channel, many passengers were drawn to her decks to gaze silently at the shimmering radiance cast by a full moon over a perfectly calm sea.

Two days later, the perfectly calm sea became a turbulent ocean and the *Oruba* was tossed to and fro by "frisky waters" in the Bay of Biscay, "the result being that one-half of the masculine passengers and nine-tenths of the feminine did not come to breakfast". By eventide, though, said William, the sea had become calm and two young India bound CMS missionaries, including Mr Phillips, his room-mate for the journey, arranged for Evensong. As he gave the sermon, based on Acts 9:6, William reflected to himself on the mood of his audience. It was large and quietly attentive, he noted, and he guessed that most of the *Oruba*'s passengers, on the first Sabbath evening of the new year and the twentieth century, felt as solemn and expectant as he felt himself.

William liked people, he liked to talk to them and study them, and the *Oruba*, filled with so many classes, and so many professions and enterprises, was an ideal environment for his curiosity. "Like the Jews and the Samaritans of our Lord's time," said William, "the First Saloon, Second Saloon, and Steerage have no dealings with one another," but fortunately, in the "Second Village", where he himself was lodged, the enormous variety of folk promised some fascinating encounters. Many of his fellow passengers were clergymen, said William, "travelling to take up churches and parishes in sparse regions of the British Empire", while others were missionaries "off to heathen lands for the Gospel's sake". From Mr Phillips and the other India men,

William learned how the Gospel was preached to the Muslims and Hindus of the sub-continent, while Reverend Mr Abel, heading back to New Guinea, told him all about the dangers of mission life in the jungles of the South Seas.

Well-to-do colonists returning from home visits to Scotland explained how life was organised on tea and rubber plantations, and "khaki volunteers who have fought for Queen and country in South Africa", complained, sometimes humorously, sometimes bitterly, about the intransigence of the Boers. "Troupes of amusement professionals heading for the Antipodes to cheer up all and sundry", described the pleasures and frustrations of their itinerant lifestyle, and "ladies who are to be married when they arrive in New Zealand" confided their hopes for future contentment. William also found himself intrigued by the daily sight of four Sisters of Mercy "mantled in flowing black garb set off by enormous starched white collars", and delighted by the hordes of children, "whose pranks and voices afford no small commotion and merriment among us".

Vesuvius, dominating the Naples skyline on a cold and sombre morning, brought back poignant memories for William of an earlier visit to the city with a much-loved and long-dead friend, and for a while he felt weighed down with sadness. It was a sadness that changed rapidly to consternation when the *Oruba* headed into open seas south of Sicily, and "our gigantic liner plunged and rolled in a frightful manner through a night of pitch darkness, shrieking winds and mountainous waves". Despite trying his best to concentrate on the fortitude of Saint Paul when the Apostle to the Gentiles passed over the same unpredictable waters, William confessed to Mr Phillips that he was not sorry to leave the *Oruba*, "still rolling from side to side", as she finally made her way to safe anchorage at Port Said. A little unsteady, and weary after his troubled and sleepless night, William set off alone from the seaport on a cold journey by railway over a flat desert landscape illuminated by bright winter sunshine, until he was finally met at the Cairo railway station by Reverend Dr Ewing who escorted him to the warmth and comfort of the city's American mission.

An ever moving, ever changing pattern

William loved Cairo. He loved the busy clatter of two horse carriages and rattling tramcars, and the complex interweaving of colour and costume that transformed the city's crowds into an ever moving, ever changing pattern. He loved to watch the loaded camels and donkeys, threading their careful way through narrow streets barbed by dazzling sunlight and dense shadow where merchants of many races hawked their wares. And his heart warmed at the sight of tall British soldiers of the occupying army, red-faced from the sun, in khaki tunics and kilts, who haggled for souvenirs in the bazaars. "I stood and watched the strange spectacle as in a dream," he wrote.

There was more colour and spectacle waiting for William in the everyday missionary life of Egypt. At Saturday evening Bible class he addressed 25 earnest young men, each wearing an identical scarlet felt tarboosh, on the "personal steps of faith that lead to salvation", while among girls at the American Mission Sunday School, he saw "heads uncovered, heads swathed in white and black mantles, and even heads beneath straw hats topped by enormous piles of artificial flowers and ribbons". At Sunday morning service he talked with Mrs Lewis, "a lady renowned for manuscript discoveries in Sinai and Egypt", and in the evening, at a Soldiers' Farewell at the Gordon Hall, he took tea with 250 Seaforth Highlanders bound for South Africa. As he wrote up his journal later that night, William noted a sad rumour that had circulated all day through Cairo, "that our beloved Queen has been stricken with paralysis".

Dr Frank Harpur, recently returned from Sudan, took William on a tour of Cairo's new CMS hospital, with its modern operating chambers, its adult wards and clinic rooms, and finally to "a lovely ward for children, the only one such in Egypt". It was deeply interesting, said William, to see how science and Christian love combined were nursing the sufferers back to life. Another of William's cherished memories of Cairo was his "first living illustration of hareem work amongst women", when Miss Thomson of the American mission led him through a "low quarter of the city wherein the streets are one half in ruins, dirty and dismal", to a narrow, upstairs room, barely furnished with a divan and several chairs. Twelve quiet women were waiting there to welcome him, all dressed in their best clothes for the occasion, and with all their children gathered around them to greet the foreign guest. As he joined their regular weekly meeting of prayer and praise and Bible study, William reflected on the wonderful diversity of the body of Christ, and how the churches of his own land and those of Egypt were joined together in holy unity.

Old and new wonders in Egypt

At Assiout, "where nearly all the missionaries of the city were gathered on the railway station platform to welcome me", William visited another of Egypt's new hospitals. Making his way through the Assiout wards, and marvelling once more at the potent healing power of modern science and Christian compassion, William stopped to gaze at a scene that greeted him in the men's surgical ward. It was a picture of wonderful and telling simplicity, he thought. In an airy whitewashed chamber, dappled with sunlight, the patients who lay in two rows of neat white beds were devoting all their attention to a blind Bible reader, his jet black body swathed in robes of brilliant white muslin, who sat in one corner of the ward. Sightless, the reader gazed calmly before him, while the fingers of one dark hand glided over the pages of a raised Arabic Gospel as he spoke the Parable of the Talents into the hushed air.

At Assiout College, said William, that had grown from Dr Hogg's little donkey stable school, "so strong is the hunger of young Egypt that nearly 900 sons and daughters are gathered here to be fed with intellectual and religious instruction". William spent as long as he could at the college, looking in on the classrooms, requesting information from teachers, and "in many cases speaking to scholars who could understand my mother tongue". It was a thrilling congregation of young life, he said, a wonder of modern Egypt and in need of enlargement in every way, more dormitories, more study rooms, more classrooms, more teachers, more funds, for the hundreds of young Egyptians "who thirsted for admission to this fountain of knowledge and truth". He promised to do what he could to ensure those funds were forthcoming.

The highlight of William's visit to Assiout was his attendance for several days at the second Annual Assembly of the Synod of the Nile. How moved he was, he said later, when that whole great assembly bowed its head in prayer, as, far away in England, Queen Victoria was laid to rest, and how proud he was to receive from the Synod its grateful thanks for the ongoing support of the Bible Lands Missions Aid Society. He would ensure the message was published in the *Star*, he promised. But, most moving of all, he thought, was to hear the representatives of Egypt's Protestant churches discussing their own missionary work in Central Africa. How the noble faces and strenuous eloquence of the Egyptian Christian leaders made him think of the early church, he said, how their unity and devotion, their faith and hope, and their commitment to prayer and missionary enterprise, made him think of the days when the Word had first gone out to the world from the lands of the Bible.

During a visit to Aswan, William's thoughts travelled even further back in time, to Pharaoh Amenhotep III, who in his own day had sought to control the Nile for the benefit of his people. "That truly royal work has devolved upon our fellow countrymen today," he said, as he described the gigantic engineering project where Sir John Aird and his team of British engineers were constructing the Nile's first modern dam. "A more novel or memorable walk I never had," said William, "first across the genuine sandy desert", and then on the massive reinforced wall "perforated with steel sluice-gates for regulating the outflow of the priceless treasure, which is the life of Egypt".

At Tanta on the Nile Delta William met Anna Watson and Caroline Lawrence, two female physicians who were the pioneers of an ambitious medical enterprise planned by the American Mission. Their meeting followed a hard-won tour of Tanta's famous mosque and Muslim college, where William feared the students bent over their *Qu'rans* resented his presence, and he was grateful to the two young Americans for raising his lowered spirits by sharing their vision for two and a half acres of bare land that would one day be home to a women's hospital. "What faith, what grace, what funds they need," said William, and encouraged by their enthusiasm he promised to open an appeal for them in the *Star* as soon as he reached home.

Galilee to Gaza

There was more grace and faith waiting for William in the Holy Land, but his time in Jerusalem, Nazareth, Hebron and Bethlehem was a round of activity and he found few quiet moments for long reflections at holy sites. The CMS and the London Jews Society, with missions from Galilee to Gaza, were keen that William should see as much of their work as possible, from the famous boys' boarding school in Jerusalem founded by Lord Shaftesbury's great hero, Bishop Samuel Gobat, to isolated village outposts. They also wanted him to see and to understand how the country seemed to be changing before their eyes, as Jewish immigrants from Russia and Eastern Europe arrived with plans to transform the ancient landscape of Palestine into modern agricultural communities and urban townships. "The missions to the Jews especially," said William, after attending an LJS service at Christ Church on Mount Zion, "must show the ancient people of God that Jesus is the Messiah, the only Saviour of the world."

After the bustle of Jerusalem, three quiet days in Jaffa gave William some time with an old friend, Miss Jane Arnott of Tabeetha School, an institution supported by the Society for nearly 50 years. Like many other visitors, William was intrigued by the famous Tabeetha visitors' book whose first entries dated from 1869 when Mr Thomas Cook, a dear friend of Miss Jane's, began making his name and his fortune by conveying western pilgrims to Christian missions in the Holy Land. Among the many well-known names, said William, he saw that of the Society's Honorary Treasurer, the Hon. A. Kinnaird, dated 1875, while "about twelve months later my own autograph appeared". William loved Tabeetha School, the airy new building, squarely built of stone and backed by fragrant orange groves, and the cheerful mix of Christian, Jewish and Muslim girls who thronged its spacious classrooms. In the evenings, he strolled with Miss Jane to the nearby seashore where they gazed northward along the sandy Mediterranean coastline and wondered about the future of Christian missions in the Holy Land.

William's last memory of Jaffa was a burning sirocco wind, bearing flying locusts, that poured into the city just as he resumed his northward voyage. Glad to escape the wind and the insects, he made the most of his time on "the calm, cool sea", by watching the passing coastline, a low sandy shore and cliffs, the cities of Haifa and Acre, and in the distance, the hot haze that loomed over "snow-crowned Hermon", until finally the steamer *Urano* delivered him to Beirut and a welcome from Mr and Mrs Hoskins of the American Mission. William had a long list of visits to make in Lebanon, to American and British work supported by the Society for many years, and just as in Egypt and the Holy Land, missionaries at every station waited eagerly to welcome him. As they described their work, recounting their successes and their hopes for the future, William continued filling his notebooks and snapping with his Kodak, eagerly anticipating the pleasure both would give to his friends in Britain and the readers of the *Star*.

The Bible and prayer, God and Jesus Christ

The Parable of the Talents, that he had heard in Arabic at Assiout, was one of William's favourite Gospel stories, and one he often used in his own sermons, but at the Sidon mission of Reverend Dr Ford, "an ardent, persevering enthusiast", William believed he saw the parable at work. Just like the workers in the Armenian orphanages, Dr Ford believed that for Christian workers to offer education without employment prospects was dishonest, that it cheated young people and cheated their nation, and at Sidon he had given 20 years of his life to building "a composite industrial, educational, evangelistic boarding institution", where students looked forward to a future based on security for themselves and service to others. "Every scholar must learn a trade," said William, and he described how the academic and religious classes were complemented by workshops for tailors, shoemakers, carpenters, furniture makers and masons, and by the hilly farm where scholars learned agriculture by raising produce for the Mission's other enterprises. What a joy it was, William thought, to see the example of Christian men like Dr Ford, who devoted themselves to the service of individuals and nations, drawing out their talents, encouraging and developing them, so a future based on spiritual and material prosperity could be shared by the nations of the world.

From Beirut William travelled by railway in the company of

Mr M. Kazun, a senior medical student at the Syrian Protestant College, "and a very pleasant Muslim", to Zahleh on Mount Lebanon, where he arrived just before Good Friday. Everything about the region and its Christian work impressed William enormously, and he wrote about it with great feeling. He described the mountainous beauty of the countryside and the lovely drives on zigzag roads with long views over "terraces of wheat, fig and mulberry, to the great blue sea on one side, and dark cedar groves on the other". The American Mission families, he said, worked in such harmony with the Lebanese Christian workers, while the students themselves were so attentive, so fond of their schools, their teachers, and their families, and so devoted to the "Bible and prayer, God and Jesus Christ".

William found more devotion to the Bible and prayer among the British women and their Lebanese colleagues who also laboured on Mount Lebanon. At Baakleen, the dispensary and cottage hospital of Miss Wordsworth Smith's medical mission served the surrounding Druze communities, while the Christian witness of Dr Ali, its chief physician, a courageous convert from Islam, made very clear his commitment to the healing powers of the Great Physician. Near Shemlan, William was led up a rugged track to an outpost of the British Syrian Schools where he met the impressive Miss Williams, "a bright sparkling lady of 80, a remarkable lonesome heroine serving Christ in such an outlandish village". And at Schwifat, he found another English heroine, Miss Louisa Proctor, "the primal force and ruling spirit" of an extensive network of schools among the Druze. After hearing "Miss P's unrivalled Scripture classes", William followed her onto the drill court, careful to record the picture with his Kodak, "where this extraordinary lady, under the burning sun without head covering, commanded the entire physical exercise class, keeping time by clapping her hands".

Dr Mary Pierson Eddy was an extraordinary American woman, the first female medical practitioner to receive an official licence to practice in the Ottoman Empire. Like Dr Ali, Dr Mary made her Christian faith quite clear, opening every daily clinic with hymns and a talk about Jesus. "Wonderful," commented one Arab male patient, "who would think a woman could preach like that?" Not many years before William's visit, Mary had suffered a long and painful illness and the loss of all her household and hospital possessions in a shipwreck, but by 1901, the call to begin work once more had led her to open a new dispensary, high in the hills above Junieh, with views of distant Beirut and the blue Mediterranean. The road outside her door was a well-used one, said Mary, and camel caravans, flocks and herds, and a thousand people, passed her surgery each day. Many of those travellers, Kurds, Armenians, Bedouin Arabs, priests and peasants, found their way into her waiting room, where her faithful Bible woman, Muallmy Leeza Taamy, comforted them with the Scriptures as they waited for the doctor.

Another of William's photographs taken in Lebanon, that appeared later in the *Star*, showed the Beirut Mission Press, where a staff of 50 produced Arabic Bibles for the American and British Bible Societies, sacred literature for evangelists and missionaries, and textbooks for Christian colleges and schools. As Mr Freyer, manager of the press, showed him the great workshops and press rooms, and the stores and vaults piled high with books waiting to be packed and sent to wherever people spoke Arabic, William reflected with pride on the Society's part in the great work and that funds from Britain were among those that sent God's word into the mountains and deserts of the Bible lands.

The Syrian Protestant College was another cause for pride. Situated on 35 acres of land overlooking the sea at Beirut, the site was covered with an assortment of "halls, classrooms, dormitories, museums, a library, an observatory, dwellings and grounds". All this, William reminded himself, had also been helped on its way by the Society, and Dr Bliss, president since 1866, recounted fond memories of his days in Britain, when he travelled with some of the Society's leading men and collected a total of £4,000 towards the foundation of the College.

"Such young, hopeful life"

The British Syrian Mission remembered the early days of the Society with gratitude too. *Jehovah-Jirah*, the Lord will Provide, was printed on all its literature, and Miss Thompson, the Superintendent, was happy to remind William how in 1860, the Turkish Missions Aid Society had been led to support the mission's founder, Fanny Bowen Thomson. There were 56 schools now, Miss Thompson told William, and three medical missions, while the Teacher Training Institution in Beirut, with eleven off-shoots, "is the great dynamo for working the spiritual machinery of the mission, carrying life, light and love into the darkness". William saw something of the entire British Syrian Mission work, including its famous school for the blind in Beirut, but his day spent among the trainee teachers, "the choicest daughters of Syria in their youthful prime", lingered fondly in his memory.

That day was also the last day of his Bible lands travels, and the British Syrian Mission laid on a celebration tea and invited William to preach to the assembled teachers and students. How lovely the girls looked in their pretty pink dresses, he thought, "a truly beautiful sight going and returning from the house of God", and how privileged he felt to share Communion with them and give the sermon on 1 Corinthians 3, St Paul's thoughts for Christian workers. He was greatly moved, he wrote later, "to address such a group of young, hopeful life".

Late that same day, teachers from the Mission escorted William to the French steamer, *Niger*, bound for London, and after he watched the Lebanon coastline sink slowly away, and as "the shades began to fall", he tried to describe in his journal what his journey had meant to him. How much there was to say, how rich and full the months had been, with so many cities visited, so many journeys undertaken, and so many fruitful meetings with workers and congregations, the good people of many races bound together by their faith in one Lord. How privileged he was to have a life brightened with so many wonderful memories, William wrote, "the medical clinics with the crowds of sick women and babes waiting for the doctor, the mothers' meetings where the women sat swathed in white veils, the schools, the Sunday schools, the solemn Sabbath services when God was so near, and all this labour being wrought out of love to our Lord and Saviour Jesus Christ".

William plans the 50th anniversary

"A right royal welcome home" waited for William at the Society's annual meeting at Exeter Hall, where he was persuaded to share some of his stories and photographs with the eager audience, although, said Lord Kinnaird, the traveller needs little persuasion to share his full story with us in the *Star in the East*. More of the story appeared in a new lantern lecture, "Old and New Wonders in Egypt", that William prepared for Samuel Gentle-Cackett. He also began to fulfil his promises to the mission workers, and in 1902, the *Star* opened a special appeal for Anna Watson and Caroline Lawrence at Tanta Hospital. William hoped it would speak directly to the hearts of Christian women in Britain, especially when they learned that women were among Tanta's physicians and that a team of trained Bible women were already recruited to work among sick women on the wards.

William spent a lot of time thinking after his return home about the many Muslims he had met during his tour, kindly and generous men and women most of them, but to his mind, lacking the inner grace of Christianity. How he longed for them to be welcomed into the Christian fold. We must pray, he told the Society's prayer circle, when it joined the week of prayer for Islamic lands called by the Evangelical Alliance in 1902, "for Muslim hearts to hear the claims of Jesus". Also in 1902, William began making plans for the Society's 50th anniversary, and among his own contributions, he told Lord Kinnaird, would be a book. His tour among the missions had inspired him to write a history of the Society's work, 25 chapters were already completed and he hoped the final manuscript would give a real insight into Christian work in the lands of the Bible.

As William drew up the anniversary plans and continued with his book, news arrived from the American mission stations in the Balkans of terrible events in Macedonia. Revolutionary groups, engaged in a war for national independence, said the reports, had begun to fight each other, and as more fighters unearthed hidden weapons and joined the bloodletting, villages considered to be on the "wrong side", were being subjected to brutal retaliation. Women as usual, are the chief sufferers, said a local missionary, but William could not bring himself to print details of the atrocities committed against them. They are, he said, "indescribable abominations".

"They tell of fearful things"

While Macedonian anarchist groups subjected their fellow citizens to a series of bomb attacks, the Ottoman Army, in attempts to destroy the rebels and their strongholds, deployed artillery

THE STAR IN THE EAST.

A QUARTERLY RECORD

Of the progress of Christian Missions within the Turkish
Empire, and also in Persia and Greece.

No. 3   JULY,   1883.

WHEN·THEY·SAW·THE·STAR : THEY·
REJOICED·WITH·EXCEEDING·GREAT·JOY

"*Look on the fields.*"—John iv. 35.
"*Toward the sun rising.*"—Joshua xiii. 5.
"*We have seen His Star in the East, and are come to worship Him.*"
—Matt. ii. 2.

PUBLISHED BY THE

TURKISH MISSIONS' AID SOCIETY,

7, ADAM STREET, STRAND, LONDON, W.C.

ABRAHAM KINGDON & Co., Printers, 52, Moorfields, Moorgate, E C.

The Star in the East, quarterly magazine of the Turkish Missions' Aid Society.
Frontispiece of issue 3.

Telegram

From Mosul Jan 19 1880 to
Sir H. Layard, Constantinople

Distress among the poor at
Mosul and vicinity now reaches
crisis and extensive relief
measures have become urgently
requisite. Misery caused by
scarcity of food aggravated by
severity of winter. Wheat
36 piastres a wazna, twelve
time ordinary price — barley
in proportion. People flocking
in from neighbouring villages
increasing the gravity of
situation. Several deaths have
occurred and children have
been sold or abandoned. No
effective steps as yet taken by
local Govt. to afford relief by
distribution of food or money.

Heads

"Children have been sold or abandoned": copy of a telegram from a TMAS member in diplomatic service in Turkey, to the British Foreign Office. Mosul, January 18th 1880.

Turkish Sins, Armenian Sorrows.

AUTHENTIC CATALOGUE FOR HARPOOT AND HER SEVENTY-
THREE VILLAGES.

Needy persons	26,990	Wounded	1,315
Houses plundered	6,029	Miscarriages	829
„ burned	1,861	Killed in fields and on	
Churches badly injured		highways	280
and defiled	29	Persons burned	56
Churches burned	15	Died (hunger and cold)	1,014
Protestant chapels de-		Suicides	23
stroyed	5	Martyrs, bishop	1
Do. badly damaged	18	„ priests	11
Monasteries burned	2	„ Protestant	
„ damaged	4	ministers	3
Forced marriages to		„ teachers	7
Turks	166	„ men, women,	
Dishonoured	2,300	and children	1,903
Forced conversions, priests	12	Total deaths	4.127
Do. men and women	7,654	Loss of property	£1,501,780

This does not include the Malatia, Arabkir, Egin, Chareau-
jak, Geglir, Palu, Choonkoosh and Diarbekir districts.

No one can imagine the extent and the degree of the desolation wrought all about us. Even we ourselves cannot take
it in. It is too vast for the human mind to comprehend.

Aside from the chapels that have been destroyed altogether,
there are some so badly damaged that no service can be held
in them until they are repaired, and the people are utterly
helpless.

Almost every surviving preacher and pastor has been
stripped of everything. We have given to a few such, as we
do to the Gregorian priests, a few shillings extra as relief, in
view of their calling. Then there are several widows of
pastors who were killed, with their children whom we must
help.

Malatia suffered much worse than Harpoot, the destitution
there is awful. We are sending money for food as fast as
we can; but the Christians are very thinly clad and the
majority are without any bedding. Arabkir, Palu, Choonkoosh are in the same condition.

Harpoot, February 19, 1896.

Printed and Published by W. M. HUTCHINGS, 38, Hutton-st, Whitefriars, E.C.—April, 1896.

Turkish Sins: Armenian Sorrows. *Star*, January 1896.

Gregory Baghdassarian, founder,
Broussa Orphanage.
Star, October 1899.

Before and after: an Armenian orphan of the 1895
massacres, on arrival at an orphanage supported
by the Society in Harpoot, Turkey; and one year
later. *Star*, April 1900.

Marash, Turkey: Armenian orphans of the 1895 massacres learn the shoemaker's trade.
Star, January 1900.

Rev. S.W. Gentle-Cackett, newly-appointed Secretary, *Star*, October 1905.

Rev. W.A. Essery, Hon. Sec. of the Bible Lands Missions' Aid Society from 1892. *Star*, January 1901.

"He often added to the impact by wearing the Arabic costumes he had grown to love."

Adana, Turkey: refugee camp, 1909. *Star*, July/October 1909.

RELIEF.

The War in the Balkans.

The non-combatants have suffered terribly. Houses and property destroyed. Thousands of Refugees homeless, the great majority are **Women and Children.** These must be fed and clothed during the winter.

"Please help us to help them."

ORPHANS.

Armenia has been somewhat forgotten. The Balkan War has attracted attention and sympathy that our Orphan Fund has become exhausted.

A speedy replenishing is urgently needed.

ESSERY MEMORIAL ORPHANAGE.

This is the only Protestant Orphanage in the whole of the Balkans. The war is responsible for thousands of orphans, but present accommodation completely inadequate. Two more centres should be opened at once.

BIBLE LANDS MISSIONS' AID SOCIETY,

LORD KINNAIRD,   Rev. S. W. GENTLE-CACKETT,
Treasurer.   *Secretary.*

392, STRAND, LONDON, W.C.

The Chichester Press, 30 & 31, Furnival Street, Holborn, London, E.C.

The Balkan Wars: appeal in *The Star*, July/October 1913.

The Armenian Genocide: the heroes of Musa Dagh, 1915. *Star*, November 1922

Dr Robert Vaughan, leader of the Bible Lands Medical Unit. *Star*, October 1917.

Miss Mary Lovell

Mary Lovell and her girls at Barachah, 1918. Mary is in the centre and Siranoush and Adele are second and third from left at back.

At home at Barachah, 1918.

against them. Caught between the rebels, the anarchists, the heavy guns, and "the Turkish soldiery let loose", said one report, Macedonian civilians who wanted to save their families and themselves, fled for their lives. Most left everything behind and as winter approached, thousands seeking sanctuary on the wild mountainsides died of starvation and disease.

Twenty thousand Macedonian refugees fled to Bulgaria, where fighting had also broken out, and Pastor Popoff and Reverend Furnajieff from the Bulgarian Evangelical Society arrived in London to plead for them. They asked their audiences to remember Saint Paul's vision of the man of Macedonia who said, "Come over and help us". One woman who did just that was Mrs Marriage-Allen, one of the Society's first female committee members, who went to Macedonia to distribute relief on behalf of the Society of Friends. "My own eyes saw 7,000 refugees in the mountains without covering or food," she wrote, "and they tell of fearful things." Those fearful things were wholesale massacres and rapes, villages plundered and burned, flocks and herds stolen, and people with nothing to eat but roots and grass. Other reports told of wounded people left lying on the ground with no medical help within reach. "Regardless of where responsibility lies, and the creed or nationality of the sufferers," said a petition for international aid, supported by the Society and presented to the British and American Governments, "the thought of whole districts weltering in blood without a single doctor or trained nurse to relieve the suffering, is too brutally revolting to be tolerated in this twentieth century."

The missionaries at Monastir in Macedonia, like those in Turkey in 1895, ignored the advice of their own governments to abandon their posts, and did whatever they could for the 50,000 starving and homeless people who made their way towards the city. Part of the Society's Macedonian Massacre Appeal Fund went to Monastir, where nearby Christian and Muslim villages alike were supplied with food until harvest and seed corn and oxen for the new ploughing and planting. A large house in Monastir was purchased with the fund too, to be a refuge for the orphans of Macedonia. It was less than 100 miles from another new venture. Dr John House, the driving force behind the Samokov Institute and now in retirement at Salonica, witnessed the Macedonian massacres with horror. As he wondered what he could do to help the orphaned children, he was inspired by Dr Ford's mission in Sidon, and also by the famous enterprises in the United States at Tuskergee and Hampton, where slaves freed after the American Civil War had developed self-supporting educational and industrial settlements. With a vision taking shape in his mind, of a Christian industrial farm colony where orphaned boys could learn self-reliance, fellowship and modern agricultural methods, despite his 60 years, Dr House bought 52 acres of land south-east of Salonica and set to work.

The Essery Memorial Orphanage

In London, William threw himself into raising funds for the new orphanage and for the Salonica farm, but as he did so, his health began to trouble him once more. His asthma, which had seemed so much better after his mission tour, seemed worse than ever, and one Friday afternoon, early in January 1904, he said goodbye to his colleagues and left the office for home. On Sunday, despite a tightness in his chest and a breathlessness that made him stop after every few steps, he felt an almost unbearable urge to visit a very old friend, Ridley Herschell, the man who preached in 1854 at the founding service of the American Mission in Egypt. Ridley's nurse, constantly in attendance to her elderly and frail employer, opened the door to William. One look told her he should be in his own home. She took him to the station herself and urged the ticket collector to fetch a chair. William died as soon as he sat down.

Samuel Gentle-Cackett opened William's office desk on behalf of the Society. Inside, carefully arranged, he found the completed manuscript of William's book, *The Ascending Cross*, the Society's accounts, neatly brought up to date, and a proof copy of the *Star in the East*, ready for the printer. "We lost him when we could least spare him," Lord Kinnaird told the Exeter Hall audience at the Society's 50th anniversary meeting.

Less than one year later, the first orphan boys arrived at the Salonica Industrial Farm Colony, while almost at the same time, the first eight Macedonian children entered the Society's new orphanage at Monastir. In memory of their late secretary, a man whose generous heart and gracious manner had touched everyone who knew him, and who had been used so much by God, the

Society named the new home at Monastir, the Essery Memorial Orphanage. Samuel Gentle-Cackett, William's assistant, wondered what the future had in store for the orphanage and the farm. All the newspapers seemed to think that events in Macedonia heralded the beginning of a greater conflict, one that would finally tear the Ottoman Empire to pieces. Given the Empire's history so far, Samuel thought, that final conflict would be a bloody one, and he wondered how the Bible Lands Missions Aid Society would be used by God to help the innocent victims. And he wondered too, whether there would be a part somewhere that he himself might play.

Chapter 6

Give Me the
Gospel
The Balkan Wars

Samuel Gentle-Cackett was just 21 years old when he joined an enormous and expectant crowd one icy winter evening in 1891. As he looked around at the dense mass of men and women, he saw on their faces expressions of many human emotions: excitement, agitation, nervousness, worry and hope. There were also some faces, he noted, that seemed to express an almost half-embarrassed curiosity. He wondered what emotion showed on his own face and decided it might be a mixture of all of the others. It would be, he decided, an expression that reflected both the question that troubled him, what was the purpose of his life, and also how much he hoped to find the answer that night, from the American evangelists, Dwight Moody and Ira Sankey, who were taking Christian Britain by storm with another triumphant revival crusade.

Ever since he was little, Samuel had had the feeling that his life was meant for a purpose. But he had no idea what that purpose was and he often felt restless and troubled, always wishing he was somewhere else but never knowing where to go. Sometimes he discussed it with his much loved father, but although the older Samuel, a solid Kentish dairyman, was wise in country lore and the ways of the farm, the intensity of his son's nature and the boy's unanswerable questions, often unsettled him. "Trust in God, Samuel," he would say, anxious to be reassuring, "when the time is right, he will lead you to your answer."

Hold the fort, for I am coming,

Ira Sankey and a massed choir sang Philip Bliss's famous chorus,

Jesus signals still;
Wave the answer back to heaven;
By thy grace we will.

When Dwight Moody called on the huge audience for decisions for Jesus, Samuel Gentle-Cackett was among the first to stand. And when the huge congregation prayed for him and he felt his heart beginning to burn, he knew he had found the answer he had been seeking for so long. He knew too, at that very moment, that God had great plans in store.

The missionary

Almost immediately, full of enthusiasm, Samuel devised his own plan. He would take up the fallen mantle of his great hero, Henry Martyn, the first modern missionary to Islam, and like Henry, he would become a missionary to the Muslim world. Ever since he had first learned about Henry Martyn, Samuel had often thought about the young East India Company chaplain and his lonely death at Tocat in Turkey, and he wondered if Turkey might feature somewhere in his own future, and whether there was a fort in that far away country that God was calling him to hold.

Academic study and a degree in divinity followed Samuel's encounter with Jesus, and then ordination as a Baptist minister. Something of an achievement for the son of a dairyman, Samuel liked to think. When a call from Africa followed, for an energetic young man capable of making careful assessments of plans for a string of new missions from the Niger to the Nile, Samuel felt it was meant for him, and with bright hopes the brand new missionary set out for foreign lands.

At first Samuel seemed set for success. In Egypt and Sudan he worked alongside graduates of Assiout College, whose courage and commitment to their Christian faith inspired him to greater missionary enterprise. In their company he acquired a passion for native dress, and an even greater devotion to the lands of the Bible and for evangelism. Perhaps it was all of those combined that made Samuel such a threat to the Muslim authorities in Libya. Whatever it was, a spell in a dank and rat-infested jail followed by deportation back to Britain, meant the door to active missionary service among the people he had grown to love, was very firmly shut.

Opening doors

Samuel was not a man to be daunted for long and when he saw William Essery's advertisement for a Deputation Secretary for the Bible Lands Missions Aid Society, he saw another door opening for him. If he could not go from Britain to evangelise the Bible lands, he vowed, then he would bring the Bible lands and their needs to Britain. It was a promise Samuel kept for a lifetime.

Other doors were opening in Samuel's life too and one day they would connect into his work with the Society and cause him to reflect with awe on how well the master planner had prepared the way. In 1902, Samuel, his wife Elizabeth, and their little five-year-old daughter, moved to Bedfont in Middlesex, where Samuel became pastor of a small Baptist congregation. "Hardly conducive to reverence," was Samuel's first comment about Sunday meetings at the Bedfont village hall, where instead of visions of God's Kingdom, the heavy atmosphere encouraged thoughts of Saturday night revelries. Within a year, Samuel's enthusiastic fund-raising efforts had resulted in a new Baptist building, the Bedfont Tabernacle, on the Staines Road, which is where Harry Fear first met him.

Harry, who later became treasurer of the Bible Lands Missions Aid Society, was a leading Bedfont businessman, and a member of many local charitable committees, and when he learned about the new minister's fund-raising successes, he decided to pay him a visit. "I was looking for the pastor," Harry wrote, many years later, "and I stopped to ask directions of a young man in shirtsleeves painting the chapel doors."

"That's me," the young man replied, setting down his paintbrush and reaching out a friendly hand. And that was Samuel, Harry said, always willing to take on any task and always giving it his all, whether it was as a missionary, as secretary of a missions aid society, international commissioner to investigate genocide, or painting a chapel door.

Samuel began his work with the Society in 1900, and just as he had vowed, he quickly began bringing the Bible lands to life in British churches with a series of lantern lectures: Palestine of Today, The Land of the Seven Churches, and Suffering Armenia. He often added to the impact by wearing the Arabic costumes he had grown to love during his missionary venture and by displaying items from his personal collection of historical and contemporary objects from Africa and the Near East. Very soon, the engaging young man, with his charismatic personality, his exotic costumes and his abundant stock of background Biblical knowledge, was a well-known figure among British Christians who supported missionary enterprises.

In memory of William Essery

William Essery's Macedonia Massacre Relief Appeal gave Samuel some sharp insights into the suffering of refugees and how life was lived in the Balkans, a life he saw more closely in 1906, when as the Society's new secretary he made the first of many visits to the mission stations it supported overseas. Despite the blow to his earlier missionary ambitions, Samuel always remained an evangelist at heart and he never missed an opportunity to preach. When his party fell among revolutionaries in Bulgaria who asked him to speak on the cruelties of the Turk, "a few very guarded remarks", Samuel said, "opened my way to preach the Gospel to them".

It was on that first trip that Samuel arrived at the Essery Memorial Orphanage at Monastir to be delighted with what he found there. The children were all comfortably housed in completely refurbished buildings and although signs of their previous sufferings were sometimes inescapable, he could also see they were flourishing in the homely surroundings created for them. Bright fires and carpets underlined with hay kept the rooms warm, and to the children's never-ending delight, modern sanitation had replaced the traditional "holes in the ground". New ranges in the kitchens meant regular hot meals, and cosy bedrooms furnished with bright rugs and blankets and pictures on the walls, encouraged a sense of security and belonging.

Samuel was impressed too, by the Salonica Farm, where the Society had already provided a brick bakehouse and a windmill over the artesian well. Other gifts of fountains and cattle troughs had been donated personally by William Essery. "I think we will never really know just how much the orphans of Macedonia and Armenia owe to the generous and quiet heart of William Essery," said Samuel, as he took part in the dedication of another memorial to his predecessor. In a comfortable shelter on the dusty public road that ran past the farm gate, weary travellers were invited to relieve their thirst at the Essery Memorial Fountain, where fresh water was piped to shiny new taps, and where an array of Scripture texts on the walls surrounded an inscription that read, "Those who rest or drink bless the memory of the beloved W.A. Essery."

Hearts riven with sorrow

Samuel also visited the American orphanages in Turkey during his first trip as secretary, and his meetings with the Armenian orphans and the shocking reality of their stories, made him more determined than ever to support them and the Armenian cause. Although there had been no repeat of massacres on the scale of 1895, a depressingly regular series of brutal acts, generally ignored by the Ottoman Government, left more Armenian adults dead and more Armenian children orphaned. "Who will be the benefactors of these children?" the Reverend R. Cole of Bitlis asked Samuel, when he recounted to him the story of little Samson and his sister, Yeghsa. The two small children, he said, who were saved when their village was attacked and burned by Kurdish tribesmen, were forcibly returned later to their home. In what remained of their house, the pair discovered the charred and rotting remains of their own parents. "They buried them as best they could," said Mr Cole, "and they will carry the memory of it for life."

Although thousands of children lived in American, German and Swiss orphanages across Turkey, they were still the fortunate few. As Miss Salmond at Marash pointed out to Samuel, thousands more children were roaming the city streets and countryside in gangs, begging and stealing. She told him about two little girls she had recently taken into Marash orphanage, their father dead since the 1895 massacres while their mother had simply given up on the struggle for life. The girls were found running wild, said Miss Salmond, and they had caused her to look more closely into the fate of the orphan children of Armenia. "We had been shutting our eyes to it," she said, "and comforting ourselves that the massacre orphans were all being cared for, but when we saw the great need, our hearts were riven with sorrow."

Samuel's heart was sorrowful too and he began to wonder if there was something that his own family could do for the Macedonian and Armenian orphans. The girls especially, worried him, he knew the likely fate that waited for them if they were left to roam the streets. "Who will help the orphans?" he asked readers of the *Star*, and went on to say, "Were I able financially, I would gladly go and father the whole family, troubling none for contributions." As he wrote, Samuel began thinking about his own adopted British children, the little boy and girl that he and Elizabeth and their own daughter Persis had welcomed into their Bedfont home, and as he did so, an idea and a plan began to take shape in his mind.

Islam: a new challenge

If Samuel had been right in 1905, when he wondered what the future had in store, if the upheavals in Macedonia were harbinger to conflicts that would ultimately destroy the Ottoman Empire, he knew too that other forces were at work in the Near East that would also play a part in giving new dimensions and shape to the region. Nor had he forgotten his earlier concerns for the Muslim world, and in April 1908, in a special supplement to the 100th edition of the *Star*, he reprinted papers from a 1907 Church Conference at Yarmouth that focused on the current state of Islam. The preface to the supplement was written by the Bishop of Durham, the Society's new vice-president, and chairman of the conference. "The present revived activity of the Muslim faith and its ambitions," wrote the Bishop, referring to a new vitality within Islam, "is a challenge to the disciples of the Cross."

Samuel Zwemer, an old friend of the Society's based at Bahrain, and a major contributor to the conference, wrote about the challenge of Islam too. "Islam has awakened to a new self-consciousness," he said, and he referred to the Pan-Islamic Movement that had political as well as religious implications in any future encounter with Christianity and the West. But Samuel Zwemer was optimistic, he saw great opportunities, particularly as technology and education opened new doors in the East, and he encouraged Christian missionaries to rise to the challenge. Perhaps, his article concluded, "the answer to those who claim that Muslims cannot be converted is this; the time had not come because we have forgotten to wind the clock, the doors are shut because we keep the key in our pockets, and Muslims are not converted because we ourselves are not yet sufficiently converted".

Now we are brothers

Samuel Zwemer also referred in his article to political changes, and to countries where "mass meetings are held where thousands are being addressed on social progress and political liberty". That Turkey itself should lead the way in those political changes, in social progress and in liberty, came as a welcome surprise and something of a shock, and caused many whose business was with the Ottoman Empire to reassess their prospects. On 24 July 1908, the Committee for Union and Progress, the "Young Turks", an underground organisation that for years had eluded the secret police networks of the Sultan, engineered a rebellion in the Ottoman Army. Under its leaders, Niyazi Bey and Enver Bey, the power of Sultan Abdul Hamid was fatally weakened, and the CUP, the new power in Constantinople, proclaimed its commitment to modernising and strengthening the Empire under Western constitutional principles. A constitution held in abeyance since 1876, that enshrined principles of equality and religious toleration, was published to a jubilant reception in all regions under Turkish rule. Western newspapers carried enthusiastic reports. Ecstatic crowds, they said, thronged the streets carrying banners that proclaimed Liberty, Equality, Fraternity and Justice. Old enemies embraced and wept tears of joy. Balkan guerrilla fighters handed their weapons to officers of the CUP. Women took off their veils and walked openly with their husbands in the streets. Armenian bishops shook hands with Muslim clerics on public balconies and Turks joined Armenians in services of remembrance for the victims of 1895. Throughout the Empire, there was rejoicing. In Jerusalem, said Samuel Gentle-Cackett, where religious liberty meant Jews were permitted to enter the Temple area for the first time since Saladin's conquest in 1187, the city was *en fête*. "Imagine if you can," he wrote in the *Star*, "thousands crowding into the Sheep Market just outside the Damascus Gate, every approach decorated with arches, bunting, flags and green boughs." Inside Turkey itself, religious liberty encouraged

Christians whose families were forcibly converted generations earlier to Islam, but whose outward obedience to the *Qu'ran* cloaked an inward and secret Christian faith, to live openly as Christians once more.

"Will it all last?" Samuel asked readers of the *Star*. He himself believed it would and he quoted a native of Jerusalem who said, "Before the Constitution we were Jews, Muslims, Christians, Greeks – now we are all Ottomans – we are brothers." Samuel was optimistic and he was encouraged by reports from the missionaries in Turkey. The Constitution, they said, had enormous implications. Everything that was previously against the law: street preaching, cottage prayer meetings, public religious gatherings, Bible distribution, new church building, was now permitted. At last, they believed, they saw in sight the final triumph of Christianity in Turkey. For Samuel, that triumph, when the citadels of Islam crumbled before the power of the Gospel, would also mean that Henry Martyn's lonely death at Tocat had not been in vain.

Plans for free compulsory education, said the missionaries, would release an enormous percentage of funds for evangelism. Freedom of publication meant great opportunities for Christian literature. Freedom to form societies, the word itself previously forbidden, meant new opportunities for Christian organisations, and the International Secretary of the YMCA, as he travelled throughout Asia Minor, called for the establishment of a branch in every large centre of the Empire. He foresaw the day, he said, when YMCA ideals of caring, honesty, respect and responsibility, would act as a beacon through the lands of the Near East.

Other voices were less optimistic. Dr Barnum, American missionary at Harpoot, said, "Here, in the far interior, the feudal chiefs find it difficult to recognise Armenians as on an equality with themselves, and no longer subject to tribute to them." Reverend A.N. Andrus of Mardin thought change would come only slowly. "The majority of the citizens are reactionaries," he said, "and will exercise a very strong passive, if not active, resistance to the measures of the new Government." There is also, he said ominously, a lack of able, honest and sincere officials to administer the new constitution.

The lure of the West

Other missionaries raised different concerns. Even as they called for more workers to take advantage of the newly opened doors, so many of their best young men and women were now heading for the West, they said, particularly for America, they were beginning to fear for the future leadership of the Christian communities. "We must train our boys and girls to be a blessing to their country," they said, and they began to devise new educational and vocational schemes and encouraged highly skilled and educated young Armenians to return from overseas to take up leading roles at home.

Samuel also recognised the powerful temptations of Western career opportunities and high wages to young people from impoverished Armenian communities and he encouraged the Society to send larger grants towards the salaries of local pastors, teachers and Bible women throughout Turkey. For their part, the missionaries did their best to support the Armenian workers who resisted the lure of the West, and they reported dedicated work by local Christian leaders. Despite the smallness of the Protestant communities, compared with their Muslim and Gregorian neighbours, said Reverend Edward Riggs, describing a mission tour along the southern edges of the Black Sea, "their influence is felt very widely in those larger communities, in moral and religious reform, and perhaps most effectively, in educational matters". Edward was also enthusiastic about the rebuilding of churches and schools destroyed in 1895. At the village of Kapou-key, he said, where he delivered a new church bell presented by friends in Marsovan, the people had raised their new church themselves. "These rough mountaineers have cut and shaped and drawn the great oak and beech timbers, sawed the planks, and split the shingles," he said, and he went on to describe how his heart was stirred when he witnessed the dedication of the new church built to withstand the violence of the winds and the drifting snows of winter, and was among the first to hear the new bell as it rang through the echoing green valleys, summoning the people to prayer.

In Armenian blood

As Samuel began preparing the July 1909 edition of the *Star*, where he planned to include more details of proposed evangelistic efforts in the new, open Turkey, disturbing reports reached him from Adana in south-eastern Anatolia. At first he found them difficult to believe, but as more news arrived and the newspapers confirmed it, he knew it was true. Turkey's new dawn had foundered and the road that had seemed to lead so securely towards a bright future was suddenly ominous with shadows. There were many among the ordinary Turks, said the Adana reports, who had expected great things from the revolution of 1908, especially immediate economic improvement. When nothing had changed, except the loss of their once superior status, those whose hopes had been dashed vented their rage in the traditional way, in the blood of their Armenian neighbours.

At Adana, Tarsus, Antioch, Hadjin, and hundreds of small towns and villages far from the centre of power in Constantinople, over 30,000 people were murdered, girls were abducted and raped, and goods and livestock stolen. Thirty-five thousand refugees, mostly women and children, were left desperate for relief. Herbert Adams Gibbons, an American writer and historian who was travelling in the region, appealed in the *Star* for the refugees. "I saw all this horror with my own eyes," he said, "men, women and children butchered without mercy, mutilated festering corpses lying in the streets and dogs feeding upon them, girls bewailing the brutal, horrible loss of their virginity, mothers seeking children, children seeking parents." Herbert wrote too about "death-doomed refugees crowded together like sardines waiting to be burned alive". Among those who died in that terrible way were 30 Armenian and American delegates on their way to an annual church conference in Adana. Desperate to escape a pursuing mob intent on butchery, the group sought refuge in a church at Osmanieh. The attackers set light to the church and helped the blaze on its way with kerosene. Every man inside was burned alive.

"Remember the San Francisco Earthquake of 1906?" asked Mr Gibbons, "how a universal sympathy for the sufferers swept Britain? Remember the Mansion House Fund, the money that poured in, the special prayers and sermons from every pulpit? Remember how day after day, the British newspapers were filled with descriptions of the calamity, the death, the destruction, the city laid low?" But, please think, he went on, "the earthquake survivors have a future. They are in the midst of a friendly country. Every hand is stretched out to help them." How much more, he said, "our sympathy and our prayers and our money are needed by the Armenians, whose sufferings have been far more horrible, whose present is unspeakably sad, and whose future seems dark and hopeless".

Once more, the Society responded to the call and opened another Armenian Massacre Relief Fund. Most of the money went to an International Committee based at Adana, where the British vice-consul in the region, Mr Doughty-Wylie, was a leading member, and where his wife, a trained nurse, took charge of the emergency hospital. The *Star* published a photograph of Mrs Doughty-Wylie in her nurse's uniform in the same issue that its very first pictures of refugee camps appeared, neat rows of white canvas tents soon to be deep in mud when Adana was hit by some of the worst storms and floods the region had ever seen. But despite the floods that caused enormous devastation and hampered the relief efforts, the camps suffered no serious epidemics and by September 1909, the Relief Committee announced it was concentrating its efforts on making small loans to enable country farmers and city craftsmen to begin the long road back to self-support. The Ottoman Government, it said, after a shameful lack of initial sympathy and response, had eventually set up a Relief Committee of its own, while the region's new governor, Djemal Bey, a man who "inspired confidence and hope, even enthusiasm", took a leading role in feeding the hungry and rehousing the homeless. Such humanitarian enterprise gave the missionaries cause to hope that the Adana massacres were the final frustrated excess of the old order in Turkey.

First aid to the wounded

At the Society's Annual Meeting in 1910, another of its vice-presidents, Sir Andrew Wingate, a retired Indian Civil Service man who had once been Plague Commissioner in Bombay, described the Society as "a first aid to the wounded, a reserve force brought up to the relief of agencies already in the field". It was a reserve force that would be much needed in the years to come, and in

1912, Samuel watched from the Society's new headquarters in the Strand, as another bloody episode unfolded in the Balkans.

The Balkan Wars ended Ottoman rule in the Balkans, but at a terrible cost. As a series of bloody battles gradually expelled the Turks from the region, each major Balkan nation attempted to gain as much for itself as possible, and as the struggles for land, power and strategic alliances progressed, Bulgaria, Greece, Montenegro and Serbia eventually turned on each other. Both Samuel and Lord Kinnaird were equally horrified and frustrated. They had hoped that democratic change in Turkey would bring a swift peace that would allow the Society to devote a greater percentage of its future funds to evangelism, and they had already begun planning their first campaign.

As part of that evangelistic campaign, Samuel had produced a special supplement for the *Star*, containing a long article about Henry Martyn and encouraging supporters to join the Day of Prayer for the Muslim World called by Samuel Zwemer for 16 October 1912, the centenary of Henry's death. But, once again, the immediacy of human suffering took precedence over missionary enterprise, and Lord Kinnaird, opening another relief fund and describing the condition of thousands of Balkan refugees, said "Our first care must be those who suffer through no fault of their own, and through no actual participation in the conflict." From Bulgaria, Pastor Dimiter Furnajieff, who had appealed for the victims of the Macedonian massacres several years earlier, appealed to the Society once more as 10,000 refugees gathered in Sophia. "The needs are appalling," he said, "the stories of suffering heartrending." Samuel threw himself into the relief effort, money for food and blankets was sent to Bulgaria, and hundreds of bundles of warm clothing were collected at his home in Bedfont and then sent by train to Bulgaria.

Samuel always had a heart for those who suffered at Christmas time, perhaps because he was so conscious of the happiness of his own growing family at Bedfont, and he liked to send something special for the orphans at Monastir and in Turkey. At Christmas 1913, he made sure another very special grant went from the Society, this time to the refugees in Bulgaria. In return, Reverend Dimiter wrote back to say, "You may not have heard any special voice in London coming from the suburbs of Sophia, but surely heaven heard the loud, rolling, thundering echo of the voices in unison, when they shouted out of hundreds of throats, 'Thank you! God bless the givers and the gifts!'" Letters from some of those givers of gifts were printed in the *Star*. "I am only a labourer in the works," said one, "but here is five shillings from my weekly wage for the poor souls who suffer so much in the Balkans." Another said, "I am just a working housekeeper, and I willingly give a tenth of all I earn, but at Christmas time I felt I wanted to give our Saviour a Christmas gift... realising what He has done for me."

The battles of the Balkan Wars were some of the bloodiest ever seen in a region renowned for bloody battles. Each conflict lasted only a few short weeks in 1912 and again in 1913, but thousands died as armies fought from muddy trenches, cities were besieged, and infantry and civilians alike were blown apart by artillery shells. The latest technology was also employed as huge searchlights allowed fighting to continue around the clock and aeroplane pilots demonstrated the lethal effectiveness of bombs dropped from great heights. A lack of field hospitals generally meant that wounded people were left to die where they fell. Others died later of the cholera and dysentery that haunted a region littered with rotting corpses. In the West, when details of the carnage appeared in the newspapers, hundreds of medically trained men and women offered their skills and set out overland to the Balkans and to Turkey. Young doctors and nurses from Britain laboured alongside American medical missionaries. Armenian doctors and nurses worked with Turkish medical officers. At the Ottoman Hospital in Constantinople, staff from the Broussa Orphanage, and workers from the Red Cross and the Red Crescent, united in the common cause of saving human life.

In Christian hospitals in the Balkans, Bible women sat with the wounded, and Bible colporteurs, carrying their books through the wards, reported hundreds of men crying out to them, "Give me the Gospel, please give one to me!" A retired missionary doctor who had become an amateur printer, used picture cards collected by the Society from thousands of British homes, to convey a message of hope to the wounded and sick. On the back of each card, in the many languages of the Balkans, the message read, "Wishing you a rapid recovery and hoping that your sufferings will lead you to love the Lord Jesus, who suffered for you, better than you have ever done before."

Of all the terrible battles of the Balkan Wars, the siege of Adrianople moved the hearts of people in Britain like almost nothing else, as for five long months the Turks refused to hand over the city to the besieging Bulgarian Army. From inside Adrianople, the Reverend Paul Dressler, of the London Jews Society, sent one of the last messages out before communications were cut. "Bring relief," he urged his friend, Samuel Gentle-Cackett. When the city finally fell in March 1913, over 40,000 people were dead of artillery wounds or starvation, and military doctors spoke later of the heavy snow that settled in January that was almost immediately stained scarlet with blood. When the aid workers, waiting for days in the freezing weather for the city's capitulation, entered Adrianople, they clambered over mounds of dead and dying people lying among ruins where cholera, dysentery and starvation were rife. Among those aid workers was Samuel Gentle-Cackett, loaded with huge quantities of blankets and food from the Bible Lands Missions Aid Society and ready to relieve the exhausted Paul Dressler.

The changing world

By the end of the Balkan Wars, thousands of new refugees had joined thousands more from earlier conflicts living in squalid conditions all over a region where boundaries and frontiers had changed. The *Star* printed a map showing new national borders and a chart showing losses and gains of territory and population. The Essery Orphanage at Monastir found itself in Serbia. Salonica, with 30,000 new refugees, where the Society planned to found another orphanage, was in Greece. Turkey, its Empire shrunk and its economy depleted by years of war, sought more help from Germany, whose banks were already heavily involved in financing the Ottoman Railway that linked Constantinople with Baghdad. Germany, the strongest military power on the planet was delighted to oblige.

Early in 1914, Samuel and Lord Kinnaird began planning the Society's Diamond Jubilee. King George's Hall at the Central YMCA in Tottenham Court Road was booked, the Society's Bible Lands Exhibition that had grown from Samuel's own collection was prepared, and Samuel and others planned to appear dressed in Arabian and Armenian costumes. Missionaries from all over

Turkey and the Balkans agreed to attend, anxious to highlight their work and raise funds for the swelling numbers of orphans and refugees. Reverend Dimiter Furnajieff would be guest of honour.

On 3 July 1914, the Society celebrated its Diamond Jubilee in London. A long day of prayer, speeches, entertainment and refreshments had been arranged for a large gathering of supporters. But, there was something new in the air of the capital, London seemed to be holding its breath. And despite their delight in being together once more, many old friends were filled with foreboding. Germany and Austro-Hungary were marshalling their forces to attack Serbia. In Russia, the army was under orders to begin a general mobilisation. In Britain, young men were talking of war.

Less than four weeks after the celebration, Austro-Hungarian artillery shells fell on the panic-stricken people of Belgrade. They marked the beginning of the Great War.

As Samuel wrote up the minutes of the September meeting of the Society's managing committee, he recorded that "Lord Kinnaird has given all his sons of age for the defence of the country". All around Britain other young men were enlisting. The committee said prayers for them all.

Chapter 7

Genocide

The Great War

"We are on the eve of great and solemn events," Samuel Gentle-Cackett told readers of the *Star* at the beginning of the Great War, and once again, he reflected on the possible outcomes of the collapse of the Ottoman Empire. An area so large, he said, so strategically situated, raises all sorts of perplexing questions. How will it be divided, what powers will gain control of it and what will be their policy towards its religious life and its missionary enterprises? Samuel also questioned what might be the fate of the Holy Land. Several nations would like to possess it, he said, and he wondered if it might ultimately fall to the Jews. "But, one thing is sure," he continued, "when the war is over the people will still be there, needier, weaker, and more depressed than ever, humiliated and hopeless. Black ruin in city and town, in shop and home and in mosque and church." Samuel could not possibly have imagined how black the ruin would be.

The Great War began in late July 1914, when Austro-Hungary declared war on Serbia and its forces attacked Belgrade. It was the opening act of a combat that would eventually spread throughout Europe and the Middle East, and would involve, in one capacity or another, almost every nation on the planet. When Britain declared war on Germany in August, waves of patriotism led young men in their thousands to join the armed forces, and British casualties on foreign battlefields were reported almost at once. The death in France of Lord Kinnaird's eldest son was recorded in the Society's minutes of November 1914. In that same month, Britain declared war on Turkey. "She has willingly surrendered herself to German control," wrote Samuel, "her army and her navy are under German officers; the Governmental policy is shaped by German diplomats." One of the almost immediate effects of the state of war was that grants from the Bible Lands Missions Aid Society to mission stations in Turkey and what remained of the Ottoman Empire came to a halt.

You may safely reassure all friends

As British missionaries were advised by their government to leave their stations in the Ottoman Empire and return home, the Americans, citizens of a non-combatant nation, seemed secure. On 10 November 1914, said Samuel, the American Board in Boston had received a reassuring despatch from its missionaries in Constantinople. "American Ambassador," it said, "with hearty co-operation of Turkish officials, has situation completely in hand. Missionaries and their work fully safeguarded. Everything proceeding as though normal conditions prevailed. You may safely reassure all friends."

As one of the most long-standing friends of the American Board, the Society tried to feel reassured. Samuel had been anxious about the fate of the Armenian orphans and thoughts of what might happen to them if the Americans left Turkey had tended to keep him awake at night. Now, he did his best to share the confidence of the American Ambassador and the missionaries and tried to convince himself there was truly nothing to fear. Hopefully, he reasoned, even if there was fighting and hunger all around them, under the protection of the American flag and in the security of the mission compounds, the children could see out the war in safety, learning their lessons, continuing their vocational training, and ready to take up adult roles and responsibilities when the conflict was over. They would be ready, he hoped, to be a blessing to their nation.

But Samuel was not entirely reassured. Some of the reports he received from Turkey made him feel uneasy. From Sivas, the Reverend Ernest Partridge wrote about the conscription which since 1908 had also included Armenians. "While the Turkish Army is gathering men," Ernest said, "the harvest, which is very abundant this year, is ungathered. Shepherds on the roadside and in the mountains are being taken, leaving their flocks uncared for and alone." It was also true, said Ernest, that the government was stealing from the people: wheat, barley, cooking pots, cotton, cloth, anything in fact that could be used by the army. And there

was something else, he said, the government was building barracks and schoolhouses with free labour. From Talas, the
Reverend H. Irwin said, "The requisition of the railroads and of
all good traction animals has stopped the movement of freight,
consequently many staples, especially sugar and kerosene are
almost impossible to find in the interior." From Moosh, an
unnamed missionary wrote, "The military are impressing into
the army every male from 20 to 45 years of age, leaving many
families without food, and only the women and children to care
for the fields." And from Bitlis, Miss Mary Uline said, "Hundreds
and hundreds of wild Arabs and Kurds from the South have been
going through the city on their horses."

There was nothing in the reports that related directly to the
Armenian people, except that they seemed to share the fate of all
Turkey, their menfolk forcibly conscripted and their families left
to go hungry. But, nevertheless, Samuel's sense of unease persisted and when he published reports in the *Star* of January 1915,
that Russian troops were laying siege to Trebizond, Erzroum and
Van, he prayed that if the Russians were routed or withdrew, that
the Armenians, so often seen as sympathisers with their
Orthodox co-religionists in Russia, would not suffer the fury of
the Turkish mobs. But how would anyone in the West know, he
wondered, what was happening in Anatolia and Armenia, to the
people who lived in those huge, remote lands. The only news from
Turkey came from battlefronts and it was all about advances and
retreats, sieges and surrenders, landings from the sea and campaigns on land. After war was declared and underway, regular
reports from the missionaries had almost ceased. Anything could
happen inside Turkey, Samuel thought to himself, and the outside world would not know.

Serbia: conditions indescribably terrible

Despite his fears, the absence of news from Turkey and the
urgency of events elsewhere, pushed the Armenian people to the
back of Samuel's mind. His main concern had become the
Balkans, home to the Essery Orphanage and the Salonica Farm,
where Serbia, Britain's greatest ally in the region, was crumbling
under an Austrian military assault. Heavy artillery shells
destroyed buildings and shrapnel tore through people. Fires

raged through factories and oil depots. When the Belgrade water-works was destroyed, sanitation and clean drinking water became a thing of the past. Cholera and dysentery took their place. Thousands of refugees sought shelter in mountain caves. The situation seemed hopeless, but eventually, desperately, at an enormous cost in human life, the Serbian Army, already exhausted by years of Balkan warfare, repulsed the Austrian invaders and gained a brief respite for their people.

Sir Edward Grey, Britain's Foreign Secretary, and author of the famous phrase, "the lamps are going out all over Europe..." urged the British people to help the desperate civilians of Serbia. He also made a special plea to the Society. Its work among sufferers of the Balkan Wars had been mentioned in so many reports to the British Government, Samuel told readers of the *Star*, "it was only natural that Sir Edward, writing from the Foreign Office, begged this Society to help in relieving the suffering and starving in the Monastir district".

Extracts from Sir Edward's letters, describing the terrible conditions in the area, appeared in the *Star*. "The mortality has been appalling," said one, "the condition is indescribably terrible." "Six to ten thousand people need relief in food, clothing and fuel," said another. "Alarming incidence of disease, principally spotted typhus"... "Medical resources of the region have proved totally unable to cope"... "Men are dying in the streets of the town, and surgical appliances so scarce that some operations are performed with scissors and pocket knives".

Please help these suffering Serbians all you can, urged Samuel, and despite their own wartime hardships, the Society's supporters responded with great generosity. Within weeks of its opening, the Serbian Civilian Relief Fund was sending blankets and clothing, disinfectant and medicines, condensed milk and baby food, to the people of Serbia, much of it transported through Salonica with the help of the Royal Navy.

The Bible Lands Medical Unit

"Could the Society also send a doctor?" asked Sir Edward Grey. The doctor who came forward was Robert Vaughan, a young surgeon who had achieved the highest academic honours as a student and whose devotion to service and to the Christian faith had been nurtured among the mountains of North Wales by his father, a vicar at St Asaph. Almost as soon as war was declared Robert had abandoned the safety of his London hospital career to work among British wounded in France, and by the time he left Britain once more, this time bound for Serbia, he had enormous experience of battlefield wounds and diseases and the trauma caused by conflict. Gathering a team around him, one other doctor and two nurses, Robert led the Bible Lands Medical Unit to the Balkans.

By 1916, despite the earlier successes of its army, Serbia was under enemy occupation. The combined assaults of Germany, Austro-Hungary and Bulgaria had brought the country to its knees. Monastir itself suffered a savage onslaught and Robert Vaughan and his team retreated with thousands of Serbian refugees to continue working among them at Florina in northern Greece. Years later, a British vice-consul who had been at Monastir spoke about Robert Vaughan. The success of the medical unit was largely due to him, he said, Dr Vaughan was a devoted and Christian man, always willing to go to those in need, no matter how tired he was or how long his day had been. When Florina itself came under attack by Bulgarian forces, Robert stayed as long as he could, only agreeing to leave when one last operation was completed and his patient made comfortable. Only then, with the advance parties of the enemy less than one hour away, Robert left his makeshift hospital, carefully hid his surgical instruments and drugs in a nearby garden, and made his way out of the city.

"The whole world at our door"

When Robert left Florina, he joined a remnant of the Serbian Army and thousands of refugees, all heading for the massive Allied base at Salonica. By 1916, almost 300,000 troops were stationed at Salonica and feeding them and providing for their welfare was an enormous logistical problem. Part of that problem was solved by Dr John House at the Salonica Farm. Despite his great age, in 1916 he was nearing his eightieth year, Dr House could not let an opportunity for aid and evangelism pass by, and as well as supplying the camps and military hospitals with milk and eggs and other fresh produce, a refurbished farm building became a popular rest and recreation centre for British,

Canadian and French troops. "I'm off home now," the British Tommies always said whenever they left camp to spend their off-duty hours at the farm. It was simple fare they received there, cups of tea, conversation and singalongs that were a mixture of Ira Sankey's hymns and the latest music hall hits, but the soldiers loved the homely atmosphere and the welcome they always received from the down-to-earth American who never seemed wearied by his great age and who always found time to listen to a man's troubles and fears.

Although the Society never achieved its aim of founding a new home for Macedonian orphans in Salonica, it supported the missionaries who worked in the city. They had never imagined it would become home to such a huge population of refugees or to one of the war's largest allied bases, but like Dr House, they did what they could and made the most of opportunities. Among those opportunities, the American missionary, Dr Cooper, told readers of the *Star*, were the regular and nourishing meals for refugees, produced each day from leftover food, collected in empty five gallon kerosene tins by soldiers and cooks of the British Army. "I suppose this war is the greatest eater the world knows of," he said, "it eats up human lives, villages, cities, millions of money, and materials of every sort. Is it not a happy thought that a trifle of meat comes forth from this great eater?"

By 1916, the inmates of the Essery Orphanage had joined the refugee throngs in Salonica. "Sometimes," said one of the city's missionaries, "it seems as if the whole world is camped at our door!" The children had been rescued by the American Red Cross from the orphanage cellars where they spent almost one whole winter sheltering from an artillery barrage thundering above them. Under the protection of a white flag, they left the Essery Home for ever. The buildings and gardens once so beautifully refurbished for them had been damaged beyond repair. Miss Matthews, who cared for the children during the siege and then travelled with them to Salonica, wrote to Samuel. Would the Society take 20 of the girls to England, she asked, where they could be trained as nurses and teachers before returning to help their own people?

Another group of orphans passed through Salonica in 1916 too. They came with Darinka Gruitch, an orphanage worker in Belgrade and an old friend of Samuel's. Darinka had no illusions about the likely fate of orphan girls at the hands of invading soldiers and when another Austrian Army crossed the Serbian frontier she gathered her 200 charges together and set out with them, on foot, walking just hours ahead of the Austrian advance parties. Months later, ragged, weary, but safe and alive, the Belgrade orphans arrived in Salonica. Darinka also wrote to Samuel, asking if the Society might take some of her girls too, to be trained in England for useful careers. Samuel raised the matter with Lord Kinnaird. "Would the Society fund a project," he asked, "whereby orphans of the Balkans and the Near East could live and study in Britain?" His Lordship was not certain if such a plan fell within the Society's remit. Supposing the answer was no, he asked Samuel, what would you do? "I'd have a shot at it myself, sir," said Samuel. Good man, Kinnaird replied, go ahead with my blessing, and should you ever find yourself in difficulties, the Bible Lands Missions Aid Society will certainly look favourably at any request for help. It was beginning to seem, Samuel thought to himself later, that the idea that first seeded itself in 1906, was beginning to blossom.

Destroying a nation

Even as Samuel began to plan ways and means to bring a British refuge for Balkan orphans into being, he was trying to come to terms with news arriving from Turkey. For some time, all through the late months of 1915, there had been rumours of atrocities and massacre, stories that caused Samuel to recall his earlier fears. But there was nothing substantial, nothing that could be verified. By the end of the year, however, and then in 1916, what had been rumour suddenly became fact. Something had happened in Turkey, Samuel learned, something that in its concept, and in its magnitude, was new in the catalogue of human barbarity.

In May 1916, under the heading Destroying a Nation, Samuel attempted to communicate to readers of the *Star* what he had learned. The sources, he said, were absolutely reliable and the accounts were "so appalling as to be almost beyond belief". They indicate, he went on, "a systematic, authorised, and desperate effort on the part of the rulers of Turkey to wipe out the Armenians". As Samuel went on to describe the reported uprising at Van, in support of the Russian invaders, that the Turks had used as the pretext to attack every Armenian community in Turkey, Samuel thought once more of his earlier fears, and how they had eventually come to pass. The Armenian people, he told his readers, were being exterminated, "sometimes through massacre, more often through torture and exile, they are being eliminated from the field; they are being put where they need no longer be considered".

"You have probably learned something of the sad condition of the Armenians from the papers," Samuel said, "but probably nothing gets through that in any adequate way portrays the desperate straits in which these poor people find themselves." Later in the year, Samuel, his readers and the whole world knew much more. The optimistic "business as usual" and "normal conditions", reported in 1914 by the American Ambassador to Turkey, had become something very different. The American missionaries, who had planned to spend the war caring for orphans and sustaining as best they could the Armenian Protestant communities, had been among the few western eyewitnesses to what actually took place. It was their reports to the American Board in Boston, and the State Department in Washington, that alerted the world to the fate of the Armenians. Later, in February 1916, at the request of Sir Edward Grey at the Foreign Office, Viscount James Bryce of the British House of Lords, and Arnold Toynbee, an up and coming young historian, began compiling the same documents into an official record for the British Government. Other information, from the American Committee for Armenian and Syrian Relief, "received through the highest diplomatic authority", appeared in the daily press. "We regret to say," said Samuel, "that it is only too true."

By mid-1916 Samuel felt himself to be a changed man. Although his missionary fervour still burned, and his passion for the lands of the Bible shone as bright as ever, they had become tempered with something else, with a resolute determination to ensure the world would not forget the fate of the Armenians. Ever since his first years with the Society, the years of the Macedonian massacres, Samuel had seen evidence of brutality on a terrible scale, but the crime of 1915, committed against the Armenian nation, dwarfed everything else. Just as never before had there been war on such a gigantic scale as was taking place in Europe, he thought, so never before had there been an attempt to exterminate a whole race. Samuel thought of William Essery's welcome to the twentieth century. "What wonders, mysteries, hopes and demands lie ahead?" William had asked. None of the Society's supporters, Samuel reflected, and probably not even William himself, in January 1901, could possibly have imagined the carnage the twentieth century would bring.

Like cattle they were made to march

As Samuel resolved to dedicate himself more fully to the Armenian cause, he began to print more details of the atrocities in the *Star*. Just like William Essery before him, he wanted his readers to feel the emotions he felt himself, the same shock, the same passion, and the same urgent desire for action. He hoped he was worthy of the people he wanted to serve, those who had died and those who survived.

Ernest Partridge from Sivas had already reported the barracks being built with free labour. That free labour, said the new reports, was in reality the forced labour of Armenian soldiers of the Turkish Army, who had been disarmed and conscripted into gangs of road and barrack builders. Most of them, when their usefulness was done, were clubbed or machine-gunned to death. Then, the Turkish authorities turned on the Armenian communities. At Marsovan, at Hadjin, at Bitlis, in towns and villages all over the country, the remaining able-bodied young men were shot while women, children and old men were rounded up and told to take only what they could easily carry. They were to be relocated. Filled with apprehension, their minds a chaotic mass of terrors, the Armenians left their ancestral towns and villages. Their possessions and their children they carried on their backs or sometimes on hired carts. Some looked back to see Turkish families moving into Armenian homes.

For days, for weeks, and for months, the Armenian people, travelling in enormous convoys, were driven through Turkey. The hired carts, loaded with everything they needed and valued most, their bedding, their clothes, the family photographs, the children's toys, were left behind when their guards forced them to walk on rutted tracks. Like cattle, Samuel said, they were made to march long distances, hungry and thirsty, under the burning sun.

Most were forced to walk southwards, into the waterless deserts of northern Syria; towards huge open-air concentration camps. Thousands died by the sides of the roads, where their decaying corpses were eaten by wild animals. Families were forcibly separated. The sick died as they walked. New mothers, unable to care for their babies, strangled or drowned them at birth. Where there were locusts, people ate them, where there were animal remains, they ate those too. Some reports spoke of starving people swallowing human remains. "According to reliable sources," Samuel wrote, "the accompanying gendarmes are told they may do as they wish with the women and girls." When the gendarmes had finished with them, many of those women and girls committed suicide.

Bandits and local tribesmen in the lands through which the convoys passed, attacked and robbed the Armenian exiles, often stealing pretty girls, while the bored Turkish guards stood by and watched. Water from wells was sold for the remaining possessions of people dying of thirst. From western Turkey, Armenians were transported on the new Ottoman Railway that ran southeast towards the Taurus Mountains. Eyewitnesses along the line reported thousands of people, cold, frightened and bewildered, often transported in cattle trucks, turned out at isolated stations on the bleak Anatolian plateau before being marched over the Taurus. Along the southern coasts of the Black Sea, Armenians were herded into boats, taken out into deep water, and thrown overboard alive. Others were drowned in the Tigris and the Euphrates.

Mouths watering to receive it

As much as they could the missionaries attempted to defend the people and the work of so many years. At Erzroum, where only 200 Armenians survived from a population of 20,000, the Reverend Robert Stapleton personally defied the Turkish troops. "You must kill me before you can touch them," he said of the 30 terrified Armenian girls who sheltered in his home. More often than not, such bravery was to no purpose, the missionaries were simply pushed or clubbed to the ground. Others watched, unable to intervene, as the orphans they had cared for and whose futures they planned so carefully, were led away, destined for Turkish orphanages and new Turkish names. At Anatolia College at Marsovan, the principal, Dr George White, and his staff, watched helplessly as their buildings were requisitioned by the Turkish Army. They could not contact their embassy, the Americans were told, and they should prepare to leave. Days of virtual house arrest followed, until eventually, Dr White, his family and his colleagues, were given half an hour to make ready for departure. Their own homes were to be left unsealed and their goods unregistered. Leaving Marsovan on bullock carts, the missionaries left behind the fruits of 52 years labour, supported by the Bible Lands Missions Aid Society since the beginning. On 37 acres of land there was a hospital and dispensary; six college buildings, a girls' school and a unit for deaf and dumb children; a cabinet making and iron working shop; a flour mill; thirteen houses; a library of 10,000 volumes and a museum of 7,000 objects. "All left," wrote Dr White later, "to a group of Turkish officials who stood with mouths watering to receive it."

At Van, where thousands of Armenians had sheltered in the mission compound and defended it alongside their American hosts, there had been a respite and the glimmerings of hope when Russian troops took the city. But, just as Samuel had feared earlier, when the Russians withdrew, the Armenians were left to their fate while the Americans were forced to evacuate. Some died on their journey to Tiflis, while others arrived "broken down with work and hardship". A few among the missionaries went with the Armenian deportees. Ernest Partridge and his wife reported their last sight of their colleague, Miss Mary Graffam. "We watched her departing figure," they said, "leading a cow, which she had taken to supply milk for the infants, and surrounded by women and children, passing over the hilltop, going south."

Christians in distress: rescue

Just as in 1895, the Society opened an Armenian Massacre Relief Fund. Most supporters, unable to aid their regular missions and orphans, had transferred their usual contributions to relief funds at the beginning of the war, and to their donations for Serbian civilians and to their prayers, they added the Armenian survivors. Most of those survivors, men and women who had somehow escaped the murders and the deportation convoys, fled to any haven they could reach, in Greece, in Egypt, Persia and the Caucasus. Most arrived at their destinations desperate, hungry, often sick, and with no possessions at all, sometimes dressed in rags unrecognisable as clothing. One relief worker in Persia described the pitiable condition of those who came across the frontier, "half naked and without any means of livelihood, while cholera, typhoid, and pneumonia did their worst among a people wasted by hardship, unprotected from the cold, and without any shelter".

Among the survivors, one group in particular, whose story made headlines around the world and who became a symbol of resistance to overwhelming odds, touched western hearts like almost nothing else and became a special concern of the Society. In the mountains of Musa Dagh, overlooking the north-eastern corner of the Mediterranean, 4,000 Armenian villagers held off heavily armed units of the Turkish Army for 40 days and nights. For almost all of those days, the Protestant Pastor, Dikran Antreassian, and other leaders of the group, made desperate and unsuccessful attempts to contact the outside world. Eventually, when they had almost given up hope, and their food and ammunition were almost gone, a passing French warship sighted their banners made from white bed sheets sewn with red crosses and pleas for help. "Christians in Distress: Rescue", read the banners.

The French ships took the rescued defenders of Musa Dagh to Port Said where the British authorities and the American Red Cross provided a "canvas town" complete with baths and wash houses. Spontaneous collections were made around the world. Children at Sunday Schools in Britain and America sent their pennies, and the Society, as well as providing a salary for Pastor Antreassian, supported a programme that provided work for almost every adult man and woman. The Musa Dagh survivors, said Samuel, were resourceful in every way, not only in holding the Turkish Army at bay. Despite fears that modern sewing machines might prove too complicated, a contract from the British Army, sewing shirts for soldiers, proved lucrative for the women and impressed the army so much that more sewing machines were provided for a succession of further contracts. More concerns proved unfounded when girls from Musa Dagh, "not a neighbourhood celebrated for the finer kinds of Armenian embroidery", proved apt and willing pupils and were soon producing embroidered and lace goods worthy of public sale. Other Musa Dagh workers made traditional Armenian rugs with waste wool shipped from factories at Axminster in England, the centre of Britain's traditional carpet industry. While their wives and daughters sewed shirts and produced embroidered goods, the men of Musa Dagh, many of them wooden comb makers by trade, continued to produce goods for their traditional Egyptian market, but instead of their own mountain hardwood, aged Egyptian orange and lemon trees proved a suitable, if not superior, replacement. Other men worked at a bakery funded by the Society that supplied the refugee camp with bread, "flat loaves, three for each person per day, 12,000 altogether daily". Another department worked day and night baking traditional Armenian buns and cakes, "30,000 every day", to supply a huge public demand that included the appetites of British, Canadian and Australian troops bivouacked nearby.

Uncounted multitudes

The survivors of Musa Dagh were more fortunate than most of their fellow countrymen. By the end of the Great War, more than one half of the total Armenian population of the Ottoman Empire were dead. Men, women and children lost their lives in the massacres and death marches of 1915, and in the slaughter and the dying that continued until the end of the war. It was murder on a grand scale, of nearly one and a half million people, who died simply because they were Armenian.

Another half million of Turkey's Armenians had become refugees. "Thousands have been saved so far," Samuel told readers of the *Star* in October 1917, "and new thousands are appearing, coming out of their hiding places, wearily trailing back from the desert regions to which they were deported, women and children in appalling numbers." And, there were other refugees too, he said, from many nations, "250,000 suffering Greeks, 1,000,000 Syrians and Assyrians in Syria and Palestine; 50,000 Assyrians in Persia; as well as other uncounted multitudes on every side, in Europe, in the Balkans, in Russia, and in so many other places." They were in camps, in city slums, in deserts, on mountainsides, and wandering the roads. Hundreds of thousands of people were homeless, workless and hungry, and hundreds of thousands mourned loved ones who had died. "Are we to see it through," Samuel asked the Society's supporters, "to keep them alive until they can get started again on the road to self-help?" Samuel knew there was only one answer.

In that same issue of the *Star*, very sadly, Samuel published an obituary for Robert Vaughan, the hero of the Bible Lands Medical Unit. Early in 1917, after leaving Salonica, Robert had returned home to Britain determined to join the fighting forces. He had seen too much destruction caused by the war, too many broken men and women, soldiers and civilians, and too many refugees. He wanted the war to be over and he wanted to be part of its end. In his urgency to reach the front he refused to wait for a commission and went to France as a gunner with the Royal Field Artillery. He was killed there, in action, during the Battle of Arras, on Wednesday 23 May 1917. Robert's colleague, Dr Grieve, went back to Greece later that year, to collect the surgical instruments that Robert had left waiting in the garden there for the day he returned to Florina.

Chapter 8

Smyrna

The 1920s

When General Allenby led the British Army into Jerusalem in December 1917, among the crowds waiting to welcome him was a middle-aged English woman and a group of blind Armenian and Palestinian girls. The woman's name was Mary Jane Lovell, and unlike many other British missionaries in the Holy Land, when war was declared she had ignored her government's advice to go home, saying simply, "I will not leave my blind girls."

All through the war, Mary was cut off from her loyal groups of supporters in America, Australia and Britain, but she trusted that God would provide for her and that relief would surely come. Years later, stories were told about her, how she smuggled boots and Bibles to British prisoners of war and how she defied the taunts of Turkish officials who claimed Britain was defeated and in ruins. Late in 1917, when rumours of approaching battle became a reality and Jerusalem woke one winter morning to the sound of gunfire, Mary knew her faith was rewarded and her years of isolation were almost over. For a whole day and night, as her girls sheltered in the cellars of her house, and as shrapnel fell into the garden and the streets all around, Mary waited. As the hours passed she carefully set each room in neat order and several times she straightened piles of very thick brown paper that sat on a big table in a long parlour, brushing the tips of her fingers over the sheets as she did so. Sometimes she sat down to study her Bible while at others she gazed from her windows towards the dust clouds and smoke that hung in the distant sky.

On the next day, Sunday morning, as a silence fell over the city and the blind girls wondered if they dared go to church, news began to spread, "The British are coming!" Mary and her girls followed the inquisitive crowds that hurried to see the victorious army, and they found a place to stand right where the weary Tommies would enter Jerusalem. "Hold the fort, For I am coming", Mary and the girls sang, "Jesus signals still, Wave the answer back to heaven, By thy grace we will." The little group sang it for the dusty soldiers trudging wearily by and they sang it for all the years Mary had spent alone in Jerusalem, trusting that God would give her the strength to survive and faith for the day of deliverance. The words could also have been the anthem for all the Christian workers in the war ravaged lands of the Bible as they struggled to bring life and hope to shattered communities and devastated people.

We will help them

"Personnel and funds are urgently needed," said a cable from Syria to Samuel Gentle-Cackett in London, "clothing for 10,000; blankets, milk, sugar, medical supplies, motor transport, shelter and training homes for older boys, orphanage for older girls... Gathering thousands more orphans." Samuel and Lord Kinnaird appealed to the Society's supporters. "With God's help we *can*," said Kinnaird's appeal in the *Star*, "and with your help we *will* help these helpless remnants, rescued from Turkish hate and cruelty." And, just as they had always responded before, despite wartime tragedies of their own, the Society's supporters gave with overwhelming generosity. Thousands of pounds were donated to the cause of the Armenian refugees.

Refugees in their thousands were gathered in northern Syria around Aleppo, the junction of the railways and roads that had taken them there from all over Turkey. They had been torn from everything that once gave their lives meaning: country, home, loved ones and possessions. They had witnessed the violent deaths of hundreds of thousands of their nation, dying during the terrible marches into Syria, or in the concentration camps the Turks set up there. Housing and feeding the traumatised and desolate survivors, and giving them hope for the future, became the task of the international relief agencies.

A thousand tragedies

Stephen Trowbridge, who had been secretary of the American Red Cross in Cairo when the Musa Dagh survivors arrived in Egypt, took charge of distributing the Society's relief funds in Syria. His knowledge of the region, and its most recent events, had led General Allenby to appoint him director of relief in the Aleppo region and also interpreter for the parties who arrested some of the worst Turkish offenders, including guards from the notorious concentration camp at Deir Zor. At Marash, Stephen witnessed the arrest of a particular henchman of Enver Talaat, Turkey's Interior Minister and the chief architect of the genocide.

Stephen became a regular correspondent for the *Star*, and in October 1918, after visiting Antoura, a Turkish orphanage north of Beirut, he wrote an article called "The Shelter of a Thousand Tragedies". Antoura was set up to house 2,000 Armenian and Kurdish children, Stephen said, the large numbers of Kurds proving to him that the policies of the Turkish Government were racist rather than religious, and when he had arrived at the orphanage, only 669 children were still alive. The rest were buried in unmarked graves.

All the young survivors, Stephen said, had terrible stories to tell. They remembered how their parents and their brothers and sisters had died on the death marches. They remembered the murders, the rapes and the mutilations they had seen. They remembered how their Armenian and Kurdish names had been stolen from them and how their languages had been forbidden. They remembered that Christian crosses were ripped from Armenian necks and that they were forced to follow the rites of Islam, instructed in Turkish ideas and customs and "the reasons for contributing to the glory of Ottoman arms and the prestige of the Turkish race". The plan, said Stephen, was for girls to be distributed among harems where they would become breeders of the Turkish race, while boys were destined for menial tasks in the Ottoman Army.

Levon from Malgara, Stephen said, a teenager whose little sisters were taken away to a Kurdish harem, was tortured when he refused to deny his Armenian nationality. After long days of starvation, rough cotton was stuffed into his throat, almost choking the boy, who still refused to "confess himself a Kurd and a

Muslim". Takouhi from Rodosto had watched her once wealthy parents die of typhus after they walked over the Taurus ranges to Aleppo, begging for food all the way and surrendering their remaining possessions for water from Arab wells. Takouhi's name was changed to Muzeyyan. Eleven-year-old Mihrdad from Adabazar near Broussa walked across the whole of Asia Minor to Aleppo and watched his father freeze to death and his mother drown in a swollen river. "Sir," said one small boy to Stephen, as he remembered leaving his mother dead beneath the blistering Syrian sun, "may you never see anyone die of thirst." But now, Stephen reassured the *Star*'s readers, Professor Stewart Crawford, of the Syrian Protestant College, had become the director of Antoura and "the best friend the children had ever had".

In Britain, Samuel Gentle-Cackett read Stephen's reports with horror. He thought about the Armenian children he met before the war and the thought of others like them, struggling along freezing mountain pathways, forced to watch their parents die, and then being stripped of their names and their religion, caused him such a mixture of grief and anger that whenever he read the reports he wept with anguish. "Hot tears fall upon the pages," he told readers of the *Star*, "and a lump rises in one's throat. Can anyone read the story of the children in Antoura without some feeling of emotion?" Samuel's own feelings of emotion led him to make a heartfelt appeal for the orphanage. "For the love of God," he wrote, "shall we not share with these children the best things we have? Shall not the BLMAS help to make the orphanage of a thousand tragedies into a home of 10,000 blessings?"

Learning the ways of peace

Samuel was anxious to turn tragedy into blessing however he could, and as 1917 and 1918 went by, a scheme that was taking ever greater shape in his mind, gradually turned into reality. The orphan girls whose lives Miss Matthews and Darinka Gruitch had saved, Samuel resolved, would soon find a refuge in Britain, where they would learn the ways of peace, be educated alongside the ordinary boys and girls of Bedfont, and be trained to be blessings to their nation. Earlier in the war, at Samuel's instigation, refugee children from Belgium had found a temporary haven at Bedfont, and he had no doubt that his neighbours would welcome girls from Armenia and the Balkans with the same generosity and kindness.

The land for a permanent establishment, Samuel told his friends, was already waiting. It was just yards from the site of his own home on the Staines Road and the Bedfont Tabernacle that sat next door. For quite a few years, he said, he had had a powerful feeling that God was telling him to buy plots of land as they gradually became available, and now, with the land secured, all that was needed was a building, large enough to function as a temporary shelter until something more solid could get underway.

"Sell huts – buy food for Russia," read a cable from the American Red Cross to a sea captain in mid-Atlantic. The Armistice in Europe and the famine that followed the Russian Revolution had led to the change of plan, and the huts, three large and two small, were hastily unloaded onto the Liverpool dockside and an advertisement placed in the British press. Within days of responding, Samuel found himself the owner of one large hut, "82 side sections, 70 roof sections, 34 floor sections and so on", and wondering how he could ever transport them to Bedfont. The solution was Harry Fear. "And, sure enough," said Samuel later, "lorry after lorry, bearing the name of 'Fear Bros, Ltd' transferred the tremendous quantity of materials to the site."

"Do not give your workmen a saw," said the construction details that accompanied the hut, and just as the directions promised, and to the great satisfaction of the intrigued Samuel and Harry, "each section fitted together as if putting up a row of shutters on a shop front". The finished building, large enough to house and sleep 20 girls and a matron, was named Bethany, for the welcome and refuge that Martha and Mary always gave to Jesus.

Samuel never forgot the arrival of Bethany's first group of orphan girls. They came via Marseilles with Mrs Mihitsopoulos, the Scottish wife of a Greek Evangelical pastor in Salonica, and were "a motley little crowd, their clothing just makeshift for the journey, their shoes long since worn out and most carrying a little bundle containing all their worldly belongings". In the most extraordinary way, said Samuel, the little group had been provided for all along their journey. At Waterloo Station a kindly woman assistant in the war canteen provided fresh coffee. Travellers and soldiers on leave supplied bread and butter for breakfast. And at Bedfont, "although there was no announcement of their coming, it seemed that everybody was near at hand and ready with a welcome".

Samuel always remembered too how the girls all suffered nightmares about the terrible things they had seen and endured. In the early hours they woke up dreaming of artillery fire or fearing that enemy soldiers hid among the shadows, but eventually, comfort and kindness and the peace of suburban England had an effect. The girls all learned English, attended the local Feltham Council School where some of them carried off top prizes, and then at training colleges they learned the skills to take home to their own lands. "The joy is so great," Samuel wrote later, "when visiting the Near East, to meet in one country or another, young women, who owe their start in life to Bethany."

Bullets whizzed above them

Despite Turkey's defeat in the Great War, the remnant of the Armenian nation were not safe. There were still Armenians left in Turkey, as well as Greeks, who also suffered at the hands of the Turks. When Cilicia, in south-eastern Asia Minor came under French control pending the outcome of the Peace Conference at Versailles, thousands of desperate refugees sought a haven there among their fellow Armenians and Greeks. But although Turkey may have finally lost its empire, under the nationalist government of its new leader, Mustafa Kemal, it had no intention of losing land from within its own boundaries. Early in 1920, Cilicia came under Turkish attack.

At the Armenian orphanage in Aintab, Miss Martha Frearson, a long time friend of the Society, found herself in the line of battle as the Turkish Army closed in. For more than a week, the children huddled together on the lower floors of the building, while bullets whizzed above them and artillery shells exploded in the grounds. Martha herself personally defied the mobs who hammered on the barricaded doors. "We are out to butcher all the Armenian filth," they shouted, "we will come here first of all, kill you, everyone, and burn the whole place down." The nights were the worst, Martha remembered later, "The heaviest attacks were always at night!" The battle for Aintab raged until Easter Sunday, "a day never effaced from our memories", when a truce was finally arranged for the orphans. Doing her utmost to appear calm while all the time pleading inwardly to God to protect them, Martha dressed every child in as many clothes as possible and gave each one a quilt and a bag of cereal to carry. "Hold them tight, don't drop them," she said. Then, with Martha and the children clustered around a white flag, and with smoke and ashes from the burning city billowing around them, the orphanage was evacuated. Utterly terrified, the little children broke away and ran as fast as they could while Martha and the older girls followed more slowly, gathering up the quilts and bags the little ones had dropped. At the Armenian barricades, the city's defenders, with tears in their eyes, made way for the orphans, and Martha hoped that at last she might have a good night's sleep. "But I was thankful to slip down and pillow my head on a girl's body," she wrote, "for the bullets were coming so rapidly through the window." Eventually, just as the beleaguered defenders began to fear for the survival of the orphans, a message came by aeroplane that the children should somehow be evacuated from Aintab. Led by Armenian relief workers, Martha Frearson, her own orphans and 900 others joined 3,000 refugees and a convoy of French soldiers who fought a way through to Beirut. "Upon their arrival," said the *Star*, "the committee of the Bible Lands Missions Aid Society cabled £600 for immediate relief."

Will you go?

When the Great War ended, the American Commission for Relief in the Near East, the successor to the Committee for Armenian and Syrian Relief, sent a delegation to Turkey to investigate the genocide committed against the Armenians. "If you are wanted in Turkey," Lord Kinnaird asked Samuel, "will you go?" Kinnaird showed Samuel the telegram passed to him that morning by the Foreign Office. The Secretary of the Bible Lands Missions Aid Society, it said, was requested by the Peace Conference at Versailles, to join the American Commission. Through Konia, Adana, Aleppo and Oorfa, travelling, sleeping and cooking in a covered railway truck, Samuel and the Commission crossed eastern Turkey into Syria. "Among all the terrible sights we saw," said Samuel later, "the one that remains with me most of all, is the one I saw in Aleppo." For the rest of his life, Samuel could never forget the bleak expressions and the haunted eyes of "the 5,000 refugees returning from Deir Zor – all that remained of the 60,000 who had been driven there across the desert."

Another request took Samuel to Turkey again in 1921, this time to Cilicia, just as rumours began circulating that French forces were planning to abandon the province. The events of the previous year, that had driven Miss Frearson from Aintab, had also broken the health of Dr Nesbitt Chambers, the American Board's senior missionary at Adana. Could the Secretary of the Bible Lands Missions Aid Society step in for three months? asked the Board. Once again, Samuel left his wife Elizabeth to care for the Bedfont orphans and the Society's London office, and set off across Europe. As he did so, he marvelled at how times were changing, "London to Constantinople, now only 90 hours by train!" Other travellers were heading back to the Near East too, among them Nurse Ash, another old friend of the Society's, in whose sitting room at Aleppo, with a British POW guarding the door, German and Turkish officers had discussed their surrender to General Allenby.

Samuel's baby chickens caused something of a headache for the customs officials of Europe. At every national frontier, they puzzled over how to categorise the chirping birds, how to record them and whether there was any duty to pay on them. To the amusement of Nurse Ash and her fellow travellers, while the officials puzzled, Samuel calmly gathered fresh grass for his tiny charges, and relied on God to find a solution. The solution, when it came, was usually a shrug of official shoulders and a comment later about the eccentricity of the English race. "Rhode Island Reds," Samuel always explained, to customs officials and anyone else who would listen, "a gift for the Farm School at Salonica." Samuel carried other gifts for Salonica too, far less a source of amusement than boxes of yellow chicks, but a more immediate and vital necessity for saving human life. Camped out at Salonica, ravaged by battlefield wounds, hunger and disease, was all that remained of General Wrangle's White Russian army after its defeat by the Bolsheviks in the Crimea. The suffering was enormous, Samuel said later, especially among the women and children who had accompanied the retreat, and the Society's condensed milk and quinine reduced the death toll from 200 to 20 per thousand per week.

Samuel was never a man to waste time or opportunity, and there were many calls on his time and talents during his months at Adana, where the town and the whole region around was packed with refugees, the remnants of the deportations from interior towns. In the city itself he took on Dr Chambers' administrative work, helped pastor the congregations and became something of a favourite with the children. Mary Webb, the Adana Station Secretary, wrote later to Lord Kinnaird to say how much everyone at the mission had valued Samuel's time with them. "In all ways," she said, "by his counsel and fellowship, he has been a help to those trying to hold the work together." She also added, "The little children of the orphanage have been delighted by his talks." At Deurt Yol, "another large centre of refugees", Samuel helped draw up the building plans for the Kinnaird Home, an extension to an orphanage supported by the Society, while nearby at Tarsus, where the Society was funding a building and refurbishment programme for St Paul's College, "my knowledge of such matters was continually in demand", he said. British prisoners of war had been imprisoned in the Tarsus college grounds during the war, and during his time there, Samuel located information for the War Graves Commission about any who had died, and later in Britain he traced relatives of the dead men. One of Samuel's most moving experiences during that time in Cilicia, was the prayer meeting he held at the new church at Osmanieh. Early in the morning, as the first sunbeams shone through the dawn mists, Samuel and a group of Armenian companions remembered the Armenian and American pastors who were murdered at Osmanieh in 1909.

Written in blood

Just after Samuel left Adana for home, as Kinnaird House neared completion and new windows and lockers for St Paul's College sat ready on an English dockside, the French abandoned Cilicia. In another Relief Supplement, headlined Written in Blood, Samuel described what had happened. "According to trustworthy information," he began, "the Armenians in Cilicia are desperate and panic-stricken over the forthcoming evacuation of the French troops. Kemalist newspapers in Bozanti, and other Turkish activities, are openly provoking massacres." The Armenians in Cilicia, as well as the large Greek community, had good reason to panic. As France withdrew its troops, its authorities in Cilicia advised any Christians, both the inhabitants of many years and the sheltering refugees, to evacuate the province. "As far as one can tell," Samuel wrote, "a stampede is taking place." The remnant of south-eastern Turkey's Christian population, who had hoped the European Powers would protect them, were attacked. Ten thousand Greeks and 100,000 Armenians were butchered without mercy while those who managed to escape fled to Syria, to Egypt, and the islands of Greece. "Now that the people are fleeing in terror and all the work will probably be destroyed," Samuel wrote in the *Star* of his months in Cilicia, the question will arise, was it worth it? "Yes," he answered, "a thousand times yes. I do not regret it, even if all my work is undone. I am thankful that God gave me health and strength to accomplish so much for the Kingdom of his dear Son, and now I pray I may still be spared to work for these persecuted, unoffending Armenians."

For a while, the Bible Lands Missions Aid Society undertook to be the sole relief agency for refugees who reached the Greek Islands, while in Syria, where it already supported others in the field, more funds were sent as old friends applied for help. Mary Webb who had escaped from Adana with several hundred children was caring for refugees in a makeshift camp. "The people are heartsick and discouraged," she wrote, "how could it be otherwise?" But, she also reported optimistically, her Armenian colleagues, preachers and teachers from Adana, were beginning to rouse their own spirits and start work once more among their people. Baynard Dodge, working in Syria on behalf of Near East Relief, confirmed it when he thanked the Society for a £500 grant towards medical work. Tremendous energy was being put in, he said, to ensure that work and homes of some sort were found for the refugees. "Many are living in little patchwork shelters," he wrote, "and are happy as long as the bright summer sunshine lasts. When the winter storms come things will be different."

Other Armenian refugees had joined Pastor Dikran Antreassian and the survivors of Musa Dagh at Port Said where the Society had provided wooden shelters to replace "the canvas town". More grants supported the camp trade schools where boys were taught carpentry, tailoring and shoemaking, and another provided a day nursery, founded so mothers could work, and covered the salaries of a teacher, eight helpers and a washerwoman. And at Broussa, near Constantinople, the orphanage supported by the Society for so many years, Armenian children still found a refuge. In 1921, a group of orphans were discovered sleeping in the yard of the town's Armenian church. Their parents were dead and the boys had walked for months, possibly for years as none seemed to have any clear memory of the past. They wore nothing but rags, "their clothes the colour of dust", and most suffered from tuberculosis. The Broussa staff took the boys in, bathed them, gave them new clothes and clean beds and the first hot meals some of them could ever remember.

In the year following the evacuation of Cilicia, relief workers in the Balkans and throughout the Near East dared to believe that a breathing space was in sight. It seemed that a hush had fallen over the region, marking the end of the violence, they hoped, and they began to speak of long-term possibilities: rehabilitation for refugees, perhaps even resettlement, more industrial programmes for the camps, schools and community centres, permanent clinics and hospitals. Samuel allowed himself to be encouraged by news from Western Turkey. The Constantinople and Smyrna stations, based in regions that had escaped relatively unscathed from the genocide, had met as the Western Turkey Mission for the first time since 1914, and two of the staff had written to say public work in education and evangelism might begin again soon. They were very enthusiastic, they said, about plans for their schools in Smyrna and they requested a grant for some particular students "who felt called to the ministry". The mission wanted to send the students to a new School of Religion in the Near East and they asked Samuel if the Society would fund the scholarships. Samuel was delighted. He knew one of the students in question and had been extraordinarily impressed by him. His name was Krikor Demerjian, or Blind Krikor as Samuel called him, and he had been a student at St Paul's College, Tarsus, "doing remarkably well in his studies despite the heavy handicap of being blind". Somehow, said Samuel, Krikor and Hohannes Abkarian, his friend who supported him in his studies, had both escaped, "rather miraculously", from the Cilician massacres and had found shelter together in Smyrna. Samuel appealed to the Society's supporters to aid Krikor, Hohannes and the other students, ten young men in all, recommended by the

Western Turkey Mission. "We trust those whose hearts have been specially touched of late," he said, "by the sorrows and sufferings of the sorely tried and persecuted Christians of the East, will co-operate in the endeavour to raise up in their midst a band of loyal ministers of the Word and true shepherds of the flock."

Lining water's edge for miles

"Details of Smyrna Calamity and Relief will be found on page 25" read a caption printed in bright red letters on a small piece of white paper attached to the front covers of the *Star in the East* dated November 1922. The twelve words signified a huge disaster, a devastating blow to all those who hoped that death had run its course and that life and a peaceful future might finally be restored to the people of the Near East.

Samuel first received the news in cables from the Near East Relief office in Smyrna. For someone who had read so many appeals for relief and so many accounts of murder and human brutality, he thought to himself, the Smyrna details shocked him in a way that startled him. They seemed so vivid and so immediate. He felt he could see, quite clearly in his mind's eye, the crowds of desperate people who lined the water's edge at Smyrna with the Turkish Army at their backs and nothing before them but the great open sea. Samuel felt he could almost hear their anguished cries echoing faintly in the streets of London.

He printed the cables from Near East Relief verbatim in the *Star*. "Fifty thousand without food or water lining water's edge for miles under broiling sun – crying with arms uplifted in pitiful supplication to be taken off – harbour crowded with bodies," said a cable of 14 September. "Fire of Armenian quarter – eventually city burned – great loss of life – Horton reports seeing Turkish soldiers with cans of petrol and petrol soaked rags thrown into Armenian houses," said another on the 15th. "Delay of Allied governments to take measures to evacuate gives Turks opportunity to deport hundreds – Armenian and Greek girls torn from families – ships come with relief supplies – but corpses in streets and harbour bring fear of plague," said another, on the 21st.

In the years following the Great War, as the victorious powers determined who would inherit the old Ottoman Empire, the city of Smyrna hoped for independent status. It seemed only right to

Smyrna's large and wealthy Greek and Armenian minorities, that the prosperous seaport, with its great western business houses, its trading links with Europe, its liberal ways and its cosmopolitan outlook, should be separate from Turkey whose nationalist government seemed more intent than ever on stamping a rigid and conformist Turkish identity on its entire population.

But, despite the optimistic hopes of Smyrna's westernised Armenians and Greeks, in the late summer of 1922, following an abortive Greek invasion two years earlier that was not without its own brand of atrocity, another catastrophe began to unfold. In early September, as the Greek Army retreated in the face of a Turkish advance, thousands of terrified Greek and Armenian civilians, most of them farmers whose ancestors for thousands of years had cultivated some of the most productive land in Asia Minor, began arriving with their possessions in the city. They joined a panic-stricken local population desperate for rescue by an Allied war fleet, French, Italian, American and British, destroyers and battleships, that rested at anchor in Smyrna's huge bay or patrolled the open Aegean beyond.

A wall of fire

The first detachments of the Turkish Army arrived in Smyrna on Saturday 9 September. Some time later, the city's Armenian quarter began to burn. Eyewitnesses reported seeing Turkish soldiers carrying petrol cans and petrol soaked rags. Others said they saw Armenian inhabitants, desperate to escape, driven back by Turkish soldiers into the fires that took such a hold on the city that eventually two thirds of Smyrna was an inferno of explosions and flame. Watchers on the Western ships in the bay described a wall of fire more than two miles long, with warehouses, churches and mosques, silhouetted against the flames and the whole city overhung with a pall of black smoke. Anyone not burned alive fled to the quayside where nearly half a million people became trapped between the burning city and the sea.

As the smoke rose over Smyrna and the sea glowed red and the screams of desperate people were heard miles away, an air of dreadful unreality descended on the once great city. For nearly four weeks, relief agencies sent food and medical supplies to Smyrna's aid workers who set up bakeries and emergency hospitals for the trapped citizens who every day were attacked, murdered and deported by the Turks. Dr Esther Lovejoy, an American physician, described the situation later for the *Star*. The old and sick died of exhaustion, she said. Some people went mad. Many, fearing their fate at the hands of the Turks, committed suicide by throwing themselves into the sea. Girls and young women were abducted or raped openly in the streets by gangs of Turkish soldiers. Armenian and Greek men were hunted down and killed. Dr Esther delivered babies on the quayside while streams of panicking humanity surged about her and the smell of dead bodies, urine, excrement and fear, drifted out to sea. And, on the sea, to the fury of their rank and file sailors, the Western ships obeyed the orders of their governments to remain as neutral observers.

Eventually, after weeks, an international agreement allowed Smyrna's survivors, Krikor Demerjian among them, to be evacuated to Greece in Greek ships. Dr Esther described how the departing refugees passed through ranks of Turkish soldiers who stole their remaining possessions.

Estimates of the numbers who died at Smyrna vary. Many died of disease or committed suicide. Huge numbers were murdered outright in the streets. Thousands burned to death in the fire. Thousands more were led away into Turkey's interior, their eventual fate guessed at but mostly unknown. George Horton, American Consul in the region, reckoned that the final estimate was somewhere in the region of just over 100,000 lives.

Three hundred thousand more were finally rescued from the "broad, magnificent quay", where Maria West once welcomed British sailors to the Rest, where the German bands and dancing girls had shocked the Reverend Mr More and where Maud Constantine and her Greek husband had worked for the Greek Evangelical Union. Behind them, in Asia Minor, the land of their ancestors, where the Turkish Army were busy dynamiting what remained of Greek and Armenian Smyrna, the refugees left thousands of years of their history and the ruins of a great seaport. As the final evening of the evacuation passed, as the warships of the great powers of the Western world sat impassively on the darkening sea, and the last Greek ships bore their sad cargoes away into exile, Smyrna, the last light of the Seven Churches of Asia, went down in flames.

Chapter 9

Homeless
Millions
The 1920s

"The need for medical aid and supplies at Mitylene is beyond description." "The Island of Mamora has 10,000 refugees who have been keeping alive eating vegetables and roots. Hundreds fallen victim to typhoid." "In the confusion, children separated from parents wander the streets, and hysterical mothers in turn search for them." "30,000 refugees at Chios; more arriving; no bread; little water; sanitation horrible."

In the makeshift camps, set up in Greece and the Greek Islands on land donated by the Greek Government, the refugees from Smyrna, in their thousands, sheltered in hastily donated tents or ramshackle constructions of battered oil drums and packing cases. They had no possessions. They had seen their homes and their loved ones destroyed. They were lost and bewildered. They were hungry, sick and bereaved. "When the winter rains come," said Pastor Mihitsopoulos, whose Scottish wife had taken the first Bedfont orphans to England, "a great dying will begin."

Aristides Mihitsopoulos was right. Despite massive amounts of money raised by voluntary contributions, especially in Britain and America, despite the work of relief agencies and the combined efforts of refugee doctors and international medical volunteers, during the winter that followed Smyrna the refugees died in their thousands. One hundred and fifty thousand died in mainland Greece alone, and from every refugee camp, sad processions of people worn down by grief carried the wasted bodies of their fellow countrymen through the rains and chills of winter to their final resting place, a mass grave in a foreign land.

No choice but God

In 1923, the refugee crisis was exacerbated by the Great Population Exchange. At the Lausanne Conference, chaired by Britain's Lord Curzon, Greek and Turkish delegates finally agreed to a peace settlement for their troubled region. Among the conditions was the wholesale removal and resettlement of ethnic populations. Over one and a quarter million Orthodox Christians were expelled from Turkey to Greece and other countries in the Balkans. Eight hundred thousand Muslims travelled in the other direction, from the Balkans to Turkey. All of them, Christian and Muslim alike, left their homes and the lands of their ancestors, and took with them only what they could carry on their backs or drag behind them in home-made carts.

By the end of 1923, there were millions of displaced people all across the Balkans and the Near East, and for the leaders of the communities, the task confronting them was of almost inconceivable proportions. For the Armenian leaders; teachers, priests and pastors, it was especially hard. Often they had been singled out by the Turks for particularly brutal treatment. They had been tortured and humiliated. They had watched helplessly as people who trusted them were murdered before their eyes. But despite their own personal torment, they knew they had no choice but to trust in God to uphold them and to carry them through the tides of despair and self-doubt, and to point them to the future.

The Bible Lands Missions Aid Society suffered a sorrow of its own in 1923. In June, the *Star* announced the death of the Society's Honorary Treasurer, Lord Kinnaird. To Samuel Gentle-Cackett, the passing of Kinnaird, whose father had sat beside Lord Shaftesbury at Exeter Hall on the day the Society was founded, seemed to mark a significant moment. He thought about the Society's early days, how Cuthbert Young and Cyrus Hamlin had yearned for the conversion of all Armenians to Evangelical Protestantism, but that as the years had passed and the world had changed, the Society had gradually developed other priorities. He thought about William Essery too, and how the outwardly placid William had burned inside for the massacred victims of 1895 and the sufferings of the survivors. And now, he thought, after so many more deaths that it was almost impossible to comprehend the numbers, there was more suffering and more refugees than ever. Perhaps, he thought, that was the real reason God had founded the Society, and the reason he had maintained it through the years; so that it could raise the fallen, succour the wounded, speak for the voices that had been silenced, and hold the fort for Jesus.

"We cannot turn a deaf ear," said Samuel in the *Star*, "to the wail of the widow or the cry of the orphan. Today thousands of refugees, survivors of Turkish atrocities are calling for help." In the face of such enormous need, that help was a slow and uneven process. "So far as I know," said a report from Aleppo, "Armenians have never been so destitute and miserable." But, gradually, with the support of the Society and the American organisation, Near East Relief, small changes, and sometimes big changes, were made. Sometimes it was wooden constructions that replaced tents and petrol can shelters as Bible Lands Rows, wooden frame buildings divided into family sections, became a feature in some camps. Sometimes it was a wooden hospital building staffed by Western and Armenian medical personnel. Sometimes a feeding station. Or a milk station for babies. Sometimes it was a new hut or a big tent used as a school.

Old faces: new beginnings

As the refugee camps became permanently established slums around the major cities of Greece, Lebanon and Syria, survivors from the same towns and regions in Turkey found each other and found ways to live closer together, an echo of the past providing a fragile structure for the future. Some camps were known colloquially by the old Armenian Turkish names, Marash, Aintab, Zeitoon, and sometimes their camp committees, where surviving Gregorian, Protestant and Catholic leaders worked closely together, were made up of familiar faces and names from the past.

Other familiar names from the past reappeared too, as Armenian and Western workers resolved that some of the most famous Armenian schools and colleges of Turkey would not die. Lucile Foreman, once a missionary with the Central Turkey Mission, reopened the Aintab Girls' High School in Aleppo as the Armenian Protestant High School. The new building was something of a challenge, she said, everything needed constant patching, the wind whistled through the windows, and everyone got soaked running through the rain from the main building to the dining room. And then there were endless stairs, "how your heart pumps when you climb those inside stairs!" But, what mattered most, she said, was the pupils, "and the girls are so wonderfully appreciative, and so happy".

Among other schools and colleges from Turkey that re-emerged in new surroundings was the Konia Institute, opening first in Aleppo and later in Beirut. Konia was founded in 1874, Samuel told readers of the *Star*, for the education of pastors, preachers and teachers of the Evangelical churches of the Konia district. He also told them how Konia's President, Dr Armeneg Haigazian, a graduate of the Central Turkey College, was murdered by the Turks in 1921. "At the present time," said Samuel, "the college property is in Turkish hands and the boys and girls that formerly attended the Institute have vanished from the land. But among the Armenian survivors are boys and girls, eager for knowledge, dauntless in their courage, hopeful for the future, and firm in their faith in God." They are doing the very best they can, he said, when he made a special appeal for Konia in the *Star*, "and no one can tell what the future holds, but we must help them in their efforts to rebuild a new nation from the remnants of the old".

In Greece too, new beginnings were being made, and another of the Society's old friends reappeared in new surroundings at Salonica where Dr George White and his colleagues vowed that Anatolia College would rise once more to be a great centre of learning. In 1924, Dana Getchell, Chairman of the Salonica Station of the American Board's Greek Mission, wrote in the *Star*, that "on Wednesday last, the new school opened in its rented location. Sixteen students and a faculty consisting of one Englishman, three Greeks, one Armenian, and three Americans, were in their places at the first chapel exercises". Three years later, in 1927, Dana wrote with more good news and to thank the Society for its help towards the project. "On the instalment plan," he said, the large rented building and four acres of land had finally been purchased. Anatolia College was underway once more.

More thanks to the Society were due, said Dana, for the truly unique renovation of another building on the college campus, an old and dilapidated wooden barracks used by French forces of the

Great War and then by crowds of poor refugees. Turning it into comfortable living quarters for 80 boarders, with dormitories, kitchens and an infirmary, "had seemed like a dream, an impossible task". But, when 20 poor students offered to undertake the work during their vacation, and local refugee workmen, "carpenters, masons and hod-carriers", queued to join them, and the Bible Lands Missions Aid Society agreed to pay all the daily wages, "it was a most happy combination!"

Before long, the work was underway, said Dana, "And tearing down partitions and erecting new ones, laying real board floors, whitewashing, plastering, painting – making new doors and windows, renovating tiles, straightening the roof, digging cesspools and building wood sheds and outbuildings – all went merrily on." The boys thrived on the work, he said, and looked forward to payday, and "each felt proud to count money that his own labour had earned". When a shower block was installed in the dormitory, he said, people flocked from the nearby refugee camp to be amazed at the latest marvel in modern plumbing technology.

And there were even more thanks due to the Society, said Dana, for London Lodge, another renovated building, and "another most useful and greatly appreciated donation from the BLMAS". At London Lodge too, he said, the students worked on the renovations that provided a home for Anatolia's college library, full of "valuable books, papers and periodicals for the daily use of students", as well as new classrooms for physics, chemistry and biology.

Everything was completed with two weeks to spare before the beginning of term, said Dana, but instead of taking a vacation, the working students preferred to put the final finishing touches to their hard work. They learned a lot during their time of labour, he said, lessons that they would take with them through life: "the value of money that is earned by the sweat of the brow, to work with and respect the common working man and the meaning of an eight hour day's work, but, most of all, they learned the true dignity of labour and that all true labour is noble and holy".

Samuel to the rescue

Samuel Gentle-Cackett was a man who believed in the dignity of labour too and in always doing his utmost for whatever task came to hand. In 1924, Miss Lena Leitzou, Principal of the Salonica Girls' School, where the Society provided refugee scholarships, described for the *Star* how Samuel had come to her rescue. She described the crowds of poor refugees, all so eager to register their girls for the new term that even though she felt overwhelmed by the numbers she could not bear to turn them away. "As you know," she said, "our school comfortably seats 150. Last year, owing to the press of refugees, we crowded in 215. You, perhaps, will wonder where we are putting our 302 this year. The question certainly kept us awake at nights!" Mr Gentle-Cackett arrived a few days before school began, said Lena, "and we laid our problems before him". The solution was simple, said Samuel, tear down that ramshackle block of disused buildings and replace them with a temporary frame structure of three large rooms. The Society, he said, would provide the funds. And then, said Lena, "Mr Gentle-Cackett got his refugee workmen together, took his coat off, rolled his sleeves up, and has been right on the job for several days."

Dr Ruth hears God's call

More grants went to Salonica when Dr Ruth Parmalee, on behalf of American Women's Hospitals, opened a maternity hospital for the city's refugee population. After being deported by the Turks from Harpoot, Dr Ruth planned a brief respite in Constantinople before heading home to America. But, when people told her about conditions among Salonica's refugees and how boats from Asia Minor were still delivering the last ragged remnants of Turkey's Christian population to its quayside, Dr Ruth heard God's call. In Salonica, the squalid conditions and the sight of "babies being born on the streets – in merest hovels", moved her to action, and with enormous determination she set about obtaining a large building and fitting it out with 100 beds. It was, said Samuel, when he made a special appeal for Dr Ruth in the *Star*, "a real life-saving campaign, and all honour is due to the brave, tired woman, who surmounted every obstacle and overcame every difficulty to start the work".

Well known at the Foreign Office

Samuel travelled a lot during the 1920s, backwards and forwards across Europe, from railway station to railway station, always anxious to devote his time, his energy and his expertise to the welfare of the refugees and orphans of the Near East and the Balkans. More than 20 years experience of working with refugees from some of the world's worst atrocities had made him an invaluable source of information and his advice was sought not only by individual orphanages and schools, but by national governments and international agencies desperate to ensure that the huge numbers of uprooted people did not cause political crises or civil unrest. "Mr Gentle-Cackett was well known at the Foreign Office," said an old friend many years later, "and his influence with men of affairs was considerable."

The Greek Government was among those that asked for help, and in 1923, at its request, the Society agreed to manage the Mount Olympus Orphanage near Salonica, based in a large abandoned monastery with thousands of acres of cultivated ground. "Now instead of six monks and one abbot who were the sole occupants two years ago," Samuel told readers of the *Star*, there are 200 orphan boys under its roof, all being cared for, educated and trained in useful trades. "We are responsible for this orphanage and shall be glad to receive special gifts towards the support of the boys," he said, "the cost is about 3s. 6d. per week for each boy, or £9 a year," somewhere in the region of £253.50 or $380.30 today. The Society's supporters sponsored every boy.

A glimpse inside

More supporters sponsored children at another Greek orphanage maintained by the Society at Corinth. A story in the *Star*, "A Glimpse Inside", told readers something about life there. Under a picture of the kindergarten children playing at bread making, an article described how the little ones had made visits to the different departments of the orphanage, "the farm, the trades, the kitchen and bakery", and how they were keen to try for themselves some of the skills they had seen. Readers also learned about life for the older children, how the Girls' League befriended and organised the younger ones and how the Lost and Found

Committee kept track of belongings. A list of talks by specially invited speakers gave an insight into the interests of the teenagers; Armenian literature, Tradition and Environment, The Power of Suggestion, Co-operation. In the boys' department, the League of Self-Expression aimed to train "Soldiers in the School of Character", and at their own request, the boys kept a record of their good deeds and read them out at weekly meetings. "A boy would make a kite," said one, "but had no paper. I gave him mine." "Someone had spit on the ground," said another, "I covered it with sand." And a third, "The end of a boy's knife was bent. I fixed it on the anvil and I sharpened it on the grindstone. He said, 'Thank you'; I said, 'Don't mention it.'"

Extensions in all directions

In 1924, again at the request of the Greek Government, the Society took responsibility for a new refugee agricultural colony at Katarina near Salonica. The success of the venture encouraged the Serbian Government, anxious to resettle Serbs still homeless since the Great War, to invite the Society to oversee another scheme, Karageorgevitch in Kosovo. Loans of £50 were made to each resettled family, "which, with a certain amount of wood, cement, nails and roofing tiles from their own governments, will be sufficient to build a house". Other loans bought agricultural implements and seed. Both schemes were successful, and "from a little start," Samuel told readers of the *Star*, "important relief works have developed along co-operative lines". At Katarina, he said, about 85 per cent of the original seed loans had been repaid, and in their turn loaned to other refugees, while at the same time, malaria, "a veritable scourge" in the district, had been almost eradicated after the employment by the Society of the Russian Dr Feldsherr.

The success at Katarina, said Samuel, "has compelled extensions in all directions", and six seed distribution and collection centres had been built in the area with money provided by the Society. However, he said, the buildings were much more than seed stores. Each one was so constructed that it doubled as a dispensary for peripatetic medical staff funded by the Society, one doctor, three assistant doctors, three pharmacists and three nurses, and for medicines each day to about £6 in value.

Referring to a picture printed in the *Star* with an article about Katarina that depicted the Bible Lands Ark, the large central seed store and dispensary based at the Salonica Farm, "many of our friends," he said, "will be interested to notice the little low roof between the end of the second building and the trees". That, he said, was the roof of the Essery Memorial Well.

The Society pioneered other successes too. In the refugee camps, small business loans provided sewing machines for seamstresses and tailors, tools and leather for cobblers, instruments for watchmakers and cameras for street photographers. In some cases, small businesses became big businesses. A £25 loom for one Smyrna refugee, for example, eventually became an industry employing fifteen others. Sometimes the products of skilled workers went to foreign markets and when Mrs Gregg, a supporter of the Society in York, advertised plants from her nursery garden and her own hand sewn items for sale, "all profits Armenian Relief", Samuel saw an opportunity. He knew that people in Britain were interested in handicrafts from overseas, that they liked to decorate their homes with exotic items from the Near East and the Orient, and that smart women loved wearing clothes with a glamorous hint of faraway places. Within a year, Mrs Gregg's advertisements had a page of their own in the *Star*, and joining the Michaelmas daisies and pinafores and hardwearing shirts from Yorkshire, were traditional Armenian rugs and needlework. "The handworks shall be made under these tents," wrote an unnamed correspondent from Aleppo, "to be sent to you with your money. I wish you could forward to me some more money for these camp works." More money was sent and British women were soon spreading Armenian rugs before their parlour fires, displaying embroidered table cloths and sideboard runners in their drawing rooms and adding pretty lace camisoles and modesty vests to their wardrobes.

The Rescue Home

Some of the Armenian needlework sold through the *Star* arrived from the Rescue Home, a secluded workshop supported by the Society in Aleppo. In 1924, the League of Nations estimated that 30,000 Christian women, abducted during the deportations, remained prisoners in the harems of some Turkish and Arab homes. Special programmes and secret networks were set up to rescue and support those who wanted to be free and the escape plans arranged for them were often fraught with danger. The *Star* hinted that the Bible Lands Secretary himself sometimes risked his own life in the rescues, and described how Karen Jeppe, the mainstay of the Aleppo workshop, ensured the "rescue car" was kept ready to leave at a moment's notice to meet escaping women at secret rendezvous and smuggle them away.

Some Armenian women had been captive since 1915, and had sometimes given birth to many babies. For most of them, it was difficult to break free. But for those who made a willing choice, the Rescue Home provided training and employment until they felt ready to face the outside world. For some that took many months, and for others it never happened at all. Some histories were too terrible and some women were too emotionally scarred. Marian, whose whole family died in 1915 on the long road from Turkey, was sold to gypsies by a shepherd who took her, a lonely child, from the Deir Zor concentration camp. Her gypsy owners violated Marian repeatedly and made her perform and steal money for them. Azniv had been at Deir Zor too. Her husband disappeared in the Turkish Army in 1915 and on the march to Syria, Azniv was forced to leave her own baby and her mother to die at the roadside. She passed through the hands of many men before being rescued by Karen Jeppe. Azniv and Marian both spent years in the embroidery room at Aleppo where they decorated the handkerchiefs and table cloths that were parcelled up and posted to the Society's offices in London.

What is life?

It was not only the Rescue Home that contained traumatic memories. In every refugee camp people dwelt on the terrible events of their exile and wondered what the future held. The Bible women, the quiet workers supported by the Society in so many countries for so many years, and whose lives, said Samuel, "are a benediction in the camps", reported that thousands of refugees suffered breakdowns and depressive illnesses. "And they constantly ask the great question, 'What is life?'" said Zmroot Babaian, a refugee Bible woman from Smyrna, "it shows in their faces almost as plain as if they were speaking it out loud."

As Zmroot and her colleagues made their daily rounds of the Armenian and Greek refugee camps at Athens, people waited for their visits, to unburden their hearts to them and to shed the tears they were ashamed to let flow before their fellow refugees and the Western relief workers. In their turn, the Bible women gave their time and ensured that needs were reported and relief delivered. Their Bible readings and prayer groups, their listening ears and open hearts, provided a little of the comfort the exiled people so desperately needed. Other comfort came from someone else. "So many people here have only a great empty feeling in the heart," said Zmroot, "but that empty place must be filled, and when they hear the message of Jesus they know it is what they want."

He heard our supplications

The message of Jesus, Samuel knew, was also being carried faithfully through the refugee camps by Armenian pastors who had survived the deportations. And he also knew, that many of those pastors had been singled out for specially vicious treatment by the Turks and that some had never recovered, physically or mentally, from what was done to them. Others were ashamed of their bitter poverty and the shabby cast-off clothing they wore when going about their Christian work. At Samuel's suggestion, the Society opened a Refugee Pastors Appeal to help the men and some of their response letters were printed in the *Star*. "Oh, dear sir," said one, "how terrible were our condition. We were praying God, thanks Him, He heard our supplications, we received that money from the hand of our Saviour Jesus Christ, thanks Him ever more." Some of those pastors had lost wives and children in the deportations, wrote Mrs J.C. Martin, an aid worker at Aleppo, "and as a worker among them," she told readers of the *Star*, "one often feels herself rebuked for lack of faith, when one hears firm expressions of trust in God's promises on the part of those whose souls have been sorely tried".

Jesus is my sunshine

Other funds from the Society went to Blind Krikor and his new colleagues at the School of Religion that finally opened in Athens.

Dana Getchell had written to Samuel to say that of all the original promising students, only three remained, the others having all been killed. "May the blood of these martyrs truly become the seeds of the future church," said Dana. After his escape from Smyrna, in a letter to Samuel, Krikor had reflected on his journey since his childhood at a Christian orphanage near Marash. "I like to believe," he said, "that God has his own plan for every individual," and he described the road from Marash to Tarsus and to Smyrna, then to a year at the Salonica Farm, and finally to Athens. He was grateful for the continued support of the Society. "And I hope," he said, "the School of Religion will teach me a great deal to contribute in return to the Kingdom of God."

Krikor began making his contribution to the Kingdom as soon as he could. From the 60,000 strong Kokkinia Refugee Camp near Athens, where the Protestant congregation had requested a grant to build a new church and school, Krikor wrote about his college vacation work there. "Although my world is outwardly dark," he said, "and in my sky there is no sun, no moon, nor twinkling stars, yet I am living in a world of luminous bodies that are much fairer and brighter. Jesus is my sunshine and my moonlight and I can very easily reflect the light of Jesus to those who are about me." Krikor went on to describe how he supervised Kokkinia's summer Sunday Schools. All the children, he said, had suffered terribly during the deportations or from other bitter experiences of the exile, but with a mixture of secular and religious education, athletic events and games, he hoped to sow in their young hearts "good seeds of Christian character and friendship". To this end as well, he said, he and his friends had reorganised the Boys' Christian Endeavour on the basis that Christian young men "can do a great deal for the coming of the Kingdom of God into this world". He marvelled to see, he concluded, the loyalty and dedication of the young people, who despite their daily hard work, never failed to put their energy into the life of the church. "The power and the glory of God are often revealed in the time of affliction and hardship," he said, and he asked his supporters in the Society to pray for him that God might do even greater work at Kokkinia through Krikor's weakness.

The power and the glory

All over the lands of the Bible, there were others too who saw the power and glory of God shining out through affliction and hardship. During one of Samuel's trips to Lebanon, where he visited one of the newest missions to join the BLMAS grant list, the Danish Birds' Nest Orphanage at Djoubeil, he received a report from Adana. A group of elderly Armenian women, it said, who had somehow been overlooked in the deportations, had been squatting for years in a derelict churchyard. The site was scheduled for redevelopment as a cinema, said the report, and the women were regularly abused by stone-throwing schoolchildren. Could the Bible Lands Missions Aid Society help? Samuel immediately arranged for a rescue. Funds from Britain provided railway tickets and the sorry little group was transported to a newly rented house at Shemlan, 20 miles north of Beirut, where Martha Frearson and Blaga, a Bedfont trained nurse, waited to receive them.

Martha Frearson never forgot the day the women arrived. "A more pitiful sight could not be imagined," she said, "eight were blind, one also a cripple, two paralysed; only one of the 18 was sound." But, by the following year the women had all settled into their new home with its clean comfortable bedrooms and its long balconies bathed in Mediterranean sunshine. In fact, said Martha, her charges were so happy and had made themselves so much at home, she had to be quite firm as well as kind in her dealings with them. It was at Christmas, though, she said, that she truly saw the happiness that a new life and a new home had given to the old women of Adana. For their dinner they had requested a favourite Armenian dish of sheep's heads boiled with whole wheat. "And what a sight it was," she said, "when all were seated in their places at the table with their individual dish of steaming food, their coloured paper bag of sweets and oranges on the white cloth before them, and their worn old faces alight with pleasure."

God's purpose for Bulgaria

Often, as Samuel made his regular trips across Europe to the Balkans and the Near East, his route took him through Bulgaria where he was always a welcome guest at the home of Reverend Dimiter Furnajieff. A close friendship between the two men had begun when Dimiter first visited Britain in 1903 to plead for the Macedonian refugees, and ever since then, during their times together, Samuel and Dimiter had discussed the Society's long involvement with Bulgaria and whether there might be some great purpose in it that God was yet to reveal. As the 1920s came to an end, Samuel and Dimiter began to believe that God's purpose was becoming clear.

Harry Fear believed he could glimpse that purpose too. Samuel's neighbour in Bedfont, who became the Society's Treasurer on the death of Lord Kinnaird, was a wealthy man by the 1920s. The road haulage company that had transported the prefabricated orphanage to Bedfont in 1918 had prospered, and Harry's shrewd business brain and sound advice ensured the Society's funds and investments prospered too. Early in 1929, as the Society approached its 75th anniversary, despite a gloomy economic outlook in the world at large, Harry was able to assure Samuel that a plan already discussed with Dimiter Furnajieff was not only possible but had every chance of success.

In April 1929 Samuel and Harry set out together for Samokov, home to the huge American Board Bulgarian mission station that owed much of its success to the vision of Dr John House, and which hosted an annual Bible Conference famed across the Balkans. But throughout the late 1920s, as the American Board felt the onset of the Great Depression, it had been forced to make cutbacks all over its huge mission field. One of those cuts was Samokov. By 1929, to the distress of the Bulgarian Evangelical Society and Protestants across the Balkans, the Bible Conference was suspended, the Institute was closed, and the site and buildings were up for sale.

After Samuel and Harry's visit to Bulgaria, they went straight to Boston. Then in June, back once more in Britain, they took the results of their Bulgarian and American discussions to a special meeting held in Canterbury where an elderly member of the Society's managing committee was recovering from a long illness. "After a splendid journey from London by motor," Samuel wrote later in the Society's minutes, "the Committee was welcomed by the Reverend and Mrs Robinson Lees. The weather was gloriously fine and the meeting was held on the lawn." On that sunny June day in Canterbury, the Bible Lands Missions Aid Society, with the hearty endorsement of the Bulgarian Evangelical Society and the American Board, agreed to commemorate its 75th anniversary with the purchase of the entire Samokov site, the restoration of the Bible Conference, and the development of a major Bible based training college for the Balkans.

Chapter 10

The Bible School

The vision for Samokov was a big one. Samuel and Harry's trips to Bulgaria and Boston had reinforced the view they shared with Dimiter Furnajieff, that God intended the Bible Lands Missions Aid Society not only to prevent the Samokov mission site falling into secular hands, but that it was to found a new college to train Evangelical Christian workers for the Balkans, Eastern Europe and Asia Minor, and also to restore the Bible Conference.

When the Society learned that the American Board's School of Religion in Athens was likely to become another casualty of the Great Depression, they saw their task as even more urgent. If Athens closed, Samuel told readers of the *Star*, and if the Society's project went ahead, Samokov would be the only Bible based college in the region and the major training centre for future leaders of its Christian communities. For the sake of those communities, he said, it was essential the vision became reality.

It was so very appropriate, Samuel said, that the Society should be called on to take up the work at Samokov. Its relationship with Bulgaria went back to its very earliest years, when Lord Shaftesbury urged the American Board to open a Bulgarian mission and promised the Society's support. And Samokov itself, he said, was a place of sacred memories, "that all Evangelical Christians in Bulgaria remember with gratitude and thankfulness to God". Dr John House, one of the Society's very best friends, laid its foundations. He purchased the land in 70 separate lots in the 1880s, drew up the building plans and then became foreman and labourer on the work. Through the years that followed, "large numbers of active Christians, pastors and laymen, were trained and educated at Samokov, revered American missionaries ministered there, and religious conferences and Summer Bible Schools by the score were held there". And as the work grew and prospered, Bulgaria itself emerged from its earlier troubles to become a country based on democratic ideals of freedom and equality. Among all the Balkan lands, said Samuel, Bulgaria was foremost in encouraging its mixed population of many races and religions to live and work together in harmony. As a site for a new Bible School there was none better.

Samuel knew Bulgaria well. During his visits to Dimiter Furnajieff, the two men had sometimes travelled together through Bulgaria's towns and country villages where Samuel's populist preaching attracted large crowds. Orthodox and Protestant Bulgarians, gypsies, Armenians, Jews and Pomaks, (Christians converted to Islam centuries earlier), and even some Muslims, were all drawn to the enthusiastic Englishman who led them in rousing choruses of his favourite Ira Sankey hymns and openly proclaimed his love of the Scriptures and his passion for the souls of his audience.

He was a familiar face at Samokov too. Except for an interval during the Great War, Samuel had been a regular speaker at Samokov's annual Bible Conference since 1912, and his talks that included, "The Bible, its Plan and Purpose", and "Old Truths and Present Day Beliefs", provoked intense interest and discussion. On the four and a half acre Samokov site, Samuel told the Society's supporters in Britain, there were several school buildings and assembly halls, dining rooms, dormitories and family houses. The whole complex could house, feed and sleep 300 people and he outlined his plan for residential family Bible conferences, a YWCA holiday camp, holiday homes for young people and a boys' orphanage. But at the centre of the plan, he said, was the proposed new training college, "an Evangelistic Centre for the Bible Training of Christian leaders for Bulgaria and the Balkans".

Soul-winning men and women

A fund-raising campaign for the proposed new Bible School was opened by the Society's vice-president, Sir Leon Levison. Sir Leon was another passionate evangelist, whose commitment to Jesus Christ had become deeper and more profound after being disowned by his father, a Rabbi at Safed in Palestine, for his conversion to Christianity. Hard and bitter times had followed, until years of study and hard work had led finally to great success, and the experience had made Sir Leon a keen supporter of young Christians taking their first steps towards future ministry. He told the guests invited to a fund-raising event at a London restaurant that the plan proposed by Samuel Gentle-Cackett, the "indefatigable secretary of the BLMAS", was intended to combat the apathy, indifference and atheism that seemed to be a feature of the twentieth century, and to train "a continual stream of soul-winning men and women, real living saints, who by their life and conduct would set a new standard in the land and bring souls to the Lord".

He knew of no people who were doing so much for Christian charity as the people of Great Britain, said Sir Leon, and he urged his listeners "to lay hold of so great an opportunity". His hopes and prayers were answered and the campaign was a huge success. The purchase of the Samokov site was completed in 1931, and Dimiter Furnajieff, on behalf of the Bulgarian Evangelical Society, became first principal of the new Bulgarian Bible School. In 1932, Samuel told readers of the *Star* that the first 16 students had completed their first year and he appealed for additional donations to provide bicycles that would enable them to minister at Sunday services in distant villages. Later that same year, he reported that 25 more students had enrolled for the following year and that every student at the school was sponsored at £10 a year by the Society's supporters in Britain.

At the end of 1933, Samuel described progress at Samokov for the *Star*. The previous year had been "a season of deep spiritual uplift", he said. The Bible Conferences were underway once more, and at the most recent, "the Divine Presence was markedly realised and a sense of 'one-ness in Christ Jesus' was very apparent". At the end of the conference, he said, "Interspersed with the very moving prayers were expressions of gratitude, and best of all, vows of consecration. Many were moved to tears and even to sobs as they recounted their experiences during the gatherings." Samuel was equally delighted to recount the progress of Samokov's new students. It was just as he and Sir Leon had hoped and prayed and the young people were following eagerly in the footsteps of their predecessors, the illustrious company of missionaries who had carried the gospel message down through the centuries and across the wide world.

Samuel told readers of the *Star* about one particular group of four young people. In the villages around Philippopolis, he said, "they were received most heartily" and before long, a growing crowd of people, hungry for the Gospel of Salvation, was travelling alongside them. Just as Jesus himself had sometimes travelled, Samuel had thought to himself. Among these new followers, he said, were some who were soon giving personal testimony of the grace of God in their hearts, and in all the villages, "people came out for Christ in the presence of their fellow villagers, and are still standing steadfast and true".

All along the Nile

Samuel also had reason to feel proud of the work supported by the Society elsewhere in the world, and to have a growing confidence in the future. Even as far away as Sudan, he said, a hunger for the gospel was growing. The missionaries of the Egyptian Protestant Church, the successors of the men William Essery met at the Nile Synod in 1901, were still hard at work in Sudan and reported large congregations and bands of new converts. Both Sudanese and Egyptian Bible women received grants from the Society and Samuel was especially proud of its support for Reverend Toobia Abd el Masih, the first Sudanese minister among his Western and Egyptian colleagues at the pioneer Doleib Hill Mission Station on the White Nile. Also hard at work on the Nile, said Samuel, was the *Elliott*, the highly sophisticated mission boat that was the personal gift of the Society's Treasurer, Harry Fear. And working alongside the *Elliott* was another craft, the *Jubilee*, an earlier anonymous gift that had celebrated the Society's first 50 years and that still carried evangelists and medical missionaries through Egypt and through Sudan. All along the Nile, said Samuel proudly, crowds still gathered at the waterside and thronged mud brick village churches to hear the missionaries preach, and Christian and Muslim villagers waited eagerly to greet the Christian doctors who travelled to them on the great river with medicines sent by the Bible Lands Missions Aid Society.

Samuel was especially pleased at the progress of Egyptian women. He had read some of the Society's early annual reports and he liked to think that if the pioneering Miss Whately herself was looking down on Egypt from heaven, that her heart would be most satisfactorily warmed at the sight of so many Egyptian girls eager for education. Especially in the major cities, Samuel told readers of the *Star*, in Cairo with its Egyptian and American Universities, and at Assiout, increasing numbers of girls were attending schools and going on to higher education. Women teachers graduating from the Pressley Institute, the female department of Assiout College, worked at schools throughout Egypt, while nurses from Assiout's Mission Hospital Training School found family welfare clinics and hospitals all over the country eager to receive them. Miss Gomar Mansour, the very first Egyptian nurse graduate of Assiout, helped manage three child welfare centres in Cairo where she inspired the girls who accompanied their little sisters and brothers to her clinics to follow in her footsteps. Some of the nurses went to Tanta Hospital, where the Christian management encouraged nurses, doctors and Bible women to work closely together to ensure "that the work is a blessing, not only physically for today, but spiritually for eternity".

Co-operation and co-ordination

At Salonica, the American Women's Hospital founded by Dr Ruth Parmalee after the Smyrna catastrophe and supported ever since by the Society had become one of the city's major hospitals and health centres. "It has been our joy," said Samuel in the *Star* of September 1936, as he introduced an article by Dr Ruth herself, "to help continuously from the Refugee days of 1922, knowing that healing the sick is part of the glorious Gospel of our Lord and Saviour Jesus Christ." As well as its work in the city, said Dr Ruth, the Salonica hospital had developed outreach work in the Kokkinia Camp, "which included the development of public health projects and a complete course in nurse training, along with a well-organised hospital and dispensary system". There had been a further development in December 1935, she said, when the Greek Government took over the Kokkinia Hospital "with the intention of using it as a model for the reform of all the Government hospitals of the country". It was a most fitting application, said Dr Ruth, "of the motto which had been adopted at our centre at Kokkinia, i.e., 'Co-ordination and Co-operation'". Dr

Ruth concluded her article by telling readers about the latest development, "a dream, which unexpectedly seems about to come true". Just the previous summer, she said, after circumstances forced the American Women's Hospital to discontinue its own nursing school and she herself "began to long for a further opportunity to aid Greece along the lines of nursing education", her colleague, Miss Emilie Williams, was offered the position of Directress of Nurses at the Municipal Hospital in Athens. Her task, said Dr Ruth, was to develop there the first Government School of Nursing!

The Farm School at Salonica assisted the Greek Government too when it began a programme to train government sponsored boys in the modern methods that made the Farm such a success. Not only would the trained boys earn a livelihood from their own work, Samuel told readers of the *Star*, but by what they taught their neighbours about modern crop production and animal husbandry, farming would improve and living standards rise throughout their regions. Charles House, the Princeton-educated son of the Farm's missionary founder, said of the Farm, "In 30 years, a few acres of mulberry trees and malaria ridden swamp has blossomed into 300 acres of orchards, vineyards and grain fields, and into a self-sustaining community." The Society had been part of that community ever since the Farm's foundation following the Macedonian massacres, Samuel reminded his readers, and it had provided some of the modern equipment that included water pumps, electric generators and dairy equipment, that contributed to its success and self-sufficiency. The Society also funded regular additions to the Farm's breeding stock and Samuel, the son of a dairyman, always chose the Jersey cattle and Black Yorkshire boars that were shipped regularly from Britain to Salonica. Samuel wrote later about the atmosphere of the Salonica Farm. It was a combination of the practical and the spiritual, he said, "It greets you when you arrive and remains with you long after you leave."

"It keeps me rather busy"

Blind Krikor believed in combining the practical and the spiritual too. All through his training at the School of Religion, the Armenian exiles at Kokkinia Camp had been part of his life, and when his college days were completed, Krikor decided that Kokkinia was where God meant him to stay. "Your Society has meant much to us," he wrote to Samuel in 1935, and he said how grateful he was, that although the world economic depression was forcing cutbacks everywhere, and even the Society's grants were sometimes less than in earlier days, its funds for churches, schools, social centres and salaries, were still the main support and sustenance of Kokkinia. Krikor's own salary, as Pastor of the camp's Protestant church, had been reduced during the worst Depression years, not an easy thing to bear with a wife and little son to support, but, he said, "We must go on bravely without any feeling of retreat and backsliding. The Lord is our Shepherd and sooner or later He will lead us into green pastures." Krikor himself, despite his blind eyes, always gazed on green pastures and he never forgot his early promise to work as hard as he could for God's Kingdom. As well as pastoring the church, Samuel told readers of the *Star*, Krikor also taught 200 children at a camp school supported by the Society, while in his off-duty hours he still ran the Sunday Schools and Christian Endeavour he founded as a student. "It all keeps me rather busy," Krikor told Samuel.

Conglomerations of wreckage

The Society also provided funds for Kokkinia refugees with tuberculosis to spend a few weeks each year in the countryside or by the sea, far away from the unhealthy conditions in the densely packed camps. At Salonica, Dr John Goldstein, a medical missionary employed by the London Jews Society, who received additional funds from the BLMAS, knew all about the unhealthy conditions that refugees endured. Many lived in the worst slums of the city, he told readers of the *Star*, in dark cellars where damp oozed through the brickwork and mildew covered their few belongings, while others spent their lives in the suffocatingly crowded camps, where there were no drains and rats infested the rubbish heaps and flies settled on every meal. Most of his patients suffered from tuberculosis, pneumonia, influenza, and "colds that never went away". But they were too poor to afford the remedies he knew they needed, and sometimes, said the frustrated doctor, "When they look at me so queerly and smile wanly at my suggestions of better housing and better diet, I feel such a fool."

As the years went by, and hopes of a better life gradually faded, some refugees saw death as preferable to endless poverty, sickness and despair. Suicide rates, said Dr Goldstein, were on the increase. Suicide rates among another group were high too, he said. A new influx of refugees was arriving in Salonica, Jewish refugees from Germany, who had left everything behind as they fled from the Nazi Government who intended to do to the Jews what the Turks had done to the Armenians. Most of the Jewish refugees who arrived in Greece hoped to travel eventually to Palestine, but for many of them, Salonica became the final end of a sad and bitter road. Adding to the refugees' troubles, said Dr Goldstein, was a new development. International tourism, he said, was a growing industry, and Salonica's city authorities and businessmen were anxious that refugees, the long established ones and the desperate new arrivals, should be kept well out of sight of the wealthy men and women who travelled for pleasure.

In Syria and Lebanon, the situation was just as in Greece. Nearly 20 years after the deportations, the Armenian refugees still lived in the camps they had once thought of as temporary shelters. The wealthy Christian nations of the West should be ashamed, said Samuel, that they had abandoned the Armenians and allowed them to exist for years in places which were "conglomerations of wreckage, habitations not fit for pigs that were harbouring refined human beings with scarcely a whole garment among them, and most of them hungry for a good part of the time". The situation is unthinkable in a time of peace, he said, "yet it exists". The unthinkable situation was made even worse by the Depression and as work disappeared, as grants from overseas were slashed, and as bread prices rose and kept rising, the hunger and poverty that had stalked the camps for years became ever more devouring. Just as in Greece, life for some refugees was so grim, so pointless and so filled with despair, that death was the most preferable thing of all. "I have never known so many suicides," Samuel said, "so many bodies found floating in the sea."

The refugee camp at Beirut, that was a quarter mile square and housed 15,000 Armenians, was a tightly packed mass of homes made from old packing cases, rusty Standard Oil tins and pieces of sacking. A blot on the landscape, Samuel called it, and he tried to convey to the Society's supporters in Britain, just what life was like for the people who had spent 20 years of their lives in the camp, or for children born there and who knew nothing else. In some homes, he said, nine or ten people lived, cooked, ate and slept in one room, twelve feet square and balanced precariously on boards just above the earth. When it rained in the winter the cold water seeped into the earth beneath the shacks. For months dirty water lay in muddy puddles in squalid streets lined with makeshift shops, "for those with money to buy", and in dark, narrow passages, musty with dampness, that ran between the people's homes. In summer the sun baked the mud into deep, uneven ruts. But despite the lack of clean water and sanitation, and despite their desperate circumstances, most people longed for cleanliness and domestic comfort and beauty. In all the tragedy, Samuel said, and in all the squalor, he sometimes saw God's face shining out from human spirits that refused to be utterly overwhelmed and from people whose dignity in the face of suffering always humbled him. He described the generous welcome he received at one clean and tidy home that was made of flattened rusty tins. A roof of old tenting was cut so a flap could let in light and air, he said, a few family photographs salvaged from the deportation had pride of place, and at the side of their one room the family had created a garden, a tiny enclosure of old netting where they grew onions and flowers.

Delinquency, crime and prostitution

"The Depression has been terrible and the reduction in grants almost unbearable," wrote a spokesperson for the Armenian Evangelical Union, the Beirut based organisation that spoke on behalf of Armenian Protestants, "yet no churches or schools have been closed." It had meant great sacrifices by the Armenian people, Samuel told readers of the *Star*, to keep open the churches and schools that helped bind their communities together, but despite all their efforts, the younger generation was causing the Union enormous concern. Poverty and unemployment were taking a toll, he said, and with so many families destroyed and disrupted by massacre and exile, and traditional community patterns broken, the Union saw many of its Armenian young people turning to delinquency, crime and prostitution. Over 1,000 orphaned Armenian girls lived in Beirut, and it was easy for them to drift into life on the streets. Other girls had children with men they had not married and only realised when they were abandoned that without a marriage contract their little family had no security. The Society, said Samuel, together with the Union, was funding a hostel for single working girls in Beirut. The rent was low, regular meals were provided, and a friendly matron ensured that evenings spent at home were comfortable and friendly. Elsewhere in Beirut, Mary Webb, once mission secretary at Adana, and her sister Elizabeth, opened the Lighthouse Mission in the city's red light district for girls who had already become prostitutes. Most of the girls were desperate to escape life on the streets and grants from the Society helped them train for regular jobs and careers, while some of the city's Western missionaries offered their support by becoming second families to them and welcoming them into their homes. Mary Webb's cook, said Samuel, had learned never to be surprised at the number or character of her employer's guests.

Karen was their final hope

Karen Jeppe continued her own rescue work at Aleppo and even in the mid-1930s, Armenian women still arrived at her door. Most came from Turkey and were sometimes carried to the Rescue Home by muleteers who knew about Karen's work and also that she would pay them. Other women walked, often from faraway places, said Karen, "to the very gates of Aleppo, and many, in fact, arrived in a condition not very different from that of the deportations". Some of them, she went on, "bring little children along with them, but generally they come alone". Karen was the women's final hope. Some of them had venereal diseases or tuberculosis or other illnesses and were treated by Christian doctors and nurses. Most arrived with desperate hopes of finding family members still alive, hopes that had sustained them through their long years of captivity, but the chances of success after such a long time were slim, although, said Karen, "miracles sometimes happen". Karen Jeppe refused to close the Rescue Home while any chance remained of an abducted Armenian woman needing her help. "We firmly believe," she said, "that our friends abroad will stand by us until the day when we can say, with a clear conscience, that now this work is finished and done."

The kindness of God's children

At Shemlan, where Martha Frearson herself was growing old and increasingly troubled by arthritis, her work increased as elderly women from the camps, most with no family left at all, arrived to join the original Adana group. Forty women eventually spent their final years in the Shemlan widows' home, with its bright airy rooms and sunny balconies where they sometimes reminisced about the long ago days in Turkey when they were pretty young women courted by handsome young men, the men who had all been swept away in 1915. In their old age, Martha told Samuel, although the Society had funded cataract operations for some, many of her charges were blind, and how it warmed her heart, she said, to see how they all lived together in harmony. The blind often read to the whole company from their Braille Scripture portions, she said, while the sighted led their blind colleagues by the hand when they set out on their walks through the local villages. "It is so good to see them sallying forth in that way," said Martha, "and its fills one's heart with thankfulness that they can thus be taken care of through the kindness of God's children in the HOMEland."

Tear down your home!

For refugees not fortunate enough to be cared for by women like Martha Frearson, as the 1930s progressed, life became increasingly uncertain. It was not only the developing city of Salonica that wanted refugees out of the way. National governments and city authorities in Syria and Lebanon had grown tired of what they saw as a continual drain on their resources, and owners of prime sites, who had once been grateful for minimal rents, wanted to sell their land for development. In the middle of the decade, as camps all over Syria, Lebanon and Greece faced demolition, the League of Nations began a loans programme to help refugees buy small homes of their own on new sites. For many refugees the scheme was a huge success. But the poorest: the old, the sick and the unemployed, who could not afford the repayments, could not bear to tear down their homes when the order arrived. "When people are so poor they do not know where their next meal is coming from," said Samuel, "we cannot wonder if they are slow in pulling down their present home, even one made of kerosene tins, packing cases and rotting planks." But, he said, if they refused to tear down their shacks in the condemned camps when ordered to do so, the police usually arrived to do it for them. "And you can imagine," he said, "the ruined fragments into which such a house is turned." When the camps are destroyed, said a report from Beirut, "it looks as though a hurricane or earthquake has struck it. Heaps of broken bricks and earth, splintered wood, sheet iron roofing, or more often gaping holes, marked the site of former houses". The poorest people, said the report, were reduced to living among the ruins.

In Aleppo and Beirut the Society made grants to refugees who could not afford the League's home loan repayments and hundreds of twelve pound donations, each one sufficient to purchase a plot of land and enough sun-dried bricks to build one room and a kitchen, were provided by supporters in Britain. One of the largest donations was made by Mrs Gregg of York, whose advertisement in 1921 was the inspiration for the Society's first trading venture. But, there was more to do in a community, said Samuel, than simply building houses. In Lebanon, he said, the demolition of the camps meant people were moving to new districts and among all the new building, the regular rows of tiny one-roomed homes that were all most refugees could afford, there were few schools, few social centres and few churches. There was little evangelistic work either, he said, and with no organised work for young people "you may certainly be sure that the world, the flesh and the devil are on the job!" In one such district, a poor area of Beirut called Trad, instead of the devil, Elizabeth Webb was on the job. With financial help from the Society, Samuel said, Elizabeth and the local Armenian community had purchased land to build a social centre, and the newly ordained Pastor Marganian had accepted a position as schoolteacher and youth worker while his new wife had agreed to work among the women. Elizabeth described the proposed new centre for the *Star*. A building of two rooms was planned, she said, to serve as primary school on weekdays and Sunday School on Sundays, as a playground for the children and as a gathering place for young people and the whole Armenian community. "We have put down our feet on this plot of ground in faith that God has given it to us for the extension of His Kingdom," she said.

Alexandretta

As the 1930s moved towards their end, other Armenians were on the move too and putting down their feet in new places. For most of them it was an unwilling journey, another episode in the forced exodus from their ancient home. Ever since its defeat in the Great War, Turkey had sought to regain those parts of its old Ottoman Empire it considered vital to its military interests. Paramount among them was the Sanjak of Alexandretta, part of the Syrian Mandate territory awarded to France in 1920, with its strategic Mediterranean seaport and land bridges through Syria into northern Iraq. As France felt increasingly threatened in Europe by Nazi Germany and in the eastern Mediterranean by Italy, Alexandretta became its bargaining tool for guarantees of Turkish friendship. When rumours spread among Alexandretta's non-Turkish majority that France would cede the Sanjak to Turkey, some of the 15,000 strong Armenian population, many of them refugees from earlier massacres and only too well aware of their likely fate, began making their way into other parts of Syria and Lebanon. In 1937, Samuel urged the Committee of the BLMAS to petition the League of Nations, the French Prime Minister and the British Foreign Office, on behalf of Alexandretta's Armenians. "We view with alarm," said the petition, "the Turkish attitude concerning the Alexandretta district." The Armenians of the Sanjak, it said, were those who survived earlier massacres when France abandoned Cilicia in 1921, and the Society, who had aided them then, feared a possible repetition if France released its hold over Alexandretta "and allowed the Turkish Government any semblance of authority". In 1939, France finally handed the Sanjak of Alexandretta to Turkey and the remaining Armenian population fled for their lives.

Palestine: lawlessness, murder and arson

In the British Mandate territory of Palestine, the refugee traffic was in the other direction. As the Nazis stepped up their campaign to exterminate the Jewish people, Jewish refugees poured into the Holy Land. But as the immigrant tide swelled throughout the 1930s, Christian missions in Palestine had reported a continual rise in tensions. The newcomers were desperate to buy land, said the missionaries, and as plots that once sold at five dollars an acre changed hands for 50, and poor Palestinian tenant farmers faced eviction when land was sold over their heads by their own Arab landlords, frustration turned to anger. And as the land changed hands, the land changed. More modern Jewish farm colonies sprang up in the countryside, the new cities that had been growing ever since the 1920s, grew larger, and the Arab Palestinians watched helplessly as their ancient landscape grew more urban, more modern and more Western.

As early as 1930, Dr Wright at the CMS hospital in Jaffa had written to Samuel about his growing concerns for the future of Palestine, the first indication of unease in the Society's literature. The hospital had acquired an x-ray machine, Dr Wright said, and not only was it the first in Jaffa, it was the first to be used for Palestinian patients, since they were unwilling to use similar machines in two Jewish hospitals in towns nearby. That was partly from resentment of the growing Jewish population in the land, he said, but also from fear of other Arabs "who are strictly boycotting the Jews".

In 1936, the *Star* reported that a nationwide strike against Jewish immigration by the increasingly bitter Palestinian population of the Holy Land had led to violence on both sides. "Lawlessness, murder and arson prevails throughout the country," said the report. Within two years the Society had opened a new relief fund, the Palestine Orphans Appeal, for innocent child victims of the violence and Samuel had suggested that some of them might join his Armenian girls at the Bedfont Orphanage.

If there is a war...

But it was not only in Palestine that lawlessness, murder and arson prevailed. Early in 1939 it was obvious that Europe was heading for a major conflict once more and in Bulgaria, the young people at the Bible School asked uncomfortable questions. Samuel's vision for Samokov had been a great success, the college was often called the Gospel Power House of the Balkans and its graduates worked all over the region. The week-long annual Bible Conference sponsored by the Society drew hundreds of delegates who came to speak and debate and to share Christian fellowship as they relaxed with their families on Samokov's spacious lawns and beneath its shady trees. But, the questions the students asked were unsettling. What do young people in Britain think, they asked Samuel, do they think there will be a war? If there is a war what will Britain do? What will happen to Bulgaria? What will happen to the Bible School?

The Armenian Genocide: Armenian orphans. *Star*, March 1919.

Graduates of St Paul's College, Tarsus, out teaching and preaching for a year in Kozolooks, a mountain village seven hours from Tarsus. Probably taken before the 1921 massacres.

FOR SALE.

All proceeds for Armenian Relief.

When ordering please mention this magazine.

◆◆◆

PLANTS.

Hollyhocks, Daffodils, Narcissus, Raspberry Canes, Tansy, Mint, Golden Rod, **2**d. each. Lavender, Thyme, Rhododendrons, Fleur de Lys, Iris, Fuchsias, **6**d. each. Bridal Wreaths and Flowering Broom (Yellow), **9**d. each. Wallflowers, Honesty, Sweet Williams, Michaelmas Daisies, Scillas and Freesias, Small Sunflowers, **6**d. dozen. *Postage extra.*

Mrs. GREGG, Branfold, Strensall, York.

NEEDLEWORK.

Men's Shirts (strong), **6/6** each. Socks, **3/6** pair. Hand Painted Text Scrolls (any verse) from **2/=** each. Poker Worked Book Shelves, **7/6**. Work Boxes, **4/6**. Glove Boxes, **5/6**. Photo Frames, **4/=**. Tea Pot Stands, **3/6**. Figure Game, **6**d. Nightdresses (warm), **6/9**. Girls' Frocks, **6/6**. Infants' Frocks, **4/=**. Petticoats from **2/6**. Boys' Knickers, **3/6**. *Postage extra.*

Mrs. GREGG, Branfold, Strensall, York.

The following from our own office :—

Armenian Lace and Embroidery Work made by Widows and Orphans in various Relief Centres.

All proceeds for Armenian Massacre Relief Fund.

Goods at actual cost price of labour and materials.

Needle Lace Doilies (round) from **1/9** each ; ditto (oval), **2/9** each. 34 yd. length Bebe Lace (suitable for handkerchief edging), **£1 2**s. 18 yd. length Lace, ⅜ in. wide, **£1 4**s. 4½ yd. length Lace Edging, ½ in. wide, **3/=**. 34 yd. length Lace, ½ in. wide, **£1 1**s. 11 yd. length Lace, ½ in. wide, **11/6**. 11 yd. length Lace, ½ in. wide, **12/6**. Crochet Camisole Tops, **5/3** each. Ditto in D.M.C., **6/3**. Silk Embroidered Cushion Squares, 14 in. by 14 in., **10/6** each. Linen Embroidered Cushion Squares, 17 in. by 17 in., **13/6** each. Round Lace Collar, **10/=**. Two Silk Embroidered Table Centres, 30 in. by 18 in., at **24/=** each. One Silk Embroidered Piano Top, at **70/=**. Silk Embroidered Table Cover, **65/=**.

The Secretary, Bible Lands Missions' Aid Society, 358, Strand, London, W.C. 2.

All Proceeds for Armenian Relief: notice in *The Star*, November 1922.

Smyrna Catastrophe

means all the help we can give
and as quickly as we can give,

OR THOUSANDS WILL DIE OF STARVATION.

OUR OTHER RELIEF FUNDS include :—

Near East Relief Fund.

This Fund embraces the whole sphere of the Society's operations—Palestine, Syria, Armenia, Asia Minor, Persia, Serbia, Greece, &c., and is allotted by the Committee according to the most urgent need.

Armenian Massacre Relief and Orphans.

Serbian Civilian Relief.

Macedonian and Serbian Orphans.

Palestine and Syria Relief.

Persian Relief (including Nestorians).

Special Jews Relief.

Contributors may specify in which section of Relief they desire their gifts used. We would, however, earnestly ask our friends to remember in their prayers and gifts the

Regular Work of the Society.

From this Fund the Committee sustain the many branches of Mission Work in Bible Lands. Unfortunately, Relief Work has the tendency of attracting money from the usual channels, and thus the Lord's work suffers.

Kindly make cheques payable to "Bible Lands Missions' Aid Society,"
and crossed Barclays Bank

358 Strand. London, W.C. 2.

" And Jesus sat over against the treasury and beheld how the people cast money into the treasury."

The Chichester Press, 30 & 31, Furnival Street, Holborn, London E.C.

Smyrna Catastrophe, 1922: notice in *The Star*, November 1922.

Salonica: Dr Ruth Parmalee with an armful.
Star, June 1923.

Greek Bible colporteur, 1920s.

Bedfont Orphanage: Samuel and Elizabeth Gentle-Cackett with their Armenian orphans.
Star, November 1924.

"The Finished Article": young men, all from Corinth Orphanage, now trained and filling responsible positions including chauffeur, carpenter, head of bakery, librarian and others. *Star*, June 1926.

A Muslim convert, now a Bible colporteur. *Star*, December 1926.

Rev. Dimiter Furnajieff, President of the Bulgarian Evangelical Society, 1931. *Star*, 1932.

Harry Fear's gift, "The Elliott", a mission boat for use on the Nile. 48' long, it was built of boiler-plate to withstand the ever-shifting sandbanks, and had a draught of only 18". It would ply a thousand miles into the interior. *Star*, December 1926.

A new congregation in Rod el Farag district of Cairo. *Star*, May 1935.

Shemlan, Lebanon: aged Armenian widows, many blind and several helpless. *Star*, September 1936.

Bethlehem, 1943: Bob Clothier (back right) with blind children. *Star*, Easter 1990.

Silwan, Jerusalem: Sister Johanna Larsen with leprosy patient.
Star, Summer 1957.

Lovell Home for blind girls, Bethlehem: Dr Helen Keller (left) conversing through touch with Miss Adele Dafesh (right). Miss Polly Thompson, Dr Keller's guide and companion, is interpreting. *Star*, Autumn 1959.

Bethlehem, Christmas Eve, 1961: Miss Adele Dafesh and her blind children paying a visit to the cave under the Church of the Nativity where, according to tradition, the manger stood. *Star*, February 1962.

London: The Bible Lands shop, Museum Street. *Star*, Spring 1963.

Chapter 11

An Age Passes
The 1940s

When a German bomb hit the Society's London offices in May 1941, Samuel resolved that despite the damage and confusion the work would not suffer. The Bible Lands Missions Aid Society had seen wars before, and nothing had ever stopped it providing relief to the innocent victims of conflict and then helping them endure the trauma and make a new start. Through good times and bad times, fat years and lean years, Christian men and women, upheld by love and courage and the Society's grants, had sheltered the homeless, healed the sick and comforted those who grieved. Even though the current war had reached Britain itself, and British cities and civilians were devastated by days and nights of German bombing, at least, Samuel reasoned to himself, the people of Britain were still free. For the Society's friends elsewhere, suffering under Nazi occupation, that was not the case, and wondering what had become of dear friends of a lifetime was hard for him. Only one month before the bomb caused such damage in London, Greece and Yugoslavia were invaded by Germany and there had been no news since from Krikor Demerjian at Kokkinia or Darinka Gruitch in Belgrade. Reports from Albania spoke of heavy fighting around Kortcha, home of the still successful school founded in the 1880s by Gerasim Kyrias. And from Bulgaria, Germany's ally in the Balkans, the last news from Samokov was that the Nazis had confiscated the Bible School.

With south-eastern Europe under enemy occupation the Society concentrated its grants on the Middle East and Sudan and sent all its funds through the Reverend Eric Bishop, a CMS missionary and old friend of Samuel's based in Palestine. Some of those funds went to a group of Armenian refugees from

Alexandretta who found refuge at Anjar in Lebanon where they were laying the foundations of a self-supporting Armenian colony. Other funds maintained the twelve pound refugee house building programme, Martha Frearson's widows' home at Shemlan, and the Birds' Nest Orphanage. Others went to the new social centre at Trad. Still more supported Danish and Norwegian missionaries working in Palestine and Syria whose regular grants were cut off by the German invaders of their homelands. Eric Bishop also went to the aid of German missionaries threatened with internment by Palestine's British authorities. One of them was a Moravian nursing sister who worked among leprosy patients. Sister Johanna Larsen, Eric was assured finally by the British Army, could consider herself interned in the leper hospital where she had lived and worked for many years.

"I will do what I can"

Just as in the Great War, paper was in short supply in Britain during the twentieth century's second great conflict, and only two issues of the *Star* were produced in the early war years. One appeared in 1940 and the other in 1942, and Samuel wrote almost everything in them himself. In the second, he reminisced for readers about the past. He recalled the years of Christian fellowship with friends at Samokov and his preaching tours with Dimiter Furnajieff through the friendly towns and villages of Bulgaria. He wrote about the time in 1921 when he crossed Europe with Nurse Ash and the Rhode Island Reds heading for the Farm at Salonica. He remembered the weeks in 1919 when he travelled with the Near East Relief Commission through Turkey and Syria and saw the 5,000 Armenian survivors who returned from Deir Zor. He remembered the relief of Adrianople, when he waited for days in the freezing winter weather with blankets and bread for the besieged population. And now, he told his readers, with the world at war once again, "just as always in the past, the Society must be on the doorstep ready to go in as soon as the way is open". He was ready to go himself, he said, and although at just over 71 years of age he no longer had the energy of a young man, "by God's help I am willing to do what I can". Samuel died on 9 July 1943. His last months were painful ones but he faced death as he had faced life, with courage and with hope. His loss to the

Bible Lands Missions Aid Society was enormous. For over 40 years he was the mainstay of the Society's work, his name was a household word in the mission stations of the Balkans and the Near East and most of the workers were his personal friends. "He has finished his course as a faithful servant of Jesus Christ," wrote Martha Frearson from Shemlan, "and has reached his reward. Blessed be his memory."

The mission to the blind

In the few years before his death, Samuel had planned to bring children orphaned by growing conflict in Palestine to Bedfont Orphanage, to join the successful procession of 83 Armenian, Serbian and Greek girls who were educated and trained in England. The Palestine Orphans Fund that would have paid their passage, was administered in Jerusalem by Eric Bishop, whose invaluable knowledge and advice, gained from many years in the Holy Land, was often in demand by missionaries, the British authorities and representatives of the Arab and Jewish communities. But no matter how busy he was, how frustrated and hard-pressed, Eric always tried to find time for the Mission to the Blind in Bible Lands, the organisation founded in the closing years of the nineteenth century by Mary Lovell, the woman who sang "Hold the fort" as the victorious British Army entered Jerusalem in 1917.

Mary's life began in Stickney, an isolated village deep in the Lincolnshire Fens, and the road to her final home in Jerusalem was an eventful one. From her earliest Sunday School days she dreamed of becoming a missionary but her eager first attempts ended in disaster when she fell so ill in South Africa that she was shipped back to Britain on a stretcher, "to die peacefully at home". At home, although Mary survived she became an invalid and her listless days were spent lying on a sofa or propped in a wheelchair where she grew increasingly sorry for herself and angry at God for abandoning her. Was he blind, she often wondered, couldn't he see how much she wanted to serve him? Sometimes on summer mornings, Mary's sisters wheeled her chair to a favourite garden corner, where an old apple tree leaned over long grass and where Mary sometimes gazed for hours across the familiar broad flat landscape that was overarched by enormous Fenland skies. On one special morning, in that quiet corner of a Lincolnshire garden, something happened to Mary. From out of a dazzling light God spoke to her. When she walked into her parents' parlour and announced to her startled family that God had called her to work with the blind, she was met with a mixture of disbelief, wonder, hope and concern. But, whatever her family felt, Mary would not be dissuaded. She knew that wherever she went from that moment onwards, a path would be opened before her. Without hesitation, she said goodbye to Lincolnshire, made her way to London and became a teacher at the Kilburn School for the Blind where the newly developed Braille code was rapidly replacing the old system of Moon's raised type. At Kilburn, Mary learned Braille, she rose to become deputy headteacher of the school, and then, almost at the height of success, she felt called to set out on a new adventure.

"I saw at Kilburn just how much blind people need holidays and rest," Mary told her friends when she opened at St Leonards-on-Sea near Hastings, Britain's first holiday home for the blind. It was a great success and as reports spread it attracted blind travellers from overseas who were passing through Britain. One of those travellers was Ghandoor Zaytoon, a blind Lebanese Druze convert to Christianity. There was some education for the blind in the Middle East, he told Mary, most famously at the British Syrian School for the Blind in Beirut, but on the whole, provision was scarce, and for girls, there was almost nothing at all. For them, he said, the situation was particularly tragic, as they were often seen as nothing but a burden and a source of shame, and many were kept hidden away by parents who had no idea what to do with them. As she listened to Ghandoor's story, Mary knew where the next stage on her journey would lead her. This time the farewells in Lincolnshire were tinged with deep sadness. The Lovell family knew they might never see Mary again. She left England in 1893 and set out for Lebanon and for the next two years she lived as companion to Ghandoor's Canadian wife and learned Arabic from the children she taught at the John Wilson Memorial School in Ghandoor's home village of Baakleen. When she felt she had mastered enough Arabic, Mary began to devise an Arabic Braille, and when she believed she had mastered enough Arabic Braille, she began translating the Bible. When she left Baakleen for Jerusalem in 1895, Mary was 46 years old and had nothing in the world except one small trunk containing a few clothes, her mother's gift of two golden sovereigns, the beginnings of an Arabic Braille Bible, and a verse from Saint Paul's letter to the Philippians printed as a cheque: "My God shall supply all your needs according to his glorious riches in Christ Jesus."

The house of blessing

After General Allenby's army settled in Jerusalem, some of the British bivouacs and camel lines were pitched on the muddy slopes of Windmill Hill, just opposite Mary's house that was home and school to more than 20 blind Palestinian and Armenian girls. The house was called Barachah, a Hebrew word meaning "blessing" and it had been the gift of an American millionaire who was puzzled when Mary assured him that God provided whatever she needed. "How strange," he said, "wherever I have gone people have wanted things, pianos, furniture, carriages, but you with your blind children want nothing." A week later the millionaire returned to Mary's rented Jerusalem schoolroom to press the keys of Barachah into her startled and thankful hands. In 1918, Barachah become a second home to some of the British soldiers stationed just across the way. Five hundred and three soldiers were adopted as sons of the home and their names were inscribed carefully on Braille lists that were kept among Barachah's most treasured possessions.

One of those British soldiers was Tom Bartlett, and much later he wrote about his first visit to Barachah. "I can never forget the deep peace of Miss Lovell's long parlour room," he said, "with its old fashioned English sofas and chairs and the embroidered text on the wall, 'Be still and know that I am God'." At one end of the room, said Tom, gathered around a harmonium, "four girls were singing 'Galilee, blue Galilee', while two others who sat at a table, with no equipment but a stylus were patiently transcribing onto sheets of very thick brown paper, another page of the Arabic Braille Bible". The two girls were Adele Dafesh, a blind Arab girl from Jaffa, and Siranoush Ketchejian, a partially sighted Armenian girl from Hadjin in Cilicia who was the only member of her family to escape the 1909 massacres. Something had prompted Siranoush's mother to allow her little daughter to set out with a group of blind girls and a young Armenian teacher for faraway Jerusalem where an Englishwoman taught blind children. In doing so she ensured her daughter's survival. The Braille Bible that Tom saw the two girls transcribing so patiently, was published in 31 volumes by the British and Foreign Bible Society over the course of nearly 30 years. In its time it was one of only three complete Braille translations, one in English, one in Welsh, and one other, Mary Lovell's Arabic Braille Bible. When Mary died in 1932, Adele and Siranoush were determined that Mary's work would continue and between them they founded the Lovell Homes for the Blind, one in Beit Jala near Bethlehem and the other in Jerusalem.

Prove me now... saith the Lord of hosts

Just before Christmas in 1939, one of Adele's friends visiting her at the Bethlehem Lovell Home warned her to be careful. The war in Europe will spread, said the friend, and you will be cut off from your supporters. She advised Adele to send the blind girls home. Adele did not know what to do. Even without the disruption of war, she was finding it hard to make ends meet. Most of the people who sent regular donations to the Lovell Homes had first supported Mary and they were growing old and each year there were fewer of them. And Adele also knew that if the blind girls went home, especially for a long period, they would forget all their careful training. But, if they stayed with her in Bethlehem, perhaps they would be cold and hungry. Adele sat up late that night, praying to God to help her. Eventually, just before she went to bed, she took up her Daily Light, a Braille text of daily Bible readings. She put her fingers on the page for the day and traced out the words: "Prove me now... saith the Lord of hosts, if I will not open the windows of heaven, and pour you out a blessing, that there shall not be room enough to receive it." Adele knelt on the floor and claimed the blessing for all her blind children.

The next morning was Christmas Eve and Adele took the girls to the Anglican courtyard carol service at Bethlehem's Church of the Nativity. As always the service was beautiful and the voices of the blind girls seemed sweeter than ever. "Once in Royal David's City"; "Hark, the Herald Angels Sing"; and, "O Little Town of Bethlehem". Adele knew she should be happy to be so close to the wonder of Jesus' birth, but her heart was heavy. Had she been mistaken the previous night? Was it really true? She knew she had no money to buy extra Christmas food for the girls and the words of her friend had returned to haunt her: "You will be cut off from your supporters." Cut off! Adele prayed once more, "Dear Lord, if You want me to keep the Home open, please send me a cake for the children's tea, as a token." Then she took the girls home and waited. During the long grey afternoon, Mary's old friend, Mr Mihran Siraganian arrived with Christmas presents. But no cake. The afternoon passed, dusk fell, and suppertime approached, and Adele slowly laid all the tables. Still, she waited. At six o'clock there was a knock at the door. A stranger stood on the steps with a cake, hot from the oven, in his hands. Someone he knew, he said, who had never supported the blind girls before, had felt suddenly moved to bake them a cake for Christmas. Three days later, Eric Bishop and a German friend arrived at Adele's Lovell Home with three Christian British servicemen. That night, back at camp, the soldiers raised a collection. They took it to Adele next day. The box was so full the coins spilled over and rolled from the table onto the floor.

Something must be done

The three soldiers were from Wesley House, a servicemen's fellowship run by the Methodist Church in Jerusalem, and it continued to support Adele and Siranoush all through the Second World War. In 1943, a young sergeant in the Royal Army Pay Corps went with two of the Wesley House men, on the rickety bus that climbed the road from Jerusalem to Beit Jala, to meet Adele Dafesh. The sergeant's name was Bob Clothier and he never forgot that first meeting. Years later he still remembered walking through the shabby doorway of a dilapidated stone house into a large room, "dimly lit and barely furnished but warm", where children dressed in cheap red clothing were singing English hymns in four part harmony. It took Bob a little while to realise that all the children, who learned their hymns from Adele, who learned them from Mary, who first learned them in Stickney Village Church, were all completely blind. Bob fell in love straight away with the blind children and he soon joined a rota of Christian servicemen who spent their off-duty hours at the home in Beit Jala. "We all used our skills to do some of the repairs which were very necessary," he said later, "and we also fetched the water, which in those days had to be *bought* by the bucketful." The soldiers also shared their army rations with the children and as they talked among themselves about the desperate needs of the homes and the dedication of Adele and Siranoush, they decided that something had to be done, and that they themselves were called to take on the task. Bob Clothier and his friends agreed that as soon as they returned to Britain, they would find a way to help the blind children of the Holy Land.

God will send the workers

For a while in 1943, the managing committee of the Bible Lands Missions Aid Society, all of them Samuel's contemporaries and all of them elderly, had wondered if the Society could continue without its secretary of 40 years. Rather like Cyrus Hamlin's evaluation of Cuthbert Young so many years earlier, Samuel Gentle-Cackett had been virtually a Bible Lands Missions Aid Society in himself. So much so that he had failed to train a successor and although the very competent Mrs Ada Blair was employed as his assistant, Ada was about to start a family and once she arranged the Society's move from the bomb-damaged offices to new premises by Victoria Station, she abandoned her job for motherhood. As the committee considered the possibility of ending the Society's work for ever, Harry Fear reassured them. He and Samuel had been fortunate, he said, in the investments they had been led to make all through the 1920s and even through the Depression years of the 30s. The Society could maintain its regular grants for some time and all that was needed was for someone to take on the role of secretary until a younger man was found. Somewhat reluctantly, the Reverend Harold Gardiner agreed. It would not be for long, said Harry, God would send the new workers, he was certain of it.

Desperate needs

As the war came to an end, tributes for Samuel poured in from all over the world. Some of the missionaries supported by the Society had no idea its secretary had died, and once peace was established, some of their first letters contained invitations for

Samuel to visit their work. When they learned of his death, it seemed to some of them that part of themselves and an age of the world had passed away with him. But, with all the kind words and fond memories, the tributes to Samuel also told stories of work that went on, despite wars and because of wars, and of people desperate for help from the Bible Lands Missions Aid Society.

Martha Frearson had more elderly women at Shemlan. "Their number is increasing weekly," said her airmail letter. The Danish Birds' Nest Orphanage had more children, "Almost daily, mothers in great need are asking for help," cabled Miss Maria Jacobsen, its missionary founder. At Assiout Hospital, there were more patients. "Our beds are full continuously," said Dr McClanahan, when he wrote to thank the Society for a gift of an operating theatre steriliser. "Your Society has reached out a hand of helpfulness to the poor and suffering of Egypt," he said, "and as I bow my head in prayer before each operation I often think of you." Other requests were met too. Many of the Society's faithful supporters had maintained their donations throughout the war, and new requests from Harold Gardiner had begun to provoke others into resuming their regular giving. And when the Society's bank account was unable to meet the needs of the overseas missions, the stock so carefully husbanded by Samuel and Harry Fear was sold. In Belgrade, Antoniye Gruitch, Darinka's son, received help for a new agricultural project among Serbian refugees. Aleppo College in Syria and Anatolia College in Greece both received grants for poor students. In the Persian Gulf, where "Bedouins whose fathers for thousands of years were herders of sheep and keepers of camels, now learn to don overalls and read pressure gauges on oil wells", support went to evangelistic work at the American missions at Bahrain and Kuwait. Missions in Alexandria and Port Said, child welfare work in Cairo, students at Assiout College, a Leper Hospital at Omdurman, Harry Fear's gift of the *Elliott*, and William Essery's old favourite, Tabeetha School at Jaffa, all received grants, while in England, at Bedfont, Samuel's widow was helped too as she cared for the remaining Armenian orphans.

From Kokkinia, Blind Krikor, alive and well, cabled desperately for funds. He needed new books for his own schools and Sunday Schools and games and educational toys for refugee children in new camps and orphanages at Athens. Greece, the nation that had opened its doors so generously to refugees in their hundreds of thousands from earlier conflicts had been devastated by the Nazi occupation, by a famine where 100,000 people had died, and then by a brutal civil war. When the German Army eventually withdrew from Greece, said Charles House from the Salonica Farm, together with everything else it stole and destroyed, it took with it most of the Farm's prime stock and left farm buildings in ruins and equipment damaged beyond repair. The civil war that followed had added to the chaos. In 1946, as Charles struggled to put the Farm back on its feet, he cabled a long list of needs to London: quinine, bandages, hymn books, agricultural implements, tools, rat poison, building materials... Harold Gardiner felt overwhelmed. He had no idea where to begin and he thought it unlikely that many of the items on the list were to be had in war weary Britain. But, with help from Harry Fear and friends at a British pharmaceutical company, everything was eventually gathered together and with the assistance of the relief agencies of the newly formed United Nations they were shipped to Thessaloniki, where Salonica's ancient name was restored to her once more. When Charles House asked for new pedigree Black Yorkshire boars, Tartur Lovely Cottage and Tartur Jack Tindley were shipped by the United Nations to Thessaloniki too.

The challenge of the Great Knight

For the Armenians of Lebanon, after the disruption of another war and the influx of thousands more refugees from Alexandretta, poverty and social problems had increased. They continued to be especially destructive of the young people, said the Armenian Evangelical Union, as it described a homeless, rootless generation, disrupted by upheaval and conflict, who had few bearings and little hope for the future. Elizabeth Webb wrote from the Beirut suburb of Trad, home of the new social centre that celebrated its seventh birthday in 1946 with a grant from the Society that completed the balance on the building fund. Trad, said Elizabeth, was "a boys' town and a girls' town. The whole place is seething with them. They are everywhere; in the gutter, in the mud, on the housetop, on the tramtops; in fact, you find them everywhere except in their own homes". It was also a region of vice, she said, "A place where murder and theft, rape and calumny do not lurk in the dark, but strut in open daylight, because they are hailed as the marks of a heroic manhood." But, in the midst of it all, she said, stood the Centre, a Christian work "whose fragrance has filled the neighbourhood". You may think that statement poetic, said Elizabeth, but "it is a fact". There was something for the whole Armenian community at the Centre, she said, for young and old, men, women, youths, children and babies. On the plot of ground where she and her colleagues had stepped out in faith in the late 1930s, there was a school, a clinic, clubs for the elderly, boys' clubs, girls' clubs, night schools, Sunday schools, a reading room, a playground, and, just recently, she said, a workshop where trades can be learned and the spirit of Christian co-operation between employee and employer can be experienced. And making sure that everything runs smoothly, said Elizabeth, we have our Knights! The Trad Knights of the Christian Endeavour, she said, were real "tough guys". Some of them were former delinquents, numbered among those who once saw crime and street life as the mark of "heroic manhood", but whose lives were turned around when they were challenged by the Great Knight Himself, the Lord Jesus Christ.

An iron curtain divides Europe

Only in Bulgaria were there problems with the Society's grants. A message from Vasil Furnajieff in the United States said his father, Samuel's old friend Dimiter, had died during the war, and that the Bible School had been seriously damaged by fire. Without Samuel, and without Dimiter, Harold Gardiner and his colleagues were at a loss what to do. As the war neared its end they had watched as Germany's Bulgarian ally was defeated by the Soviet Red Army, and then as Bulgaria, Albania and Yugoslavia became satellites of the Soviet Union. The leader of Bulgaria's new pro-Soviet government and Secretary of the Bulgarian Communist Party, was Georgi Dimitrov, once a poor student at the Samokov print shop that was originally established with the Society's grants. With the new government firmly in control of Bulgaria, the Samokov Bible School site was expropriated by the Bulgarian Republic for use as offices and a school, and in 1948, as the Cold War gripped Europe, and the Iron Curtain divided East from West, all religious organisations in Bulgaria were banned.

Found in the London phone book

In 1946, Bob Clothier and his British Army colleagues who had befriended Adele and Siranoush convened a meeting at the Methodist Central Hall at Westminster. There they founded the Lovell Society to raise support for the Mission to the Blind in Bible Lands. The meeting was enthusiastic, but Bob was beginning to realise how big the task was. Since returning home to Britain he had made it his business to investigate every aspect of blindness, its causes and its treatment, and how blind people were educated and trained in the West. It was a new field for him but he had very quickly realised that although the children at the Lovell Homes were well cared for and happy, the world was changing, and in Britain and America, blind people were moving out of institutions and into the mainstream life of the world. If something similar was to be done for the blind children of Palestine, he reasoned, it would take a great deal of money, time and expert knowledge, and he wondered just how his little group of comrades were going to fulfil the task they believed God had set before them. The more he thought about it, the bigger that task seemed.

As Bob set about producing leaflets and appeal letters for the Lovell Society, he remembered something Eric Bishop had told him in Jerusalem. The Bible Lands Missions Aid Society, Eric had said, was founded to support Christian work in the lands of the Bible, and for almost 100 years, from its offices in London, grants had gone to missions from Bulgaria to Bahrain, from Armenia to Egypt and from Beirut to Jerusalem. Bob found the Society's address in the London telephone directory and wrote to the secretary, describing the work of the Lovell Society and the needs of the blind children of Palestine. The Society's minutes of 27 June 1946, record the request, and that the managing committee agreed that if a favourable report was received from Eric Bishop, £100, approximately £2,407 or $3,610 today, would be sent to the Lovell Home in Jerusalem. More requests, and then meetings between Bob and Harold Gardiner followed, and in October 1946, the Society agreed to assist with the complete "reconstruction" of the Mission to the Blind.

Help us to help these blind children

In the *Star* of 1947, the only issue published that year, there was a photograph of Adele and the blind children at Bethlehem. "Will You Help Us To Help These Blind Children?" said the caption. Beneath the picture, Adele told the story of Mary Lovell and the Mission to the Blind. Mary, she said, although praying constantly in her final years for someone from Britain or America to continue her work, had eventually come to believe that it would not survive her for long. "But when she laid down her arms in 1932," said Adele, "I, unworthy, weak and helpless, simply had to carry on." And she and Siranoush, a blind Palestinian woman and an almost blind Armenian woman, had been carrying on ever since. "Between 40 and 50 blind children, or even more, have passed through our hands," she said, "some from Muslim families and some from Christian." Most of those families are very poor, said Adele, and many of them "think that a blind child is as good as dead, so they put them somewhere they can be looked after and then forget about them altogether". But, she went on, we try to educate them as best we can and teach them to be useful and happy. Right now, she said, we have 22 children in the Homes, two teachers who work for practically no money, and Im Jaleel our housemother who serves us simply for the love of God. Please help them, added Harold Gardiner at the end of the article, please send me your gift!

By 1948, the Society had rented new premises in Bethlehem for Adele and both homes, in Bethlehem and Jerusalem, were receiving some of the specialised educational equipment they needed if their work was to develop. In October, Bob Clothier was invited to join the Society's committee together with two of his Lovell Society colleagues, Reverend Leslie Farmer who had been Chaplain at Wesley House, and Reverend Harold Keys. It was with considerable relief that Harold Gardiner welcomed them. He had done the best he could for the Society, he had tried to raise funds by speaking at London churches, he had written letters by the score, and published four editions of the *Star*. But he was not a fund-raiser, or a publicist, and his heart was not in the work. He also felt responsible that since 1946, he had overseen the sale of thousands of pounds worth of stock, Samuel and Harry's careful investments, and that by 1948 there was an overdraft on the current account and some of the Society's old friends were receiving only three-quarters of what they needed in grants.

The changing world

As the 1950s opened, only two members of the Society's pre-war committee were left. Harry Fear was one of them, but he was an old man and he asked to be relieved of his duties as treasurer. He never told anyone how much he missed the old partnership with Samuel that had made him feel so enthusiastic and so alive, and although he agreed to become the Society's president he never attended another meeting. Harry died in 1954. Harold Gardiner resigned from the committee when it was suggested that the BLMAS and the Lovell Society should work more closely together. Leslie Farmer, and then Bob Clothier, became secretary of the BLMAS, and as the Society looked towards its centenary, there was no one left on its committee who remembered the years before 1946. An age of the world really had passed away with Samuel. The world was changing and the Society was changing too.

When the Society was founded, nearly 100 years earlier, its original aim was to bring the Armenian people into the Evangelical fold from where it hoped they would eventually emerge as missionaries to Islam. Instead, it had been among the witnesses who saw the Armenian nation almost completely destroyed and the remnant driven from its homeland. Although the Society's work expanded to support many aspects of relief work, educational provision and medical care, and included work in large parts of the Balkans and the Middle East, it always stayed faithful to the Armenian people. It remained a constant witness to the genocide, it stood alongside the survivors in the refugee camps, and it upheld the new generation and helped them lay a foundation for their future. Cuthbert Young, William Essery and Samuel Gentle-Cackett had all been passionate about Armenia. Bob Clothier and his friends looked towards Palestine. And, just as the eyes of the world in 1854 were on Turkey and the Ottoman Empire, from 1948 onwards they focused on the Holy Land. As the new state of Israel was created there, the Palestinian people fled from their homes, and a conflict began that would rock the Middle East and threaten the peace of the world.

Chapter 12

Dispossessed Palestine
The 1950s

When Mary Lovell and the people of Jerusalem welcomed General Allenby in December 1917, many of them believed the British Army came as heralds of independence. Their hopes were fuelled when Allenby declared that Britain's wartime object in the East was the establishment of national governments and administrations that derived their authority from the initiative and freewill of the people themselves. What Allenby failed to mention, was that in November 1917, despite conflicting promises made earlier to Arab leaders in the Near East, Britain's Foreign Secretary, Arthur Balfour, had written to leaders of Britain's Jewish community assuring them that the British Government desired to see established in Palestine a national homeland for the Jewish people. When Britain received a mandate from the League of Nations in 1922, to govern Palestine and Transjordan, what was later known as the Balfour Declaration was written into its preamble.

Under British administration, and encouraged by the increasingly militant Zionist movement, Jewish immigration to Palestine rose steeply. And as it rose, tensions between the new arrivals and the indigenous population grew deeper and spread wider. Palestinian protesters, the British authorities, and Zionist terrorist groups whose aim was to drive the British from the Holy Land, became locked in a spiralling round of conflict. In the three years before 1939, during the Palestinian Revolt, 5,000 Arabs, 463 Jews and 101 British lost their lives. The Palestine Orphans Fund, created just before the Second World War, and administered in Jerusalem by Eric Bishop, had been another result of that violence. As the War ended and the extent of Nazi crimes against the Jewish people was revealed, emotional support across the world for a Jewish national homeland was enormous. Six million of

Europe's Jews had been murdered, and in the face of that crime, committed in Europe by Europeans, the wishes of the Palestinian people were ignored. More Jewish refugees flooded into Palestine. They were desperate for security and desperate to ensure they would never be victims again. No matter what it cost! Under intense pressure, the newly formed United Nations drew up a partition plan where over half the country was awarded to less than one third of the population, who despite immigration and land purchase owned only six per cent of the land.

The birth of Israel

On 14 May 1948, in Tel Aviv, an Israeli State was declared. Almost immediately it was recognised by the President of the United States of America and on the next day, 15 May, Britain withdrew from its Palestine Mandate. A mixture of emotions greeted the birth of the new state: relief, satisfaction and expectation in the West, apprehension and fear in Palestine and the Arab world. But, despite mixed reactions elsewhere, in Palestine itself the violence intensified as newly born Israel immediately began seizing land not assigned to it under the UN plan. And, as Israel seized the land, Palestinians began leaving their homes. Some believed they would suffer the same fate as the villagers of Deir Yassin, where 250 Palestinians were massacred in the month before the declaration of the Israeli state. Others were forced on their way. In Lydda, on the fertile Mediterranean coast, 30,000 people were driven from their city by the well-armed fighters of the Israeli Army. The refugees fled towards Ramallah, situated in the area assigned by the United Nations to the Arab inhabitants of Palestine, a three-day journey across a barren, stony wilderness where the temperature was over 100 degrees in the shade and the sand and rocks too hot for hands and feet to touch. Some accounts suggested that over 4,000 people died of exhaustion and thirst. As the Palestinians left Lydda behind, Jewish immigrants, many of them traumatised survivors of the Nazi genocide of the Jews, moved into houses filled with the treasured possessions of the evicted people stumbling across the burning hills towards Ramallah.

Despite the intervention of Arab armies from surrounding countries and a war that lasted a year, the much better-armed

Israelis triumphed and by the time a ceasefire was brokered, only 23 per cent of Palestine remained in the hands of its own people. Over 400 Palestinian towns and villages had been depopulated, some villages had disappeared entirely, and one million Palestinians were refugees. A new agency, UNRWA, was set up by the United Nations specifically on the refugees' behalf. In 1950, the Knesset, the Israeli parliament, passed the Law of Return that said Jews anywhere in the world could claim citizenship of Israel. The dispossessed Palestinian people had no such right.

Consequences

For the Society, and for many people in Britain, the events of 1948 were uncomfortable. The BLMAS had always worked closely with Christian missions to Jews, Sir Leon Levison, its pre-war vice-president, who had been honoured internationally for his work for refugees of many racial origins, was a passionate Zionist, and throughout its history, the Society's leading figures, from Lord Shaftesbury to Samuel Gentle-Cackett, had believed the return of the Jews to Palestine would herald great events. None of them had given much thought to the consequences of Jewish return for the Palestinian people.

For some other organisations and people, the consequences were becoming only too clear. In 1949, the Society received an appeal from the American Community in Beirut. The refugee crisis, it said, "pronounced by the United Nations as the greatest relief need in the world today", was not receiving the attention it deserved, and it went on to detail the latest statistics: 88,000 refugees in Jordan, 72,000 in Syria, 61,000 in Lebanon, 9,000 in Egypt and 237,000 in what had once been Palestine. They had sought refuge with friends, relatives and fellow Arabs, they were "sleeping in schools, mosques and churches, or under the seats of moving-picture houses. Many thousands have no shelter at all". They were homeless, workless and hungry and the world's richest and most powerful nations appeared to have little interest in their plight. But it was a crisis, said the report, that would not go away.

An appeal of a different kind arrived at the Society's offices from the Council of the Arab Evangelical Church in Palestine and Jordan. The Christian church in Palestine, it said, was experiencing a crisis of its own and Christianity in the land of its birth was under threat. It was true, said the Council, that church buildings had suffered damage during the fighting, but it was the scattering of the congregations that made the future appear so bleak. An age-old Christian community had been fractured and displaced, robbed of home, possessions and livelihood, and driven to the refugee camps of Jordan where so many Palestinian Christians, "who loved their church and had given generously in the past", were now destitute. To help them, the Council had borrowed money to provide food, clothing and blankets and now it was itself in need. "Brethren, pray for us," the report concluded, "that out of the present miseries and distresses, our Church may emerge purified and strengthened to be a more fitting instrument in the Holy Land for the furtherance of the Gospel of Jesus Christ."

Just as it had always done before, the Society opened another relief fund and photographs of Palestinian refugee camps appeared in the *Star*. But, while Bob Clothier felt deeply for the refugees, and highlighted the humanitarian aspects of the crisis in the *Star*, he was uncomfortable with an issue that had such enormous political and theological implications. It was his concern for the blind children of the Lovell Homes that had led to his involvement with the Society, and the injustice done to the people of Palestine never produced in him the outrage that had once greeted Turkey's murderous treatment of the Armenians. Bob felt no urge to produce articles in the style of William Essery's "Sorrowful Asia Minor", or Samuel's "Written in Blood". He believed the Society should concentrate its resources on improving life for the most disadvantaged people in Middle Eastern society, most especially the blind, and that involvement in political issues would alienate supporters and bring the Society into disrepute. From time to time, an article appeared in the *Star* that indicated an uncomfortable awareness that the unresolved issue of the Palestinian refugees was potentially explosive, but like many people throughout the world, Bob Clothier felt ambivalent and uncertain about Palestine and preferred not to dwell on what the future might hold.

Bob Clothier's vision

Although the Society's pre-war grants had mostly been maintained, Bob and his colleagues had made the needs of the Lovell Homes a priority. The conflicts that followed the birth of Israel had disrupted their work and it had taken some time for Adele and Siranoush to find settled accommodation for their blind children. Siranoush in particular had moved several times. In 1950 she had found herself in Jerusalem's no man's land on the Israeli Jordanian frontier, in the house of Mary Lovell's old friend, Mihran Siraganian. In 1951, in the retaliations that followed the assassination of Jordan's King Abdullah, Mihran received immediate notice to quit and after a day of desperate searching, all that could be found for Siranoush and the children was one tiny flat on the Mount of Olives, while their furniture, books and specialised educational equipment were stacked in the open cloisters of St George's Anglican Cathedral. Despite the disruption, the Society did its best for both homes, both of them now in the Arab state of Jordan, and as far as possible they were comfortably furnished and upgraded and the children cared for. Bob Clothier ensured that specialist educational equipment and games for the blind were sent to the homes and Siranoush travelled to Britain to develop her teaching and vocational skills at English training centres. Children and staff received regular doses of vitamins and cod-liver oil and the children were all seen by ophthalmic specialists. But until permanent premises were found, it seemed to Bob that the continuing upheavals of the Middle East would frustrate all the Society's best efforts and he wondered if the Society's centenary in 1954 might be the opportunity to raise funds for a new Lovell Home permanently settled on land of its own.

Bob had other reasons too for wanting a more secure establishment for the Lovell children. Although one or two of the most outstanding girls had advanced to further education, it was becoming increasingly clear to him that even the less academic majority could no longer be treated as they were in the days of Mary Lovell, as cherished long-term dependants. Other young blind children, many of them living in refugee camps, needed the opportunities provided at the Lovell Homes, while for the adult blind, opportunities in the world at large were widening. In the West, blind people received training for independent living and rewarding jobs, and if something similar could be pioneered by the Society in Jerusalem, he thought, it would be a wonderful commemoration of 100 years of work in the lands of the Bible and a witness to the Christian faith itself. It would signify light in the darkness and a resurrection into the fullness of life for those who were often considered outcast and worthless. Bob's vision was for a permanent vocational training centre, where blind girls would learn mobility and independent living together with hand-icrafts, typing and telephone switchboard skills. With such accomplishments, Bob believed they could work in sheltered workshops, Christian offices, and perhaps, even as homeworkers in their own villages. He knew it would be a hard task in a land where most blind children were not valued and where the tradi-tional status of women remained low, but in an optimistic ges-ture he set the vocational process in motion by shipping a weaving loom and several knitting machines to Siranoush's cramped flat on the Mount of Olives.

Bob's vocational training project was encouraged by Dr Helen Keller, the world's most famous campaigner for the blind, who visited both Lovell Homes in 1952. For Adele Dafesh, Helen Keller was the most inspiring person alive, almost rivalling Mary Lovell in her estimation, and she thought it wonderfully appro-priate that a woman who had overcome deafness as well as blind-ness to achieve great academic success and the acclaim of the world, should visit the work Mary had begun so many years before. Adele wrote an account of Helen's visit to Bethlehem for the *Star*. Miss Keller met every blind child at the Home, she said, "And by her feeling of them, and by the touches on her arm of her companion, Miss Polly Thompson, this great lady not only learned about them and their work, but was quickly in commu-nication with them." Through Polly, Helen told the children the story of her own life, about the little girl whose world was a mass of confusions and terrors until the day God sent the teachers to her who turned her silent darkness into a world of light and hope. It was her dear wish for the Lovell girls, Helen had said, as her visit reached its end, that they should live fulfilling and useful lives too, and in their turn become beacons of light to others.

The leper home

In 1953, just as Bob opened an appeal for the proposed new vocational training centre in Jerusalem, he received a request from Eric Bishop's old friend, Johanna Larsen, the German missionary sister of the Moravian Church who was interned in 1939 among the leprosy patients she had served since the end of the Great War. Sister Johanna was an old friend of Adele and Siranoush too and they had encouraged her to contact Bob. Tell him your story and your needs, they advised, and the Bible Lands Missions Aid Society will almost certainly help you. The first Moravian leper hospital in Jerusalem, the Jesus-Hilfe, was built near the Jaffa Gate in 1867, Sister Johanna told Bob, after German Christian hearts were moved at the sight of "the unfortunate ones" who lived and begged in the shadow of Jerusalem's walls. By 1948 the Jesus-Hilfe had become a modern leper hospital serving Jews and Arabs alike, but when the city was divided and the hospital found itself in the Jewish sector, its Arab patients became desperate to be among their own people. Despite her own misgivings, said Sister Johanna, and the concerns of the Israeli doctors, her poor patients were so distressed she felt she had no alternative but to take them to Jordan. "I go to prepare a place for you," she told those who were fearful at being abandoned, and despite her advancing years, she had set out to seek a new home. One month later, she met her Arab friends again at the Mandelbaum Gate, Jerusalem's only crossing point between two hostile nations, to take them to the only place suitable for leprosy patients that she could find. She was almost afraid to tell them where it was. After the modern hospital they had become used to, with its sophisticated equipment and doctors always on call, their new home was to be the derelict Turkish leper home at Silwan, the Biblical Siloam, at the south-eastern corner of Jerusalem. Only a few stone huts were still standing, Sister Johanna had told her Arab friends, rocks tumbled down the hillsides whenever the rains came, and they must spend their nights alone as there was no room for Sister Johanna and her nursing colleagues. Never mind, the mostly Muslim lepers said, we know God walks beside you and that therefore he will look after us.

Dispossessed Palestine

The small country of Jordan, which was home to Siranoush and Adele, and now to Sister Johanna and her leper friends, had taken the bulk of the 1948 refugees, and the small desert hamlet of Zerqa had become home to 10,000 exiled Palestinians. There was little work and not enough local food, and most refugees lived on rations provided by UNRWA. But like the Armenian survivors of the deportations it was not only unemployment and hunger that attacked the Palestinians. They were traumatised by the loss of homes and homeland, and the trauma created and exacerbated physical and psychological illness. Tuberculosis and pneumonia were widespread and depression and suicide were common. A British Christian woman, Miss Winifred Coate, had founded a Rehabilitation Centre at Zerqa and appealed to the Society for funds. Her aim, she said, was to provide training and to make loans for small scale work projects where some skilled individuals such as potters and brushmakers could set up in business and become self-supporting once more. Other men, she said, were employed in ceramic and brick factories, while clothing and knitting workshops provided employment for women.

"Though our desire is to concentrate our energies on training and rehabilitation," Winifred told readers of the *Star*, "day after day more than 1,000 refugees enter our direct relief centre and many of them are miserably in need of comfort and friendship." Foremost among that group were Palestinian peasant farmers, she said, who found it more difficult than most to adjust to life in the camps. They came from ancient communities, deep rooted in the soil, where life was dictated by the customs of centuries and where the main focus for women was family: births, marriages and deaths, while their menfolk concentrated on olive harvests and the village orange groves. Winifred had established a small farm at Zerqa, but it was no substitute, she said, for the almost mystical attachment most Palestinian farmers had for the land they had been forced to leave. There was one old man in particular, who was losing his eyesight rapidly and whose lined features were often in Winifred's thoughts. "Sometimes," the old farmer had told her, his cloudy eyes misting with memory, "I dream at night that I am back among my olive trees and then I see those olive trees so clearly."

As the years after 1948 passed, the Palestinian refugees discovered, again as the Armenians had discovered before them, that when traditional family and community patterns were disrupted social problems increased and multiplied. In 1953, Sister Gwen Green of the Nazareth Hospital wrote in the *Star* about the increasing numbers of children, perfectly healthy but abandoned and unwanted, who were being cared for in the hospital's children's ward. It was becoming quite common, she said, for two babies to share one cot and even for the ward's enamel baby bath to be used sometimes as a crib. Some of those children were uncollected after mothers died in childbirth, while others were illegitimate. Just recently, Gwen told readers, a Palestinian matriarch had arrived at the hospital with a large basket on her head. Nothing extraordinary in that, she said, but when the old woman took the basket down and removed the cover, "we found not the grapes or loaves we might have expected, but a baby girl just six hours old". Little Afifeh was born to unmarried parents, Gwen explained, "a great offence here and the child would have been killed had the brave old grandmother not taken her and walked several miles with the baby hidden in the basket". Afifeh was now taking up a cot in the children's ward, said Gwen, "and sometimes we feel we are an orphanage as well as a hospital".

Inspiration from the past

As Bob Clothier read Gwen's report, he thought about the orphans of Nazareth. He also thought about Sister Johanna and all the other appeals for help that were arriving in London from the lands of the Bible. He realised he had known very little about the Society when he first joined its managing committee, and that his main concern had been to help Adele and Siranoush. But, as he read the literature which dated back to 1854 that described the enormous magnitude of the work and how great needs had always been answered, Bob resolved that the Society's second hundred years would be just as effective as its first. He knew he was different from William Essery and Samuel Gentle-Cackett, that some of his priorities were not the same as theirs, and that he was certainly no clergyman, but he was beginning to believe that God had sent him to the Society for a reason. And perhaps the reason was, that in order to go forward into the future, the

Society no longer needed a clergyman at its helm, but a layman and a businessman. A man just like Bob Clothier.

By 1954 Bob had increased the Society's income substantially, but although he sent out regular postal appeals and ran advertising campaigns in national newspapers and the Christian press, attracting new supporters to replace a rapidly disappearing older generation was a problem. It was a problem he knew his predecessors had faced and he began to wonder if restoring the position of Deputation Secretary, Samuel Gentle-Cackett's first post with the Society when he travelled the country with his magic lantern, might be a solution. He raised the matter with an old friend, a vicar with some experience of the Middle East who was just about to retire from a ministry near Brighton. It turned out to be just what the Reverend Henry Wilkins wanted. He had been facing retirement with foreboding, fearing a loss of purpose and fellowship, and he accepted Bob's offer eagerly and threw himself into the work. He compiled a list of Christian organisations: Mothers' Unions and Young Wives, Youth Clubs and Pensioners' Clubs, Christian Endeavourers and Hospital and Factory Christian Unions, and armed with a collection of 35mm slides and a slide projector, Henry set out to build for the Society a completely new generation of supporters.

As Henry Wilkins travelled around the country, he was something of a sensation. Few ordinary people in 1950s Britain had travelled much beyond the shores of their own land, and although television was finding a place in some homes, Henry's own travellers' tales and his colour slides of Middle Eastern scenes and the children at the Lovell Homes, brought the Society's work to life. The people who listened to his talks and gazed at his slides began to feel an affinity with the children whose faces they saw projected onto screens in church halls around Britain, and as they did so they wanted to know more about them and how they could help them. One way they could help was based on another idea from the past. As Bob read about Emma Baghdassarian's sponsorship arrangements for Broussa and how William Essery raised support for the Armenian orphans after 1895, he realised that people loved personal contact and that Christians in Britain would enjoy writing letters and sending birthday gifts to Palestinian children, and that in return, the children would feel valued and excited by the interest. By the mid-1950s, the Society's first modern sponsorship scheme was underway, helping to support children at the Lovell Homes and at St Margaret's Home in Nazareth which had become an orphanage for the children abandoned at Nazareth Hospital.

The past provided another inspiration for Bob when he reinstated the Society's trading operations by importing flower decorated greetings cards and mother of pearl jewellery made by refugee workmen in Bethlehem. When he found himself whistling carols as he drew up a Christmas advertisement for the *Star*, he began wondering whether people in Britain would buy gaily coloured song sheets at Christmas that showed pictures of the Lovell children alongside favourite carols. He followed a hunch and produced the first sheets for Christmas 1954. They were so popular that supplies ran out as over 100,000 Bethlehem Carol Sheets were sold to churches and schools throughout Britain, British Army bases overseas and to Royal Navy ships around the world. An appeal beside the pictures of Lovell children raised hundreds of pounds. When half a million sheets sold in 1955, Bob sensed that God was encouraging him to step forward in faith. With one and a half million carol sheets as his target, a catalogue of Christmas cards and gifts, and a private deal with God that if all went well he would establish a commercial organisation to help fund the Society's work, Bob headed for Christmas 1956. It was an overwhelming success, the Society made a huge profit and Bob rented a warehouse near his home in High Wycombe and founded Bible Lands Services and Supplies.

Pilgrims

In 1958, Henry Wilkins extended his 35mm slide collection when he travelled to the Bible lands with the Society's first pilgrimage. Bob hadn't been quite certain of how supporters would respond to a small advertisement in the *Star*, "A Tour of the Holy Land – if sufficient support is forthcoming – write for particulars", but he knew that pilgrimages that included Christian missions in their itinerary had been popular ever since Thomas Cook first had the idea in the 1860s. To his great satisfaction, it was another success, and the Society's first pilgrims, ranging in age from 16 to 73 years of age, came from all parts of Britain and as far away as Canada. "In the best tradition of pilgrimages, there was a certain amount of roughing it," Henry wrote in the *Star* when he described how the modern pilgrims travelled by train, boat and coach across Europe and the Mediterranean to the Holy Land where they stayed at St. Margaret's in Nazareth and the YMCA in Jerusalem. For most of the travellers, walking in Jesus' footsteps had been a dream of many years, and gazing over hushed Galilee in the breaking dawn, or standing quietly in the Church of the Nativity, was an experience that words could hardly express. But for most of them, said Henry, it was the sunrise service at the Garden Tomb on Easter Sunday, where blind children from the Lovell Home joined their worship, that "remained the most sacred memory of all".

Old friends: new departures

The Bible Lands Missions Aid Society had many sacred memories of its own and as Bob grew increasingly familiar with its history, and ever more aware of how wide and deep the scope of its earlier work had been, he did his best to ensure that the remaining links with the past became closer and more friendly. There were some disappointments. The American Board, the Society's partner of so many early years was unmoved by suggestions of renewed acquaintance. The Bulgarian Bible College remained cut off by the Iron Curtain. And the Bible Lands Exhibition, items collected by Samuel Gentle-Cackett and his friends over many years, had been sold to another Christian organisation. But, other outcomes were happier and although some of the old names were gone, new workers who had stepped into their places were glad to be drawn closer once more into the Bible Lands family. At Shemlan, Elizabeth Parkissian continued the work of Samuel's old friend, Martha Frearson, "one of the great servants of God", who died in 1950. New missionaries and doctors were grateful for the Society's help as they continued to travel the Nile on Harry Fear's gift of the *Elliott*. The Hamlin Memorial Hospital, the modern tuberculosis hospital that began life as Mary Eddy's wayside clinic, sent thanks for a new x-ray machine and operating theatre equipment. Scholarships for poor students at Anatolia and Aleppo Colleges, among them the grandchildren of some very old friends of the Society, were provided from interest on funds invested in London since the 1800s. From Birds' Nest Orphanage,

Maria Jacobsen wrote for the *Star* about the Armenian refugees who had lived in camps for 50 years and whose families and young people had seen too much of poverty and spiritual death, "the fruit of massacres and deportations", and she said how much the Armenians valued the long years of the Society's friendship and support. The Farm School at Thessaloniki valued the Society's long friendship too. "Pigs may seem remote from the Gospel," Bob wrote in the *Star* when he sent three black boars to Bruce Lansdale, the Farm's new director, "but by providing stock for this fine agricultural Mission School we are helping young men who will return to villages throughout Greece with not only sound, practical, agricultural knowledge, but a faith that will witness to thousands."

Bob hoped the Society's centenary project, the Vocational Training Centre for the Blind that was finally established in Jerusalem in the mid-1950s, would witness to thousands too and that in future years it would be compared with the Essery Orphanage and the Bulgarian Bible School. He was disappointed that the project hadn't moved ahead as swiftly as he had planned and that despite great fund-raising efforts by supporters in Britain, costs had risen at such unprecedented rates in the Middle East that the final total was nowhere near enough for a new building. But as the first vocational training centre of its kind was opened in a rented flat on the Mount of Olives, Bob remembered the dilapidated house where he had first met the blind children who sang so sweetly but whose lives were so limited, and he thanked God for the distance they already travelled together. The next step, he knew, would be to train the blind girls for lives of rewarding employment and successful living in the outside world.

Bob also thanked God that the Society was planning to support the Moravian Church in its efforts to provide Sister Johanna's lepers with a new home too. She had done her best at Silwan, where the Society had funded new bathrooms and a laundry, but the anxieties of leprosy patients who spent their nights alone at Silwan where more rocks than ever tumbled down the hillside, and the stress to the sisters of living in Bethany and driving to their patients each day, had caused great heartache. New leprosy cases caused heartache too. Some of them had been brought to light, Sister Johanna told readers of the *Star*, when sufferers hidden away by their families were forced from their homes into the crowded refugee camps, and although new drugs could treat the disease, very disfigured people could not live comfortably in the outside world. The new home, she said, at Star Mountain near Ramallah, would be a self-sufficient colony where the Moravian sisters and their patients would be joined by leprosy sufferers who needed 24 hour care because of other disabilities. She was already working closely with the architects, she said, and in her spare moments, together with her sisters, she was planting 10,000 pine trees and fruit trees that would eventually make their Star Mountain home a green and shady haven for the unfortunate ones.

The conflict to come

The United Nations designated 1959 the Year of the Refugee, and the *Star* published a special article by Henry Labouisse, a former Director of UNRWA. Henry referred to the continual outbreaks of violence in the Middle East and said his outlook was pessimistic. The refugee problem, over a million Palestinians still homeless, was the bar to future peace, he said, and with the air of the region so charged with tensions and hatreds, claims and counterclaims, deadlock had been reached. But, some day, somehow, the deadlock must be broken. Not just for the refugees, he said, but for the sake of peace in the Middle East and peace in the whole world.

In Lebanon too, Mr Labouisse said, there were growing problems, since the influx of the mainly Muslim Palestinians could upset the delicate religious equilibrium in a small country with not enough resources for so many new people. As Bob Clothier read the report, he thought increasingly about Lebanon and increasingly about resources. In 1957, the Armenian Institute for the Blind and Deaf in Beirut, the only school of its kind in the Middle East where Armenian children were taught in their native language, had been added to the Society's grant list and Bob had great hopes for it. But, although work with the blind was progressing in Lebanon and Jordan where some young blind people were looking forward to fuller lives and a place in the wider world, he was increasingly aware that for too many others there was little to look forward to. All over the lands of the Bible, Bob knew that thousands of physically and mentally disabled children and adults were trapped in huddled refugee camps or in tenement rooms where they received little or nothing in the way of professional care and where they faced a bleak future. More and more he was beginning to believe that the Society's work with the Lovell Homes and with Sister Johanna was just a beginning, and that with its finances on a firm foundation once more, God wanted to use the Society for a new great work. Throughout its long history, in peace and in war, it had always ensured that Christian love in action was at work in the world's darkest places, and if there was to be future conflict in the Middle East, Bob thought, who else would God use to ensure that the weakest and most vulnerable were cared for, but the Bible Lands Missions Aid Society.

Chapter 13

Trail Blazers

The 1960s

In 1962 Bob Clothier reviewed his years with the Bible Lands Missions Aid Society and felt a deep sense of satisfaction. The organisation that had seemed near the brink of collapse in the late 1940s, as the 1960s opened was flourishing; its finances were healthy, its supporter base was growing, and nearly everything in its literature suggested well being. The sponsorship scheme that had begun with the two Lovell Homes and St Margaret's in Nazareth had widened to include children in Lebanon and also Sister Johanna's leprosy patients. Bible Lands Services and Supplies had developed lucrative links with a friendly printing firm to produce bulk supplies of coloured magazine covers showing Holy Land scenes, New Testament flowers, and people in colourful Middle Eastern costumes, that churches throughout Britain bought for their newsletters, service sheets and parish magazines. The *Star in the East* had acquired something of a parish magazine flavour itself. As well as a regular "Around the Missions" feature that nearly always included pictures of smiling children, there were crosswords, children's puzzles, recipes for Middle Eastern dinners and homilies on the value of Christian giving. An almost inexhaustible series of articles on the geography and natural history of the Bible lands included Mountains of the Bible, Birds of the Bible and Flowers of the Bible, while arrangements with national publishers resulted in stories about the childhood of Jesus by the children's writer, Enid Blyton, and contributions to a series entitled "In the Steps of Our Lord" by a popular writer for women's magazines, Patience Strong. Henry Wilkins wrote a regular column about his travels around Britain and the people who welcomed him back year after year. From the Ladies' Fellowship at Heath Street Baptist Church in Hampstead, to the Girl Guides at Yately near Camberley, the Sunday School that met in the Sea Scouts Hut at Chadwell Heath, and the Nurses' Fellowship at the Middlesex Hospital, Henry signed up new subscribers for the Society and new "aunties" and "uncles" for children in the Holy Land and Lebanon.

As he surveyed its success and stability, it seemed to Bob Clothier, just as it had seemed to William Essery in the 1890s, that the Society was rather like a large, sprawling, international family, that was comfortably at peace with itself and hopeful for the future. Part of Bob's hope for the Society was that the vocational centre in Jerusalem should finally achieve the centenary goal of a building of its own, where its work could expand and develop. And another part was his desire to gather as many as possible of the Middle East's disabled young people and adults into the big family that was the Bible Lands Missions Aid Society.

Bob Clothier faces a crisis

But, as Bob thought about his hopes for the future, he also knew he faced a big problem. Where would he find time for the work that was necessary? Ever since his return from Palestine in 1945, he had done two almost full-time jobs. One was with the Society he had grown to love, while the other, that provided a substantial income for his growing family, was with a successful manufacturer of motor car tyres. Eventually, he admitted to himself, and deep inside he knew he had known it for several years, if the Society were to grow as he planned, either he must abandon his business career, or he must relinquish the Society to someone who would make it a total vocation.

Bob thought about the problem for months. He thought about what might happen to the Society in the hands of another man. He thought about his wife and about his growing children who were just reaching the age when there was so much they needed. He thought about Adele and Siranoush and the children at the Lovell Homes. He thought about the Vocational Training Centre and the new knitting machines he was planning to send to Jerusalem. He thought about Sister Johanna and the leprosy patients. He thought about the manufacturer of motor car tyres and the rewards in store for loyal employees with a flair for business and hard work. He also thought that God might tell him what to do. He was still thinking about it when the tyre company's managing director offered him a very senior sales post with fringe benefits and a company car. "It's a wonderful opportunity," Bob heard himself say, "and I'm grateful for your faith in me, but I've got other plans and I'm about to resign." Then he went home to tell his wife.

In the summer of 1962, with the enthusiastic backing of his whole family, Bob Clothier became full-time secretary of the Bible Lands Missions Aid Society. At the same time, he rented a shop in Museum Street in Bloomsbury, close to the British Museum, to be the public face of Bible Lands Services and Supplies, and filled it with books, colour slides and filmstrips on Middle Eastern themes, and exotic goods from the Bible lands. He also moved the Society's headquarters out of London to the Old Kiln, a large house in High Wycombe close to the trading company's warehouse. Later he shortened the Society's name, so that in keeping with the spirit of youthful self-assurance permeating 1960s Britain, the Bible Lands Missions Aid Society with its echoes of high Victorian earnestness, became the Bible Lands Society, an organisation open to new possibilities and ready to embrace the future.

"Those girls are real trail blazers"

The Vocational Centre in Jerusalem, which in 1960 was named after Dr Helen Keller, encapsulated exactly what Bob meant about new possibilities and future hopes. The unit that had opened in the mid-1950s in one Mount of Olives flat had moved into several others, one of them Sister Johanna's old apartment at Bethany, and by the early 1960s, its pioneering work with the blind was setting new standards in the Middle East. The success was prompting the Society to consider seriously the long-term future of the students. All of them were ex-pupils of the Lovell Homes, but while some appeared more suited for a working life in the Society's own sheltered workshop in Jerusalem, others were more adventurous and were considered likely candidates for a more independent lifestyle. Bob's earlier vision was almost ready to take shape, and rather than continue the tradition of life-long dependency, the first fully trained blind girls were signing purchase agreements on easy loan terms for their own knitting machines and looms, and were about to return to their families and communities as highly skilled workers.

Bob, Siranoush and Adele, together with Christine Holmes, the young English woman who became director of the Vocational Centre in 1959, prayed hard for the girls. "Those who desire to be homeworkers needed strength and determination," said Christine in the *Star*, "for it is certainly not an easy option." Perhaps most importantly, she said, "is whether a family wants their daughter to return to them". It may sound strange to you, she went on, "but here it is a shame to have a blind child in the family; and an even greater shame if that child is a girl. With no chance of marriage, the family are generally at a loss as to what to do with her." There was also the problem of accommodation, said Christine. Since most village houses had only one or two rooms where large families lived and slept together, it was only where a homeworker could find a private corner, if not a separate room, that could accommodate a work table and store cupboard and give privacy from small children and the demands of family chores, that there was any hope of success. The homeworker's village should also be readily accessible to the supervisors who delivered new supplies, collected finished goods and monitored quality, said Christine, something not always easy in a country where some homes were reached only on foot or by donkey. And finally, she said, there is the character of the homeworker herself. She would need a pleasant manner that cultivated friendships easily with other villagers, confidence in her ability to work alone, determination to be successful, and above all, patience and a sense of humour. A formidable list! And not one met by every girl. But for those who did meet most of the criteria, said Christine, who were willing to take the risk, whose families were supportive, and who overcame initial frustrations, there were some startling results. Just as Bob had hoped would happen, in the villages of Jordan, whenever the Helen Keller trained girls returned home with their looms and knitting machines, perceptions of the blind began to change. They were often viewed with an initial incredulity that sometimes changed almost to envy, as those who were once cast aside returned as educated members of their communities, often the only ones who had learned a trade, and sometimes as the major breadwinner of a poor family. "Those girls are real trail blazers," Bob said proudly, "they are breaking down barriers and changing lives wherever they go."

Other Helen Keller girls were breaking through barriers and changing perceptions too. Bob Clothier knew that the more widely the work of the Vocational Centre was known, the more readily the girls would be welcomed into their families and communities, and just before Christmas 1964, at the United States Cultural Centre in Jerusalem, the Centre held a week long public exhibition. "As the opening day approached," wrote one of Christine's assistants, "and we finalised our collection of samples, photographs and explanations, and translated all our notices into Arabic, there were many late nights and we wondered would we ever be finished in time?" But with the help of the Centre's Commercial Manager, Major Wadia El Far, a retired Jordanian Army officer, and Abu Salah, the Centre's driver, an exhibition in five sections, consisting of Training, Home Industry, Workshop, Equipment Used by Blind People, and The Future, was set up for the citizens of Jerusalem. "We were very nervous," said Zakiyeh, a trainee homeworker from Bethany, "and even though our teachers said they trusted us to help set up the exhibition, we did wonder how everything looked and whether anyone would come." But, just as the curious townsfolk of Broussa had flocked to see the work of Emma and Gregory Baghdassarian's orphans in 1876, so the intrigued citizens of Jerusalem turned out nearly 100 years later, to see what the Helen Keller blind girls could do. Hundreds of adults, lots of school parties, city dignitaries and foreign ambassadors all filed past photographs, bilingual posters and plans of a proposed new building, to finally gaze in fascination at the blind girls who seemed to work in little pools of tranquillity as the crowds surged around them. Zakiyeh demonstrated how stool seats were made while her friend, Khadeejy from Amman, wove sea-grass trays. Najiyeh and Leila, both of them machine knitters, worked alongside displays of knitted pullovers and jackets, children's clothes, baby clothes and pram sets. Other girls made rugs and cushion covers on small looms. At the end of each day, at home in Bethany, the triumphant girls described to Christine Holmes, "who had very trustingly said she would leave it all in our capable hands", how the crowds of visitors had lingered alongside them, totally entranced it had seemed by the clever fingers and subtle minds of young women who used senses other than sight to produce complex and beautiful objects.

New homes for old

The plans for the new building, that visitors to the exhibition had seen displayed under the heading, The Future, depicted the new vocational centre that was finally under construction at Beit Hanina, just north of Jerusalem. The foundation stone had been laid earlier in 1964, and its inscription read, "To the glory of God and to honour the name of Helen Keller". That stone had been a milestone for Bob Clothier in a long journey where he had needed all his reserves of faith to sustain him through years of uncertainty. After the original amount raised at the centenary appeal more than ten years earlier had all been swallowed up in rents and equipment, there had been times when Bob thought the new building would never rise in Jordan at all. When the estimated cost of the new centre rose from £24,500 to an eventual £56,000, some £700,000 or $1,050,000 today, he had been even more dismayed than ever. But, the dismay had prompted him to be imaginative and bold and to look for new sources of funds, and rather than relying wholly on the Society's supporters, a large part of the new centre's building fund came from an international array of churches and charities. Part of the fund came from the British charity, Christian Aid, and another from a new type of charity, the Oxford Committee for Famine Relief, commonly known as Oxfam, that had received such overwhelming responses to its appeals for famine relief in Africa that it had made some funds available to other organisations working overseas. Profits from the sale of brick bungalows at Bedfont that had replaced Samuel Gentle-Cackett's prefabricated Bethany Orphanage, also went towards the new centre that was not far from the Bethany where Jesus had so often stopped to rest among his friends.

The corner stone of the new Moravian Leper Home at Star Mountain bore an inscription too, a verse from Matthew's Gospel: "Come unto me, all you who are weary and burdened, and I will give you rest". For Sister Johanna and her colleagues, after the cramped quarters and tumbling stones of Silwan, Star Mountain was the haven they had longed for, a place of open doors to every leprosy sufferer seeking care and healing, and a home where their weary patients could find not only rest but deep peace and a renewal of the spirit. "From Star Mountain," said Sister Johanna, "you see the land stretching out before you with the vault of heaven above as a sign of God's love and mercy to all mankind, and in response, in the strength of Christ who first loved us, we will daily endeavour to serve those who are in our care." That service, Sister Johanna hoped, would also witness an end to the terrible disease. "May God grant," she said, on the day she moved permanently to Star Mountain, "that this disease completely disappears from the Holy Land."

Until that day arrived, Star Mountain would remain as a sanctuary for the unfortunate ones. Some of them, who were very old, like Hanun, Chamis and Kasim, whose lives had been bound up with Sister Johanna for many years, liked to linger on the sunny terraces of their new home where the clean winds of heaven bore the scent of newly planted pine trees. There they reminisced over times past, gossiped about their fellow inmates and the sisters, dozed gently and sometimes played the fool and told jokes. "Chamis especially has a good gift of imitation," Sister Johanna said, "and one laughs almost to the point of crying when he gives a performance." She often found herself reflecting on the bright spirit within the old man she called her happiest patient, that refused to be crushed by his years of pain, his blindness and his terrible disfigurement.

Star Mountain's younger and more able-bodied inmates, the sisters included, worked hard to make the home a largely self-sufficient community as they tilled the land, cultivated grain and vegetables and raised livestock. "Our harvested corn is lying on our washing place which is cemented," Sister Johanna told the *Star*, "and the donkey tramps round and round on it. It takes some time, but this old Biblical method of threshing works." Then, in the evenings, she said, with all the workers weary from long hours in the open air, "We like to hear Miss Lemjeh play." Miss Lemjeh was Star Mountain's only Christian patient, and the Society had provided for her what she most longed for, an electric organ that she coaxed into music with the stumps that were all that remained of her hands. "A hush sometimes falls over our home," said Sister Johanna, "as the other women gather quietly with their knitting to listen as Miss Lemjeh sings the old songs that tell of the wonderful trust she has in her Saviour."

Bob meets some old friends

When Bob Clothier became full-time secretary of the Society, he was able to do something he had dreamed about for a long time. He had always enjoyed reading old copies of the *Star* and speculating about the people and places who emerged so vividly from their pages, but although he had maintained dutiful contact with them and ensured their grants were paid, he had never had time to visit them. But, as a full-time worker, and with cheap and frequent air travel becoming commonplace, he knew he could finally fulfil an ambition to see for himself the people and places that had stirred his imagination for years.

At Thessaloniki he visited the Farm School and met Bruce Lansdale. He also saw for himself the famous Black Yorkshire boars, lean pigs now to suit a new public taste, not fat as their predecessors had been, who had unknowingly played such a vital role in improving the pig stock of Greece. At the Farm he saw the fruits of the Society's latest grants as he visited a plant where fresh milk was packaged automatically into thousands of hygienic cardboard cartons and met adult Greek farmers upgrading their skills on specially sponsored courses. A fellow visitor, Mr F. Harvie, a Bible Lands supporter and veteran of the Great War, recalled for Bob the days in 1915 when he spent his off-duty hours with John House at the Farm's Rest and Recreation Centre or in quiet reflection in the comfortable shade of the Essery Memorial Well.

It was at Kokkinia though that Bob met the person whose story had most intrigued him. Krikor Demerjian had never wavered in his resolve to fulfil what he believed was God's plan for his life and he still remembered every detail of the miraculous escapes, from Cilicia and from Smyrna, that had led him to the School of Religion and then to his life's work in the Armenian refugee camps of Greece. Bob was fascinated as Krikor recounted his remarkable life story, especially when he described how he lost his sight at the age of twelve years and how St Paul's College at Tarsus had at first refused him entry on account of his blindness. "But I quoted *Pilgrim's Progress* to them," Krikor told Bob, "and said I was on my way to the Celestial City and that God himself would find my way." How could they then refuse me, Krikor had said, smiling. Krikor had gone on to tell Bob about his family, and about the special pride and joy he had in his son, who had become a surgeon and worked at the State Hospital at Athens. "My boy's eyes are so clear and sharp," Krikor had said, "and he uses them for the glory of God's Kingdom." Krikor's eyes were clear and sharp too, Bob had reflected to himself as he listened to the old man's words and watched his face, but Krikor's eyes were inward eyes, he thought, the inward eyes of a faithful servant of the Kingdom who gazes constantly on the glory of the King.

In Lebanon, Bob saw other missions that had been part of the Society's long history. The Lebanese Evangelical School for Blind that was founded in 1868 as Fanny Bowen Thomson's British Syrian School, had been the first institution in the Arab world to educate the blind and hundreds of its mostly male students had gone on to become successful teachers and businessmen. As Bob considered how for almost 100 years the Society had supported the school with occasional grants he began to see the new vocational centre in Jerusalem as part of a long procession that wound its way down the years, of Christian workers from many lands who worked together in harmony as they devoted themselves to their less fortunate fellow human beings.

At the Home for Armenian Old People and Widows, Bob thought about Miss Martha Frearson and regretted that he had never met the remarkable woman who led the Aintab orphans through the smoke of battle to eventual safety. He thought Miss Frearson would approve of the new buildings, funded by the Society, that had transformed the old home into a small village, where pretty white houses draped in flowering vines, and a community nursing home, were surrounded by gardens and trees. He thought she would have approved too of the children who scampered across the grass and who shouted with pleasure in the playgrounds created by younger widows who lived beside their older sisters. Some of those older women, Bob noted, used their own individual gardens for grazing sheep that were probably destined for cooking pots at Easter or at Eid ul Fitr, the breaking of the Ramadan fast.

Casa Materna

Bob also took the opportunity as he travelled to visit some of the Society's more recent project partners. The Casa Materna

Orphanage that had joined the Society's grant list in the 1950s was founded when the same voice that encouraged Gregory Baghdassarian to found an orphanage at Broussa spoke in Naples in 1905. "I heard a voice that spoke to my heart," said Riccardo Santi, a young Methodist minister, who had taken two hungry children he found sheltering beneath a railway arch home to a sympathetic wife, who just like Emma, had fed them, taken them into her own home and then helped her husband found an orphanage. It was Riccardo's son, Dr Emanuele Santi, who had ensured that Casa Materna's children were among the first in Italy to receive the newly developed anti-polio vaccine, who told Bob, "Our children now, the present inmates of our orphanage, are more the victims of family breakdown and alcohol and drug abuse, as much as poverty," and he had recounted some of their unhappy stories. Little Maria's parents, he said, had abandoned each other and their little daughter for new partners and left her with elderly grandparents who treated her like a servant. Maria had never been to school, all day long she cleaned the old people's apartment, she never played with other children and never had any fun, and when she arrived at Casa Materna "she was a picture of despondency, without much grace, with big eyes and thin legs". Massimo's mother had deserted her family, and the boy's father, an unskilled labourer who worked long hours, was unable to care for his son. Carlo's father killed Carlo's mother, and was in jail for 20 years. But, at Casa Materna, said Dr Emanuele, slowly these damaged children begin to flourish again, "and here they can begin to make something of their lives".

Christian voices through the airwaves

Radio Voice of the Gospel was founded in the early 1960s. It was supported by the Near East Council of Churches and broadcast its message of hope from powerful transmitters in Addis Ababa to listeners in Africa, Asia and the Middle East, and just as William Essery had once been impressed by the Beirut Mission Press, so Bob Clothier was equally impressed by the Beirut head office of RVOG. "Mission staff there," he said, "reply to 300 letters every month, nearly half of them from non-Christians!" After the *Star* opened a special appeal for RVOG in 1964, Bob told readers that the station's Gospel message, its encouragement to churches and its promotion of education and culture, "gives strength not only to those who can live their faith in the open, but to thousands of believers who listen in secret on their transistor radios".

The newly developed transistors, said Bob, small enough to be portable and cheap enough to be readily affordable all around the world, were opening new channels for the Christian message, especially in countries where it was illegal to preach the Gospel to non-Christians or even to admit being a follower of Jesus Christ. But, despite doors that were once open being shut fast, even in those closed places Christian workers, local and foreign, "are maintaining an unobtrusive but faithful witness". Some of the believers lived in personal danger, he said, and were "living by prayer and by faith, uncertain of what tomorrow held, but trusting in God", and their letters to RVOG showed how desperate was their need to know the outside world remembered them. He had seen some of the secret communities on his travels, Bob said, and although for their safety he couldn't name them, they all needed the prayers and support of their friends in the West and the Christian voices that travelled to them over the airwaves.

Gathering in the outcasts

During a trip to Beirut early in 1967, Bob met some people who heard no voices at all. "They were misunderstanding and misunderstood," Father Andy Andeweg had told him, when he described the "tribes of outcast deaf mute men" he had discovered living in rundown areas of Beirut's waterfront and docklands. Most of them had been half wild, aggressive and fearful, and it had taxed all the young Dutch clergyman's skills and patience to gain the confidence and trust of men who had been rejected and humiliated and sometimes abused. Months of careful work had followed the first meetings until Father Andy, a trained teacher of the deaf, had finally gathered the men into a community and opened a Deaf Club for them in a central Beirut apartment block. News of the success spread, and as parents with deaf children began to plead with him for help, assistance from Dutch electronics companies who provided specialist amplifying equipment enabled Father Andy to open a School for Deaf Children in Beirut and another at Es Salt in Jordan. There the children learned signing and lip-reading and studied a regular educational curriculum.

For the older students there were also vocational studies, watch-making and carpentry for boys, dressmaking and hairdressing for girls, all designed to ensure that none would suffer the indignities and humiliations of the men who once lived as outcasts on the Beirut waterfront.

Bob was delighted to add the Deaf Club and the schools to the Society's grant list. It marked the beginning, he hoped, of the addition of other areas of disability to its existing work with the blind. He was also delighted that Father Andy's work included people from the many faith communities that made up Lebanese society. If Lebanon was to escape the potential violence that had so concerned Mr Labouisse when he wrote for the *Star* in 1959, then it seemed to Bob that the Society should do its best to support organisations that encouraged friendship and conciliation between the three great religions that had their roots in the Middle East. Half the Deaf Club members were followers of Islam, but just like Sister Johanna's Muslim leprosy patients, they all respected Father Andy's deep faith and liked to join him and their Christian comrades for Sunday evening chapel followed by a shared meal and fellowship. Bob wrote an article for the *Star* about one memorable Sunday evening when he joined that worship and fellowship. "The minister was assisted by deaf men," he said, "and the choir rendered sign language hymns. But most moving for me, especially knowing their history, was the men's manual description of how they had recently paid for and organised an outing for the Deaf School children and had taken them up into the snowy Lebanon mountains for a ride in the ski lift." The men had been so proud and happy, said Bob, and the memory of the evening would remain with him for many years. It was during that evening of fellowship that Father Andy told Bob about a local voluntary committee who helped and supported him in his work. One of the members, he said, was Mr Nadeem Shwayri, director of a sheltered workshop for the disabled called Al Kafaat, and whose "love and devotion towards the handicapped is a real inspiration". Father Andy promised to introduce Bob to Mr Shwayri.

During that same visit to Beirut, a visit to another newly supported project convinced Bob that the Society's work was extending one step further in the direction he believed God had planned for it. For some years, the Armenian Evangelical Union had been concerned that as educational provision became more sophisticated, the gap between those with most intellectual ability and those with less would grow wider, and that those with least intellectual ability of all would be left out altogether. Children who were mentally disabled, the Union believed, who often suffered great distress when they watched their brothers and sisters leave for school each morning, should be a special concern of Christian teachers, and with the Union's support, the Armenian Institute for the Blind and Deaf opened a department for the mentally handicapped. Bob wrote for the *Star* about the first ten children to attend the unit where they learned personal skills and covered a simple curriculum. "Their joy in their achievements is sometimes so great," he said, "that even though the work may tax the love and patience of the most dedicated teacher, the pleasure in seeing the human spirit shine through makes everything worthwhile." Bob promised the Society's support for the Institute's planned building extension and was thankful that despite the fears of Mr Labouisse in 1959, Lebanon remained an oasis of tranquillity in the troubled Middle East.

The Six-Day War

While Lebanon remained at peace, the Holy Land was once more torn apart by conflict. "Once again," said Bob to readers of the *Star* in the Autumn of 1967, "a substantial part of the area of our work has been plunged into war." After winning a war on three fronts that lasted just six days, that was hailed by many in the West as a victory of awe-inspiring proportions, Israel occupied the land that had remained to the Arab Palestinians in 1948; Gaza and the West Bank of the Jordan, and took the Golan Heights from Syria. The Society's new vocational training centre, Helen Keller House at Beit Hanina, together with the Lovell Homes, Star Mountain, and other Christian projects in Jordan, found themselves in occupied territory with many of their students cut off by new frontiers. Thousands of refugees, some of them refugees for the second time in 20 years, headed for squalid and already swollen camps in Jordan.

Around Jordan's capital, Amman, the Palestinian refugee camps lined the major routes into the city and sat on the hills all around. Sybil Rippin, the Society's child sponsorship secretary in

Britain described in the *Star* her visit to one camp shortly after the Six Day War. Many "old" refugees, she said, who had been there since 1948, lived in appalling poverty. They earned just enough to buy food and second-hand clothing and to rent one of the densely packed cramped dwellings of sand "composition" that covered the hillsides. When you go there, she said, "you climb up narrow twisting alleys, past thinly clad children who run barefooted, and women, looking old before their time, who trudge up the hilly roads with their vegetables on their heads". The weather was cold during Sybil's visit, late in 1967, and she recalled seeing hundreds of people, "seething along the main roads that were deep in mud after heavy rains". Most of them could afford only simple plastic sandals, she said, and although some had oil heaters or a charcoal fire, most had nothing at all. Now, with so many "new" refugees, said Sybil, despite the efforts of relief agencies, the situation could only deteriorate.

Bob Clothier knew that opinions regarding the war were divided, that even among Christians there were bitter differences, and as the Society opened another Palestine Refugee Appeal he did his best to emphasise the humanitarian consequences of the conflict. "Arguments as to the causes and responsibility for this second fearful tragedy within two decades may occupy politicians for a long time to come," he wrote, "but they do not help even one of the people or children who suffer." But, whatever people's opinions might be, Bob remembered how ten years earlier he had come to believe that God was encouraging the Society to be ready to care for the Middle East's most vulnerable people throughout conflict to come. Now that conflict was beginning.

Chapter 14

The Victory of Life
The 1970s

When Bob Clothier returned to England from his trip to Beirut in 1967 he had with him several leather bags made at the Al Kafaat workshop of Mr Nadeem Shwayri. Most of the bags, each one with a long shoulder strap and two outside pockets, were displayed at the Society's shop in Museum Street, while a few more went to another of Bob's commercial ventures, The Souk, in London's fashionable Oxford Street. At both shops the Society sold a range of clothing, jewellery and handicrafts imported from the Middle East, Afghanistan and India by Bob Clothier who seemed to have a sixth sense for fashion trends about to break on London. Lindsay Fulcher, who later became assistant editor of *The Lady*, one of Britain's most well-known magazines for women, worked at the Museum Street shop in her student days. "We sold camel saddle stools from Lebanon," she remembered, "olive wood boxes from Bethlehem inlaid with mother-of-pearl, green and blue glassware from Hebron and tons of cheap tourist jewellery from Egypt." Downstairs, the basement was stuffed with Afghan coats, "with Afghan insects still lurking inside", kaftans and cheesecloth dresses from India, and "wonderful old Jordanian embroidered wedding dresses". The shop was a magnet for anyone looking for theatrical props and costumes and Lindsay remembered the day that film director, Ken Russell, and his wife, "with black geometric hair and a floor length black and white animal skin coat", came looking for Indian cheesecloth dresses for their latest film. Although Lindsay didn't get "discovered" as she had hoped and never made it to the cinema screen herself, she did see the actress Dorothy Tutin, in Ken's film *Savage Messiah*, looking exotic in dyed Museum Street cheesecloth.

Lindsay also remembered how the Al Kafaat bags all sold

within days and how London's teenage trendsetters kept clamouring for more. More bags sold just as quickly and before long, Nadeem Shwayri was taking on more workers at Al Kafaat and Bob was supplying Al Kafaat "safari bags" to leading fashion stores in Britain, the USA and Canada. Until 1975, when their popularity finally dwindled, an average of 10,000 bags were sold every month. The profits paid the rent on the Society's London shops and helped fund the expansion of Al Kafaat.

We are all disabled in some way

Bob's first visit to Al Kafaat, where several of Father Andy Andeweg's Deaf Club members were employed, had impressed him enormously. "I found that not only were the deaf employed there," Bob told the Society's annual meeting in 1968, "but there were several blind men from the Beirut Mission School there as well as other men and women with every conceivable kind of handicap – physical and mental." However, he went on, although every worker was disabled in some way, none of the stores that bought quality goods from Al Kafaat, including the famous fashion stores selling safari bags, realised the workshop was anything other than a normal business enterprise. And the reason for that, said Bob, was because Al Kafaat was, in almost every way, a normal, if extremely successful, business enterprise.

Part of the reason for Al Kafaat's success, said Bob, was "very efficient management, competitive buying, stringent workmanship standards and expeditious freighting". But, perhaps even more important, he went on, was the name "Al Kafaat" that explained the whole philosophy of the unit's founder, Nadeem Shwayri. Al Kafaat means capabilities, said Bob, and Nadeem, a man of deep Christian faith, who liked to say "we are all disabled in some way", believed that all human beings were filled with untapped potentials and were capable of far more than society generally gave them credit for. Nadeem valued each employee, regarded them as professionals, treated them with dignity and ensured their labour was well rewarded. But, as well as the self-esteem that derived from financial rewards for a job well done, said Bob, Al Kafaat workers also took pride in the knowledge that the profits of their own labour helped fund other enterprises, a workshop for the manufacture of braces and artificial limbs, a vocational training centre for girls at risk, and a school for 45 child victims of polio.

Nadeem's philosophy and his desire to release the untapped abilities of the disabled echoed Bob's own beliefs that underpinned the Jerusalem Vocational Centre. They also echoed the beliefs of Helen Keller who had been such an inspiration to the Lovell girls, the beliefs of Mary Lovell herself, of Adele and Siranoush, of Father Andy Andeweg, and of many more Christian workers who saw the potentials of creative human beings trapped in impaired bodies and impaired minds.

By the early 1970s Bob Clothier was working closely with Al Kafaat, adding his own business ingenuity to the already successful enterprise. The workshops with their disabled workers, fuelled by safari bag profits totalling thousands of pounds, increased their staff to 80, many of them workers with multiple handicaps. The children at the "polio school", most of them from very poor families, joined the Society's child sponsorship scheme that by 1970 totalled 400 children in eleven homes throughout the Middle East and Italy. At the "polio school" itself, additional classrooms reduced the waiting list, while elsewhere in Beirut, a school for deaf children and a vocational catering school were founded and a unity chapel was built where everyone, from Nadeem to the youngest disabled child, was invited to unite in worship and prayer.

Blossoms not discarded litter

"Blossoms not discarded litter," read the little placards carried by a string of 80 disabled children who filed past the Prime Minister of Lebanon in January 1972 as Al Kafaat's new buildings were dedicated. "Human Beings with Potentials not Handicaps" said another placard, carried by an adult epileptic man who headed a procession of his fellow workers. Among them were people in wheelchairs and on crutches. They were blind, deaf, amputees and paraplegics, as well as some with severe nervous disorders. It was a deeply moving occasion, Bob Clothier told readers of the *Star*, as before an audience of national dignitaries and representatives of rehabilitation projects worldwide, the Prime Minister awarded some of Lebanon's most prestigious honours to disabled workers who had come wearing their workers' overalls straight from the Al Kafaat workshops. Bob also described to readers how many in the audience had wiped away tears during the occasion, especially as the "little blossoms" passed by.

Bob had wiped away tears himself when Charles Johar stood up, confidently holding his Braille notes, to address the Prime Minister of Lebanon. As Charles began speaking, his fingers carefully tracing the words, Bob remembered the years long before when little "blind Charlie" had been the only boy in the Bethlehem Lovell Home and he himself had been a young serviceman eager to fix the worn old building and carry water for the children's baths. "Mr Prime Minister, Your Excellencies, Ladies and Gentlemen," said Charles Johar, "my hands have contributed towards the cost of building the premises on which we are pleased to greet you today – they also help towards the rehabilitation of the blossoms of young physically impaired children you have seen. I help to increase our country's income with my competitive work and I pay taxes. Who then could say I am 'handicapped'? I may be blind with my eyes but I 'see' perfectly well with my other faculties including my intellect and spirit. I am a human being with potential capabilities, capable of sharing the same fellowship with God and my fellow men as every other citizen. Through love we strive to change the old values. Begging hands have changed to productive arms. Disability has changed to Ability."

The deaf are concerned about these things too

Other voices in Lebanon affirmed the disabled too and continued to speak on their behalf. Father Andy said, "If the world does not reach out a loving hand to the deaf, and communicate with them, they become excluded from the human family and from the communion of thoughts. Then a great gulf opens between them and the people around them, and their own thinking becomes ever more silent." As all around the world, in Britain, the USA, Germany, Switzerland and Holland, Christian organisations worked to ensure that Father Andy's deaf friends never lost touch with the human community, at the Deaf Club in Beirut the sign language conversations were increasingly about the problems of the unsettled Middle East. "Perhaps it has not occurred to you," said Father Andy, "that the deaf are concerned about these things too and need to talk about them." Another issue of immense concern to the deaf, he said, was their dealings with the police and other authorities. It was a fraught area, filled with possibilities for misunderstanding, and sometimes for hostility, and members of the Deaf Club carried special identity cards with contact numbers of hearing friends. The cards, said Father Andy, were also beneficial for deaf people who arrived in Lebanon as refugees, mostly from Palestine, with no official papers and who often found themselves caught in an incomprehensible world of bureaucracy, indifference and obstruction.

In the summer of 1970, the *Star* published an article by Daoud Yousef, Executive Secretary of the Joint Christian Committee for Social Service in Lebanon. It concerned the Palestinian refugees. In 1948 they had fled north, said Daoud, by land from Galilee and by boat from the Palestinian coast. Eventually they had arrived at Tyre, Sidon or Beirut. And more than 20 years later, they were still there, most of them in the makeshift camps that had been their first shelter. Although some professionals had found work, said Daoud, the Lebanese economy, with its emphasis on commerce and trading had been unable to assimilate the huge numbers of refugees from rural Palestine. There had been real success in Southern Lebanon, he said, where refugee farmers had made significant contributions to agricultural development, but on the whole, most Palestinians remained dependent on UNRWA relief. Where the able bodied among them sought to supplement their rations with casual or seasonal work, they found themselves competing with unskilled Lebanese workers. The Joint Committee, said Daoud, was concentrating resources on vocational training, to enable young Palestinians to take advantage of the developing economies of Saudi Arabia and the Gulf, but for those who remained unskilled, the outlook was gloomy. And even though UNRWA spent 40 per cent of its budget on education, 30,000 Palestinian children in Lebanon left school each year with no skills. Because there was little work, most became unemployed, under-employed and dependent on relief. It was, he said, "a tragic waste of human potential and a personal tragedy for each refugee".

Black September

A tragedy for the entire Palestinian people followed the events of Black September 1970, after guerrilla fighters of the Popular Front for the Liberation of Palestine highjacked three Western aircraft and forced two of them to land at a remote Jordanian airfield where the passengers were held hostage. Millions of people across the globe, captivated by the sight of the grounded aircraft worth millions of dollars shimmering in the desert heat haze, watched the drama unfold on worldwide television. When the PFLP eventually blew up the planes, minus their passengers, the act represented the world's first broadcast act of terrorism.

"Tragic events in Jordan," said the *Star*, "major clashes between Palestinian guerrillas and Jordanian government forces – thousands killed." The crisis that followed the hijacking exacerbated a conflict that had been growing steadily since the 1950s between the government of Jordan's King Hussein and the increasingly frustrated Palestinian groups who sought the liberation of their homeland and the return of the refugees. Just as Henry Labouisse had predicted in the *Star* in 1959, the refugee crisis, where more than a million Palestinians remained exiled from their homes, was proving a barrier to peace in the Middle East. In that same year, a group of young men, whose leader was Yasser Arafat, had founded Fatah, the Palestine Liberation Movement, that had quickly been followed by a stream of similar groups, many of them based in Jordan. But by 1970, the growing Palestinian powerbase was seen as a threat by the country's government to Jordan's long-term peace and stability, and in the struggle to drive out the Palestinian fighters, thousands of innocent people died. Accusations of betrayal were hurled at Jordan and at other Arab nations by the bitter Palestinians, who after seeing their comrades killed and their bases destroyed in a year of bloody fighting, eventually sought sanctuary in the Palestinian refugee camps of Lebanon.

No crossing the Jordan

Once again, the Society raised funds for those caught up in conflict. The *Star* highlighted humanitarian issues, especially the "aid needed to relieve hunger and privation by handicapped and other needy children" and Bob Clothier reflected that "There still seems little sign of reconciliation between men or any relief of the suffering which years of hatred has caused to so many innocent people." He went on to wonder how long the world would wait for the peace of Jerusalem. Sister Johanna Larsen thought the world might wait a very long time if it chose to ignore the issue of Palestine and she pointed out that for the Palestinian people violence of one sort or another was an everyday experience. The experiences of her own leprosy patients whose homes were in Jordan were particularly hard, she said, since they must either be separated from the Leper Home or from their families. Some were so desperate to be with their loved ones, but reluctant to face the questions and hostility of Israeli soldiers at border checkpoints, that they often lingered too long at home without their drugs and allowed the disease to take hold of them once more.

Some of Star Mountain's leprosy patients whose disease was controlled by successful modern drugs, or was "burned-out", longed to be part of the world once more. As they watched its vibrancy and drama on their television screens, what had once seemed remote and far away, now appeared almost within reach. Perhaps, they hoped, just as attitudes towards disability were changing, attitudes towards leprosy might be changing too. Sister Johanna was doubtful, but she gave her support to Mahmoud and his wife, Khadijeh, her patients for 25 years, when they were the first of Star Mountain's patients to venture into the outside world. The couple bought a little house in Mahmoud's family village, and full of hope they opened a petrol station. They were back at Star Mountain after just four months. The outside world did not want them, they said, it was still afraid of leprosy and feared to look at deformed faces and the stumps that were once fingers and toes. Mahmoud and Khadijeh's sad experience was a blow for other Star Mountain residents who had hoped to return to the world one day, although others were content to remain within its sheltering walls. Miss Lemjeh, the Home's oldest patient by 1972, was happy at Star Mountain where Sister Johanna loved her dearly for her courage. "Leprosy has given our sister Lemjeh many years of pain and anxiety," said Sister Johanna, "deformities, blindness and a lonely life, and yet she lives constantly in the Strength of the Lord."

It was not only Sister Johanna's leprosy patients who faced difficulty in crossing the Jordan. When Dina, a partially blind resident of the Jerusalem Lovell Home, announced her forthcoming marriage, her parents were refused entry permits to Israeli-occupied Jerusalem to attend the celebration. "Although some things are changing here," commented Siranoush, who had acted as matchmaker, "and some of our blind girls are courted and can look forward to marriage, if parents can't be present on the big day then that gives us cause for sorrow." But, fortunately for Dina, Siranoush went on, the proper rituals went ahead when a distant uncle "insisted that she go out as a bride from his house". Siranoush described the occasion for the *Star*. Dina had travelled with her old school companions to her uncle's village near Ramallah, she said, "where his two wives and other womenfolk greeted them very heartily and lustily in the traditional way". Then the Helen Keller minibus, crammed full with nine occupants who spent the journey "drumming on the native drum and singing traditional bridal songs" had led the bridal procession while all the passers-by joined in with cheering and clapping.

Siranoush had witnessed other changes too during her long life, in the developing work of the Lovell Homes and in the lives of the Holy Land blind. As well as an increasing number of marriages, more Lovell girls were training for useful careers. Dina herself worked as a dental nurse and her new husband, who was also blind, was a teacher of the blind. At the Bethlehem home, under new leadership since Adele retired to England in 1970 to be near Bob and his family, and also in Jerusalem, teams of specially trained teachers of the blind educated the younger children, while all the older students with the ability to do so, spent their days among sighted students at regular secondary schools. Schoolbooks for them, and for blind Palestinian children all over the Holy Land, were transcribed into Braille at a workshop based at the Helen Keller Vocational Centre, where sometimes, as Siranoush breathed in the scent of warm paper and sensed the intense concentration, her thoughts returned to Barachah and she almost felt the presence of Mary Lovell herself, gazing with satisfaction on the work she had begun so long ago.

Forget your disability – all you who enter here

There was more satisfaction at Helen Keller House too where blind vocational students were becoming more confident and self-sufficient and more eager for independence and a place in the outside world. Bob's original trailblazers had set new standards, and although the world could still be a frightening place, especially in the unstable Middle East, the girls who followed Zakiyeh and Khadeejy of the 1964 Jerusalem exhibition, knew they trod in the footsteps of successful sisters. New independent living skills were learned in a specially converted self-contained hostel at Helen Keller, where under the supervision of a British couple, seven blind girls had rooms of their own and learned to cook and clean, to iron and mend, and how to entertain their teachers and friends to lavish Arabic suppers. "I do lots of cooking and frying now," said Najiyeh, a machine knitter, "and although once I was afraid to light the gas ring, now I can light the oven too." Ida, a Braille copier said, "I'm doing things for myself now that once I never dreamed I could do. Cleaning my own room, ironing my own clothes and entertaining my friends to dinner." As a gesture to the future the girls pinned a notice above the hostel door: "Forget your disability – all you who enter here".

A most vital Christian witness

Although the mentally disabled could not forget or overcome their disability in quite the same way as the Helen Keller girls overcame blindness, just as in Lebanon, Christian workers in the Holy Land were reaching out to help them. The Anglican Church in Jerusalem began a new venture at Nazareth when it converted the St Margaret's Home from an orphanage into a specialist centre for Arab children with severe mental disabilities. "We see this as a most vital Christian witness," said the Church, in an article in the *Star*, "among a poor, mainly Muslim population." The Palestinian people of Galilee, the article went on, were battered by war, unemployment and the inflationary Israeli economy, and had neither the resources nor training to care effectively for their mentally disabled children. But family links were loving and strong and St Margaret's aimed to lay the foundations for successful adult lives lived within local communities. "The children have made remarkable progress," said Bob Clothier after a visit in the mid-1970s, "and they are taken out into the local community as much as possible, which not only helps to get them behaving acceptably in public but also gets the local people accustomed to behaving acceptably to them."

Other Christian schools in the Holy Land also tried to compensate for the increasing impoverishment of the Palestinian people, and among them were two institutions that were as old as the Society itself. The Evangelical Lutheran School in Bethlehem, close to the Church of the Nativity, was founded in 1856, and many of its boys, from Christian families in isolated Palestinian villages, were descendants of the school's nineteenth-century pupils. Most of the families were very poor, said Mr Azar, the school's housefather, and he hoped that as additional funds were received from the Society's sponsorship scheme, standards of comfort and care could be raised. But, he went on, as Palestinian society on the West Bank crumbled beneath the weight of poverty and the Israeli occupation, the parents of his boys suffered increasingly from physical and mental illness and were unable to pay even minimum contributions towards education. A similarly depressing story was reported by Talitha Kumi School at Beit Jala that was founded by the Deaconesses of Kaisersworth in 1851. Talitha Kumi girls came from the same Christian families and remote villages as the Lutheran School boys, and the head-mistress, Mrs Najwa Farah, endorsed Mr Azar when she told readers of the *Star* that although families were desperate to see their children become educated, they found great difficulty in making any contribution towards the cost. As an example of their poverty, Mrs Farah said that although boarding girls were supposed to arrive with all their necessary clothing, "some children start the term with a summer dress and sandals, without even a change of clothing, let alone warmer clothing for the cold weather". This is an area where we are grateful for the sponsorship payments from the Bible Lands Society, said Mrs Farah, and for the regular supply of uniforms from Zerqa Refugee Industries, blue and white cottons in summer, and warm, red woollens in winter.

We refuse to die

Early in 1974, Bob Clothier went to Cyprus. He wanted to see for himself the work founded on the island by George Markou, a close friend and colleague of Nadeem Shwayri, that had helped inspire the vision of Al Kafaat. George had opened a school for the deaf in the 1950s and when his graduates were unable to find skilled employment he had gone on to found one of the world's first co-operative ventures for the disabled, a furniture factory that by the time of Bob's visit had an annual turnover of £200,000 and produced quality products that were in demand all over the island. By 1974, government support had enabled the school to move into a new building, "a dream school", George called it, and grants from the Society had provided industrial equipment when the co-operative moved into brand new factories. But just months after Bob's visit, the factory was a bombed-out ruin and the school buildings had become barracks for the Turkish Army that invaded Cyprus after the island's president, Archbishop Makarios, was deposed in a military coup. When a ceasefire was negotiated by the United Nations, and a partition line drawn between Cyprus' Turkish and Greek Communities, the school and what was left of the factory were in Turkish Cyprus, and the students, workers, and George Markou, were in refugee camps.

"We refuse to die on our 21st birthday and necessity compels us to overcome our pride and ask for help," said George Markou, from the tent where he spent the 21st anniversary of the School for the Deaf. Bob Clothier was among the first to respond and within weeks of the Turkish invasion, grants from the Society ensured the school was living and working under canvas and that 100 acres of rented land were under cultivation. Despite the worst winter in living Cypriot memory, when tents were blown down or buried deep in snow, George Markou and his deaf colleagues placed their trust in God's providence, worked for the day at hand, and planned for the future. As they did so, the land they ploughed and planted produced vegetables for their food and for market, their chickens laid eggs by the score, a "Bible Lands goat herd" provided milk and cheese, and a Bible Lands brick built kitchen became a centre of community activity. By 1975, George Markou's faith and hard work and the determination of the Cypriot people were reaping rewards. "I had seen the foundations for the new multi-purpose school building being laid just the Wednesday before," Bob Clothier told readers of the *Star* at Christmas 1975, "so imagine my surprise on the following Saturday when I saw the complete iron framework had been erected, the chipboard walls fitted, and that the workmen were just putting on the corrugated roof." Although Cyprus remained divided on ethnic lines, a UN monitored peace was maintained and a huge international effort rehoused 200,000 refugees. To the satisfaction of George Markou and the deaf workers, a new co-operative factory, funded by generous loans, replaced the bombed ruin and was soon fulfilling a flood of orders from new homes, from offices and international embassies, and from the hotels and restaurants that served the burgeoning Cypriot tourist trade.

A war to tear their country apart

Lebanon had been a tourist destination too. Its breathtakingly beautiful landscape, its elegant hotels and its sophisticated French restaurants, drew visitors from all over the world, but, as peace returned to Cyprus, war broke out in Lebanon. In April 1975, four members of the right-wing Christian Phalange were killed during an assassination attempt on their leader. Blame fell on Palestinian guerrillas, many of them men who had fled earlier from Jordan, and as retaliation for the original killings led to more violence in return, the death toll began to mount. Ever since the years of the French mandate, the relationships between Lebanon's faith communities had been an uneasy one, and Henry Labouisse's warning of 1959, of the potentially disruptive effects of massive Palestinian immigration, had been echoed by other observers. But, in 1975, few among Beirut's citizens, sheltering in their homes from the street battles outside, imagined they were witnessing the beginnings of a civil war that would tear their country apart.

As the war began, almost immediately the buildings of the Institute for Armenian Blind and Deaf came under fire. Rounds of machine gun bullets shattered its windows and pockmarked its walls. At Christmas 1975, Mr Samuel Khatchiguian, the Society's sponsorship secretary in Lebanon, wrote via Jordan to Bob Clothier to say that fierce fighting had gripped the streets of Beirut. "And the roof of my house got blown off by a rocket," he said, and also there were no telephone lines out of the country, and no mail, and he was worried that sponsorship would stop and the schools would all close. "And by the way," Mr Samuel continued, "Mr Carpentier, Father Andy's deputy, was kidnapped by armed men." Fortunately for Andrew Carpentier, although he was robbed, his life was spared.

By Easter 1976, as Lebanon headed for its second year of civil war, and every attempted ceasefire failed, Bob Clothier determined that none of the schools supported there by the Bible Lands Society would close. He reflected how war was never far from the Society's work, and once more he recalled the late 1950s when he had first sensed God's warnings that terrible violence lay ahead and his urgings for the Society to be ready. When the *Star* published an eyewitness report by Geoff Renner of the American organisation, World Vision, who travelled with Bob to Beirut in 1975, Bob hoped it would convey some idea of what the "terrible violence" really meant for the people of Lebanon. Many recruits to the various militias, said Geoff, who were dividing the city between them on confessional and ideological lines, did not really understand the divisions of the conflict, but were sucked in by bribery, "40 Lebanese pounds for carrying a gun for one night" or by a thirst for power, violence or "adventure". Just weeks before his arrival with Bob, he said, thousands of innocent Muslims had died at Quarantina, a slum in Beirut's northern suburbs, "where infantrymen had surged through the streets shooting helpless civilians and burning and looting everything in their path". In the same week, "left-wing Muslims attacked Damour, a Christian town on the coast south of Beirut. They massacred the town's male inhabitants and machine-gunned survivors trying to flee in small boats". And one of the results of the violence, said Geoff, was that all over the country, "people who once lived in mixed areas, Muslim and Christian side by side, have been forced to leave their homes when the opposing groups gained dominance in the area". And as people moved, they left their jobs. As the militias gained control of the streets, factories and businesses closed and buildings were looted and burned. Trading and commerce came to an end. Communications broke down. And Lebanon began a descent into anarchy.

A miracle

Despite the violence and chaos that surrounded them, and although their programmes were irregular and the news they sent out was sporadic, most of the Christian-led projects supported by the Society kept going. Andrew Carpentier, writing from the School for the Deaf, said the staff had all agreed to work for whatever was offered. "It seems that something has bound them together," he said, "I would like to call it love and care for handicapped children, and a mutual respect for each other, and this itself could be called a miracle in a country so divided by religious and political strife."

Something miraculous also inspired the schools to look to the future whenever they found themselves in the line of fire, under attack, their buildings occupied and looted, and sometimes used by snipers or as gun emplacement points. The best remedy for ruin and despair, they seemed to have decided, was faith in God, a willingness to clean up the debris, replace the glass, repair the damage as best they could, and begin work once the situation was safe enough.

Throughout the civil war, the Society did its best to maintain support for its project partners in Lebanon. Funds were often carried into the country as packages of dollar bills by Bob Clothier, and then delivered, sometimes under artillery fire, by the seemingly indestructible Mr Samuel. Large sums of money also went to the Institute for Armenian Blind and Deaf, who despite its premises being occupied by the Lebanese Front and then damaged in grenade attacks, became a major centre for relief distribution to the whole city. Felix Zeigler, who worked at the Institute throughout the war, described for the *Star* how the relief system worked. "Co-operative shops are set up in local churches," he said, "and every family receives coupons, called bons, to be exchanged for the goods they need." The scheme worked so well that all sorts of organisations bought the bons and stamped them for use by their own people. "Imagine the situation," Felix said, "when bitter enemies from opposing factions, right-wing Christians, the Communists and members of the Islamic Progressive Front, meet in our churches to collect their groceries and sometimes remember that once they lived at friends."

Seven years after Jordan's Black September, the PLO forces that had regrouped in Southern Lebanon were at war with other political factions there, a situation exacerbated by Israeli shelling and finally by the invasion of the Israeli Army. Two hundred and twenty thousand refugees, among them the Palestinian farmers who had contributed so much to Lebanon's agriculture, fled to Beirut and other northern areas where people became afraid to leave home in case refugees squatted in their absence. In the same year, the Armenian community, that had tried desperately to avoid the conflict, came under attack. "The fighting has been intense and unbearably shocking," said one observer, "Armenian homes and shops have been attacked and the people were robbed and killed." Thousands of Armenians fled to Anjar where they were sheltered by the community that had once been the refugees who fled Alexandretta.

The victory of life

Al Kafaat's buildings, located in Christian East and Muslim West Beirut, as well as right on the line that divided the city, came under fire time and again. Several times they were occupied by opposing militias, often they were used by snipers and for gun emplacements. Many times they were damaged seemingly beyond repair. Nadeem Shwayri confessed that when the conflict began he became so depressed he was ready to abandon Al Kafaat for a life of safety in France. "It was Bob Clothier who saved me," he said later, "who went into no man's land, braved the sniper fire, and then phoned me to say, 'I saw Al Kafaat's main centre. It is damaged. But not in ruins as you think. Bible Lands is by your side. Don't worry, get back soon.'" After that, said Nadeem, "I learned to live under fire and now our first thoughts are for the children. We bring them back as soon as we can, and although they are all completely traumatised by war we must show them there is something better than fighting and killing." Nadeem also thought about the victims, disabled by bullets and bombs, that he knew would need Al Kafaat when the conflict was over. Despite the seemingly endless warfare all around him he began planning new ventures, a vocational scheme where the newly disabled could train as radio and television technicians, as well as a village for the disabled, where they could live "according to their own rhythms of life".

"The Victory of Life" was the heading for Nadeem's article in the *Star* at Easter 1979. "Thirty missiles per minute for the last eight hours," it said, "and now I know what hell is, and what the Apocalypse will be." We live from day to day, he said, we have no sanitation, no phones, and the electricity and water are on/off. But life has to go on and we didn't choose the broad and easy road and we cannot betray those who support us or the children and families we serve. With God's help, said Nadeem, we will endure, and he wished the men of violence would make their example the children who played together in peace on the grassy lawns of Al Kafaat. "Humanity," he said, "will realise one day what a long route it took to discover its oneness and holy unity in God."

Chapter 15

The Faith that Sustains Them
The 1980s

"We don't usually mention these things in our letters," wrote Audeh Rantisi, Principal of the Evangelical Home for Boys in Ramallah, "but the people here are suffering under occupation, and have very little hope for the future." The people of the West Bank were angry, he said, increasingly frustrated and bitter at the injustices levelled constantly against them. And, as the anger grew, more Palestinians joined the demonstrations "in support of students imprisoned without cause, and against Israel's policy of building more new Jewish settlements on confiscated Arab land". The curfews and closures of schools and universities, imposed by the Israeli authorities in their turn, hit the children and young people hard. They were desperate to learn, and when their opportunities were taken away, their resentment and hatred grew deeper. "As we seek to teach the children in our care," said Audeh, "we need to be constantly reminded to pray for Peace."

By the 1980s an increasing number of Palestinian orphanages and schools located in the occupied territories of the West Bank and Gaza had been added to the Society's grant list. Although the origins of some dated back many years others had been founded more recently by Palestinian Christians, and as they raised their voices on behalf of their people, the Society very slowly began to give more space in the pages of the *Star* to the stories they had to tell. Bob Clothier had often felt ambivalent and uncertain about the political and economic pressures that fuelled tensions in the Holy Land and about the conflict between Arabs and Jews and he had been anxious to avoid exacerbating the high feelings that existed among some of the Society's supporters who felt more strongly for one group than the other. He did his best to focus on the Society's service to the most vulnerable, particularly the disabled, but as the 1980s progressed and a new generation of Palestinian Christian leaders such as Audeh Rantisi emerged, they began to relate the poverty, the lack of resources, and the frustration that led to violence among the West Bank population, to the effects of the continued Israeli occupation.

The faith that sustains them

Audeh was a minister of the Arab Evangelical Church and Deputy Mayor of Ramallah, who had learned from personal experience the bitter history of Palestine. As a child in 1948 he had been among the thousands of refugees driven from their homes on the fertile Mediterranean coast, "three days over the mountains, a terrifying journey without food or water, aeroplanes swooping overhead, and people falling to the ground from exhaustion and fear", until his family finally found shelter in a Red Cross tent near Ramallah. With his father worn out by the loss of his home and the traumatic journey, and too old to find work, young Audeh helped support his family by selling matches and kerosene on the city streets, until eventually he found a refuge at a Ramallah Christian orphanage. It was there that he "first came to know the Lord Jesus and hear his call". Jesus' call led Audeh first to Wales and a degree in theology, then to the United States to study sociology, and eventually to Sudan as a missionary of the United Presbyterian Church. In 1965, after a narrow escape from death after civil strife broke out in Sudan, Audeh returned home to Ramallah. There, in the front parlour of the Evangelical Home for Girls, during a visit to the elderly Welsh ladies who had first inspired him to study, Audeh began his life's work. "Praise the Lord," his old friend, Ceturah Morgan, had cried, when Audeh outlined his plan to open a boys' home in Ramallah. Ceturah went on to tell Audeh that just days before she had felt moved to take into the Girls' Home an abandoned three-year-old boy who could not bear to be parted from his twin sister. "Your first child," said Cetunah with satisfaction. The Evangelical Home for Boys had begun. Just one week later Audeh received an anonymous cheque for $1,000. The accompanying note simply read, "For the boys' work".

"Our children are living under pressure and fear," said Audeh in 1980, "and it is only through the sure knowledge of Jesus

Christ as Lord and Saviour and Coming King that we can continue our work." Audeh's message was confirmed by other Palestinian Christian leaders as they wrote about the hardships of work in a fractured and impoverished society and of the faith that sustained them. At Jeel al Amal Orphanage in Bethany, "the alternative for the 130 boys crowded into a space just large enough for 60, would be life on the streets or in caves", wrote Alice Sahhar, who founded the home with her husband Basil. Most of the boys in the Sahhar's care were "orphans, children abandoned, sons of prisoners, of prostitutes, or of parents whose mental stability has collapsed under the strain of pressure and uncertainty. They are unwanted, illegitimates, the ultimate evidence of the tragic situation of the Arab poor in the occupied West Bank", said Alice. Some of the boys were filled with a seething resentment, she explained, when she wrote for the *Star* about Samir, an unemployed young man who arrived one day at Jeel with his little brother, Mohammed. The rest of their family were killed at a Jordanian refugee camp, bombed after Black September, where the baby Mohammed was discovered three days after the attack, lying under rubble and still trying to feed from his dead mother's breast. "It's hard for me sometimes," said Alice, "giving hope to these boys who have seen so much brutality, but God wants me to do it, and he gives me strength to carry on."

Salwa Zananiri, Principal of Rawdat el Zuhur School in Jerusalem, wrote for the *Star* in the early 1980s about the poverty of her pupils' families who mostly lived in Jerusalem's Old City, a maze of narrow, twisted alleys between high walls and crumbling old houses where whole families lived in one room and shared a common dusty courtyard. "It is something of a miracle that our children find space and time to study," said Salwa, "but their parents know the value of education and they are eager for their children to escape the poverty they suffer themselves." Life was hard for most Palestinian families, she explained, they were paid such low wages they could barely survive in the inflationary Israeli economy with its emphasis on all things Western, and just recently, she said, the poverty of some families had become so oppressive that the teachers at Rawdat, unbeknown to their pupils, were adding to the sponsorship funds that arrived each month from the Bible Lands Society.

One way tickets to the West

Audeh Rantisi mentioned the Israeli economy too. "The rate of inflation is probably the highest in the world," he said, "and here on the West Bank, with low wages and no social security, more and more people emigrate to the West." Just as Armenian Christians had once been concerned when their best-educated young people left their troubled homeland for peaceful and prosperous futures elsewhere, so Palestinian Christians, the most highly educated group in Palestinian society, were leaving too, mostly for America. It was just as the Arab Evangelical Church had predicted in 1948, Christianity in the land of its birth was suffering a crisis as the generation who once would have been its leaders-in-waiting bought one way tickets to the West.

Others told a similar story. At the Four Homes of Mercy, also in Bethany, Henrietta Farradj, daughter of the home's founder, Kathleen Siksek Farradj, continued her mother's work among the Palestinian poor. Kathleen Farradj, described by a Governor of Jerusalem in British Mandate days, as "the best beggar in the land", had dedicated her life to the creation of safe havens where disabled adults and children, vulnerable pregnant women and the elderly could be cared for. Two orphaned children, Kathleen's first inmates, had been followed to the Malja, or Refuge, by a sick and elderly couple escaping a home too damp to live in. Then came a young bride-to-be whose fatal slip on a tiled floor just days before her wedding left her paralysed for life. When the long stream of needy people who followed the first inmates were joined in 1948 and 1967 by refugees who camped in tents around her walls, Kathleen never doubted that God would aid her and guide her. "Faith comes into every part of our story," said Henrietta, "as does determination, love and endurance. Now we need these qualities more than ever as so many sick and elderly have no sons or daughters left to care for them. The best of our young people are forced abroad to find work or a safe life with a future for their own growing families."

From Lebanon too, after years of civil war, the educated middle classes were leaving. The once magnificent city of Beirut was in ruins. A gash a quarter of a mile wide, "the green line", ran through its centre, from outlying suburbs right down to the docks, and divided Muslim West from Christian East. Few dared

Radio Voice of the Gospel, Addis Ababa, Ethiopia. This short-wave radio station began operations on February 26th, 1963, and was soon broadcasting to millions of listeners in Africa, Asia and the Near East. *Star*, Christmas 1964.

Salt, Jordan: Father Andy (the Rev. A.J. Andeweg) welcomes King Hussein at the opening of the School for the Deaf. *Star*, Summer 1965.

High Wycombe, England: Bob Clothier in his den, 1968. *Star*, 1969.

Heller Keller House, Jerusalem: 1st year blind girls learning to cook. *Star*, Summer 1970.

Al Kafaat, Lebanon: Lebanon's Prime Minister decorates disabled workers, 1972. *Star*,
Easter 1972.

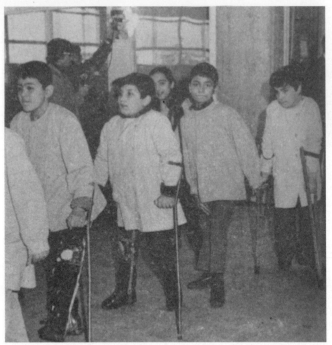

Al Kafaat, Lebanon: "Blossoms, not discarded litter." Polio-afflicted children at the opening ceremony for the new workshop, school and chapel building. *Star*, Easter 1972.

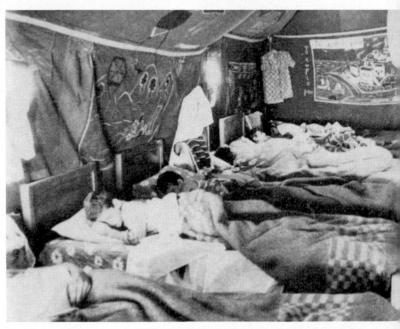

Turkey invades Cyprus: tent dormitory for deaf child refugees, Cyprus. *Star*, Summer 1975.

Civil war in Lebanon: elderly Armenians fleeing their burning home.
Star, Easter 1976.

Ramallah: Audeh Rantisi and his family. *Star*, Summer 1982.

Egypt: Menouf Hospital, with Magdy, fully recovered. *Star*, Autumn 1992.

Al Kafaat, Lebanon: Nadeem and Lily Shwayri with a child from each department. *Star*, Autumn 1983.

Zabbaleen Village, Cairo: a boy returning to the village with his donkey cart loaded with rubbish. *Star*, Easter 1986.

Beirut: a happy moment in the middle of the ruined city as boys and girls from St Luke's Centre pose for a photo. All have learning difficulties which they are overcoming with help from specialist teachers. *Star*, Autumn 1993.

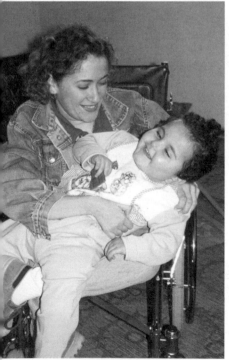

Beirut, 1999: Special education teacher Pauline is herself disabled.

Cairo, Egypt: signing the Lord's Prayer, April 1999.

Cairo, Egypt: Bishop
Mouneer Anis, newly
ordained at All Saints
Anglican Cathedral.
Star, Christmas 2000.

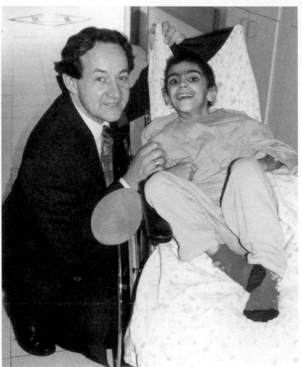

Current Director Nigel
Edward-Few at the
Bethlehem Arab Society for
Rehabilitation Hospital,
2002.

Following a major head
injury, seven weeks in a
coma and nine months of
intensive medical and
rehabilitation treatment,
Dallal (pictured right)
returned to her home where
she continued to receive
outpatient care.

cross the line. Days and nights were punctuated by the rattle of gunfire and the thud and smash as rockets fired by opposing groups ploughed into the city. Every ceasefire had been broken, and every peacemaking initiative had failed. The self-appointed militias, Lebanese Muslims and Christians, and Palestinian factions based in Beirut and South Lebanon, each wanted victory for their own cause, and as the opposing fighters fought to gain control of the city streets and vast swathes of countryside, the civilian population suffered. Thousands of innocent people had died, thousands were wounded, thousands were homeless, and thousands more, the most highly skilled and educated, packed whatever they could carry, and left for more peaceful lands.

The men of the militias

All the Christian schools and homes supported by the Society had spent the years since 1975 in conditions of uncertainty. Children were scattered as their parents moved closer to their co-religionists or fled for their lives. Some children were killed or maimed by shrapnel, by car bombs or by booby traps. But, despite the disruption, and although classes were cancelled when buildings were damaged or occupied by militias, most of the schools tried to expand, "and not close as would seem to be sensible". When Bob Clothier made a visit to Beirut in 1981 he wrote for the *Star* about how the Armenian schools co-operated to ensure the welfare of their combined student body. "The children all have good health care, medicals, eye and dental check-ups and clinic referrals," he said, "as well as a common curriculum for Christian education, daily Chapel, Sunday School, Bible Club or Christian Endeavour." Despite the war, he said, standards were high, and most children learned Armenian, their mother tongue, Arabic, the language of their country, and English. He also noted how every Armenian school was alive with colour and decoration. "Armenians are exceptionally gifted in handiwork," he said, "and the classrooms and corridors of the junior schools are filled with pictures and pattern." Even in Beirut, torn apart by five years of conflict, teachers ensured that life and colour triumphed over death and despair. But despite the enthusiasm and hard work of teachers, said Bob, the scanty resources and irregular funds that were a constant worry for most schools were made worse by the

demands of the militias. Although the government no longer collected taxes, he said, "they are imposed by whoever is in power
locally. One school estimates it pays a regular £200–£300 in protection money to various militias".

Nadeem Shwayri was no stranger to the men of the militias.
Some of them had disabled brothers or sisters, or children of
their own, at Al Kafaat, and when fighters from opposing factions
crossed paths as they collected relatives for weekend visits home,
sometimes they recognised old friends and shook hands, or even
embraced, before going their separate ways. Nadeem recalled one
incident when two old comrades, a Muslim imam and a Christian
priest, had met while collecting their mentally disabled children.
The adult pair waited in silence, staring at everything except each
other, until their two children arrived, holding hands and unwilling to part. "I don't know who is the most mentally handicapped,"
Nadeem had told the two clergymen, "your children or you." It
was examples like that, Nadeem said later, that fuelled his resolve
not to divide any of Al Kafaat's twelve independent centres on
confessional lines. Despite the pleas of some colleagues, he said,
and although he agreed to concentrate the work in East Beirut,
"until the killing stops", all through the war Nadeem insisted that
Al Kafaat's staff and students came from all over the city, and Bob
Clothier made sure that the Society funded enough new buses,
some with special hydraulic hoists for paraplegics, so that
Muslim drivers could head west and Christian drivers head east.

"Al Kafaat is my conception of human brotherhood," said
Nadeem in 1985, "where the dignity of man is upheld in people
discarded as marginals and treated as the garbage of our society."
He was speaking to Mr Berri, leader of Amal, the Shi'ite militia
that had occupied and looted Al Kafaat's main centre for the second time in two years. "What do you want me to say to those people," Nadeem asked the militia leader, "what shall I tell the
mothers of our handicapped children? Should I tell them how
your men have invaded the sanctity of our missionary enterprise,
how they have adulterated its campus and profaned our chapel?
Should I tell them 'the place where once the outcast found the
road to independent life has been turned into a Garrison of
Violence?'"

Three times Nadeem had been searched by bodyguards as he
was led to the militia leader's bunker and he refused to sit down

until Mr Berri apologised. "Do you think I have an army of mentally disabled people hidden in my coat?" he had asked, and he went on to point out that in Beirut's Shi'ite sector of half a million people, many in that population were disabled. If Al Kafaat was forced to close, Nadeem asked Mr Berri, where would those people go? "When I left," said Nadeem, "he himself escorted me to my car and shook my hand." Later, when Mr Berri's wife set up a rehabilitation programme for wounded Shi'ite fighters, Al Kafaat trained her staff. "We need to live our Christianity," Nadeem said afterwards, "we are a small minority in the largely Muslim Arab world, and unless we live our faith and witness, unless we live it as real missionaries in deeds, in accepting the others, in going towards the others, we cannot survive."

Eager for the message of Jesus

In 1982, Israel invaded Lebanon again and laid siege to Beirut in a campaign that culminated in the massacres by Christian Phalangist militiamen, under Israeli protection, of Palestinians in the refugee camps of Sabra and Shatila. Only weeks before the event, students from the Lebanon Evangelical School for the Blind had demonstrated their karate skills on national television. Viewers had also learned about the school's long history, that dated back to Fanny Bowen Thomson's British Syrian Mission of the 1860s that had provided aid and support to victims of a much earlier conflict. More than 100 years later, viewers learned, blind victims of another war were learning the educational, vocational and social skills that would enable them to live out the remainder of their lives with dignity and hope. George, once a military firefighter in the Lebanese Army, told viewers about the grenade that blinded him when it exploded in a burning building. "I thought my life was over," he said, "that I was good for nothing. But now, I am training to become a telephone switchboard operator and very soon I will be back with the army again. Who would have thought that there would be a place for a blind fireman?" There was a place for the spiritual side of students' lives too and despite its own share of occupation and looting, damage from car bombs and a forced relocation to safer premises, the Lebanon Evangelical School continued the traditions that went back to its earliest days. Even as death and destruction surrounded them, the school's Braille transcribers worked on a new version of the Arabic Braille Bible, and whenever he could, Ayoub Naim, the school evangelist, made his way through Beirut's shattered streets to visit former students in their homes. "I often find their neighbours waiting for me too," Ayoub said, "gathered in the homes of my blind friends, eager for the message of Jesus."

At Nazareth Hospital evangelists were hard at work too. The hospital's relationship with the Society dated back to 1860, when the Armenian Dr Kaloost Vartan, who trained as a doctor in Edinburgh, founded a clinic in Nazareth. Over the long years since then, the Society had made occasional grants to the hospital's medical personnel, to its evangelists and Bible women, and had funded soup kitchens for its poorest patients. In 1924 it contributed towards the cost of a new modern hospital. By the 1980s, Nazareth was the last British missionary hospital in Israel and in 1984 it was the focus of one of Bob Clothier's last trips as secretary of the Bible Lands Society. Bob had never forgotten that his predecessor, Samuel Gentle-Cackett, had led the Society into his seventieth year and that it had almost collapsed when Samuel died, and reluctantly, but knowing in his heart it was the wisest course, he had finally agreed to retire at 67. As he presented leather bound Bibles, each inscribed with the recipient's name, to Nazareth's graduating student nurses, he recalled William Essery's comments after his visit to the British Syrian Mission in 1901. William had been "greatly moved", Bob remembered, "to address such a group of young, hopeful life". That was just how he felt himself, he said, "moved almost to tears to see the eager young faces before him, and terribly sad to be leaving it all behind". Privately Bob wondered how he would get through the years ahead without the love of his life, the Bible Lands Society, that had been his constant companion for over 40 years.

A return to Egypt

Ever since events in 1956 that followed the Suez Crisis, when Israeli forces with support from Britain and France had attacked Egypt, and Western Christian workers were expelled from the country in retaliation, the Society's presence there had been minimal. Mostly it had continued to support small groups who maintained social projects of the Anglican Church although virtually nothing about them ever appeared in the *Star in the East*. In the mid-1980s, however, as tensions between Egypt and the West relaxed, the Society began to renew its relations with Egyptian Christians, and in 1984, David Izzett, Chairman of the Society's Council of Trustees, returned to Cairo where he had worked as a young missionary 50 years earlier. The city was much changed, he told readers of the *Star*, as he bemoaned the overhead dual carriageways and traffic-choked thoroughfares that had replaced the fine avenues he remembered where two-horse carriages had plied for trade and trams had clattered cheerfully along central rails. That seems to typify Cairo, said David, more cars, more noise, more dust, more smog, and, of course, more people. Egypt's population was increasing by a million every eight months, he said, and where 50 years earlier overcrowding and poverty had been a problem, now it was reaching epidemic proportions.

David described the people he met in the Boulac slum, a densely populated part of Cairo where donkey carts threaded their way along dark narrow lanes that ran between tenement blocks seven or eight storeys high, where washing drooped overhead and litter and seeping drains lay underfoot. Most of the inhabitants of the tenements, said David, lived in single rooms, that were dark, and often damp, and only reached by flights of winding stone stairs with no rails or protection of any kind. In one of those tiny homes, with only enough space for two double beds wedged into a L-formation, he met a widow in her thirties with five children, whose husband had been killed in a road accident. In another he was greeted by "an ageing couple, where the wife was bedridden; stricken with arthritis and confined to her small room where only one little ray of light penetrated from the gloomy street outside". Most Boulac families were Coptic Christians, said David, "and we went into their much loved and ancient church, rising up in the one open space among the tenements".

The Boulac Christian Social Centre, said David, "can only hope to touch the fringes of need in this great slum, but it is a hive of activity". On the morning of his visit, he said, "a packed Fellowship Meeting of over one hundred women, all sitting on the floor, was drawing to a close". In the room next door "handicapped children were receiving care and attention", while "up on the roof we were delighted to listen to the singing of the children from the infant school during their break". Later, he said, all the children at the centre would receive a meal while groups of volunteers took hot lunches to the elderly housebound who waited eagerly for the visitors who always found a little time to stay and talk. Just before he left, David saw the needlework on sale that was produced by Boulac's homeworkers, intricately embroidered tablecloths and bedspreads that followed transfer patterns sent regularly by the Society from Britain.

Do not be afraid: keep on speaking

At the Mansiet Nasser Zabbaleen Community that lay at the foot of the Mokattam Hills on the edge of Cairo, David saw rubbish far in excess of anything seen in the narrow alleys of Boulac. At Mansiet Nasser, rubbish lay underfoot and everywhere around. It was the livelihood of the zabbaleen, the name by which they were known in Egypt that simply means "rubbish people". Just over ten years before David's visit, the Christian groups who became the zabbaleen had been forcibly moved to seven settlements on Cairo's outskirts after their traditional way of life, as keepers of pigs, was ruled an offence to Muslim society. By the 1980s, the 21,000 Christians, desperately poor and mostly illiterate, had become the major collectors and processors of Cairo's rubbish. It was a hard and demoralising life, and each day, seven days a week, fathers and their children rose in the dark early hours to trek with their donkey carts into the city to collect garbage thrown out from restaurants, from wealthy homes, and from every floor of tenement slums. Returning home, they sorted and recycled the rubbish: tons of vegetable waste, animal bones, discarded paper, jagged empty tins, and broken glass. Even plastic was smelted down, the toxic fumes from tiny furnaces a sharp and acrid contrast to the heavy scents of organic rottenness. Babies and pigs rooted among the rubbish, women cooked and children defecated. There was no running water in the village, half the children died before the age of five, and as unregistered people without birth certificates the zabbaleen qualified for no government relief. The entire community depended on discarded rubbish and Christian charity.

Reverend Sam'aan Ibrahim, a Coptic priest who began a Christian work among the zabbaleen in 1981, told David how it came about. As a printer, Sam'aan said, he earned a good living, he had a modest comfortable house in a quiet street and a prosperous future was assured. Sometimes he had talked about his Christian faith to the man who collected his rubbish each day, but when the rubbish collector began to ask Sam'aan to visit his village, and to tell the same wonderful things to the people there, Sam'aan began to wish he had never begun. It took two years of urging before Sam'aan agreed finally to visit the zabbaleen. But even as he agreed, he was planning his escape. "I was like Jonah that day," Sam'aan told David, "I was called to the village but I planned to catch a bus in the opposite direction." But, despite his horror at the rotting garbage, the rooting pigs and the stench, Sam'aan eventually became a regular preacher to the zabbaleen. They were Christian in name only, he had quickly realised, and they had no real knowledge or experience of the faith, and as the months passed, and as the people of the zabbaleen became familiar to him, something began to urge Sam'aan to do more for his new friends. The idea frightened him and he pushed it to the back of his mind. But, one windy day a piece of paper blew into Sam'aan's printers' workshop. He had kept it ever since and he showed it to David, unfolding the worn sheet from the safekeeping of his wallet. The paper that blew through Sam'aan's workshop door was a page from the Bible, and words there had spoken straight to his heart: "Do not be afraid, keep on speaking, do not be silent, for I am with you, and no one is going to attack you and harm you, because I have many people in this city." Not long afterwards, Sam'aan was ordained into the Coptic Orthodox Church, and with his wife as his most loyal helper, they set to work. Together they founded a school, they began adult literacy classes and they began to build up the church. Each year they took the zabbaleen children for holidays by the seaside, away from the stink and the flies, where they played on Egypt's long sandy beaches, splashed in the clean salty waves and gazed at a brighter future.

It was rather a shock

After David left Cairo and the zabbaleen and made his way northwards through the Nile Delta, it was a relief, he said, after the noisy, smoggy city, to see "green fertile fields filled with long rows of sugar cane, broad beans and potatoes, and the palms and tall trees that ranged the long horizons". He remembered that he stopped to photograph a blindfolded donkey turning an ancient, creaking, wooden waterwheel. The day was sunny, the air was clear and David breathed it with great contentment. "But, then we came to Menouf," he said, "and that was rather a shock." He remembered later how he wondered if the roads of Menouf, "Nile mud tracks, deeply rutted and by no means free of garbage", were an indication of the standards he would find everywhere in the Delta town of 200,000 inhabitants. But, to his delight, at Menouf's Christian hospital, David found "a bright atmosphere of hard work and living faith, where everyone believed that medical skills and nursing care should be a joint witness to the love of God which is proclaimed in Jesus Christ".

Menouf Hospital was founded as a CMS hospital by Frank Harpur, the missionary doctor who was William Essery's 1901 companion in the Cairo children's ward, but after a spell in the 1950s as an Egyptian Government hospital, it was finally abandoned and its buildings left to disintegrate. It returned to life in the 1970s, when a group of Egyptian Christian doctors and nurses, led by Dr Mouneer Anis, had a vision for a Christian hospital in Menouf that would serve the city's poor and most vulnerable. "When we began," Dr Mouneer told David, "we wanted to make our hospital as big and as modern as any you can see, but after a little while, we changed our minds. This is a town of poor people, mostly farmers and fishermen, and poor people feel intimidated by big sophisticated buildings, by lots of complicated technology and by too much bureaucracy. We are here to serve the poor, and so we need basic equipment and well-trained staff who offer an excellent service in ways poor people can receive as equal partners." The aim of Menouf Hospital, said Dr Mouneer, "is to bring healing, hygiene, and the Love of God to those we serve". It was an aim, said David, that together with the aims of the workers at Boulac and those of Sam'aan Ibrahim and the zabbaleen, should inspire the Society to work once more with the Christians of Egypt and to stand alongside them as they faced the great challenges that lay ahead.

Intifada

Bob Clothier finally retired as secretary of the Bible Lands Society in 1985, a few months before the death of Sister Johanna Larsen. Her prayers had been answered and her work was done, she had told friends in 1980 when leprosy was finally declared eradicated from the Holy Land. After a brief and contented retirement, where she saw Star Mountain become a leading centre for the mentally disabled, Sister Johanna spoke her last words on earth. "Now I am going home," she said. Krikor Demerjian died in 1987. In the years just prior to his death he was a great support to his colleague, Mher Khatchiguian, who ran a refugee centre in Athens for Armenians fleeing persecution in Middle Eastern countries.

Just a few short years after Bob's retirement, new violence shook the Middle East. In 1987, the "pressure and fear" that Audeh Rantisi had written about, Alice Sahhar's "tragic situation of the West Bank", erupted into renewed violence. The *Intifada*, the "shaking off" of the occupation, a spontaneous uprising that followed the deaths of three young Palestinians in Gaza, was met with massive Israeli retaliation. Palestinian schools and universities were closed. Palestinian towns were sealed off by tanks and roadblocks. People unable to work or buy food went hungry, and young men, students with no classes to attend and the unemployed with no future to look forward to, built barricades and directed endless volleys of stones at the well-armed Israeli soldiers. "In return, there are rubber bullets, tear gas and finally live ammunition," wrote Ida and Ada Stoltzfus, the American twin sisters who ran the Evangelical School for Boys at Hebron. "Many have died," they said, "hundreds, no thousands, have been taken into custody and kept for months without trial. Others have been beaten with clubs or iron bars. There are many in hospitals or in their homes, incapacitated for weeks."

What doesn't kill us, strengthens us

Two years later, in 1989, the Lebanese civil war, after a lull in the fighting, burst into activity when a period of shelling that would last six long months began in Beirut. Syrian and Muslim Lebanese forces attacked East Beirut, and Christian Lebanese forces attacked West Beirut and the Druze-controlled Shuf area south-east of the city. Two thousand shells fell every night and 100,000 people fled for their lives. Nadeem and his wife Lily returned from a brief holiday on Cyprus with George Markou only days before the main building of Al Kafaat "got its sad share of the intensive shelling". Damages are enormous, said Nadeem. "For days and weeks," wrote Lousadzin Takavorian, from the Armenian Social Centre School at Trad, "rockets and shells fell on the houses as if it was raining shells." But, just as they had done ever since 1975, the schools opened their basements as community shelters, and began preparing lessons for students, and the elderly Mr Samuel, after being trapped for days with his invalid wife in the basement of his house, "took to his bicycle to travel about encouraging the leaders of the schools and homes".

"Trusting God, we hope to start school as soon as the bombing stops," wrote Armine Amadouni of the School for the Deaf, "and even if we cannot do that, we will take homework to our pupils, so they remember what the war has erased from their minds and hearts." In October, Al Kafaat was the first school in Lebanon to reopen. Just as he had done so many times before, Nadeem had cleared away the shrapnel, mended the bomb damage where he could, and begun work once more. "What doesn't kill us, strengthens us," he said. By Christmas 1989, all schools in Lebanon and the Holy Land were back at work once more. "Praise God," said Peter Emmerson, the Society's new secretary, "that so many have been preserved in both countries and that schools have been able to reopen." Let us pray, he added, the violence in the Middle East has finally come to an end.

Chapter 16 **Of Peace and War**
Towards the Millennium

He was in "his den" that night, 17 January 1990, catching up on correspondence. Life seemed to get busier as he got older, and it was only in the silent hours, heading towards midnight, that he found time to think about all the old friends he liked to keep up with. Before beginning his letters he liked to let his thoughts wander, back through the years, picturing faces, remembering voices, and travelling in his imagination with people whose lives were moved by faith, who combined their fragile humanity with great trust in God, and who tempered their dreams with determination and their visions with persistence. As he dwelt fondly on one old friend in particular, his dog, sitting at his side, nudged his hand. The friendly touch brought him back to the present. A short walk, he thought, taking up his scarf and the dog's lead, a short walk in the starry January night, for a last breath of air. A neighbour found him, slumped at the base of a thick beech hedge, its crinkled leaves rimed with frost, his dog sitting quietly by his side.

The old friends all honoured Bob Clothier. In Jerusalem a special memorial service was held at St Andrew's, the grey Scottish church that looks over the Old City. In Britain, hundreds of people thronged the crematorium at Amersham in Buckinghamshire, where David Izzett, a friend since wartime years together in Palestine, spoke about Bob's long years of service to the Bible Lands Society. He told them about his first meeting with Bob, their journey together on the ancient bus that climbed the steep road to Bethlehem, and his own introduction to Adele and the blind children. It was that vision, David said, of a simple Bethlehem home where a group of poor blind children gathered trustingly around their devoted teacher, that had spurred Bob Clothier to dedicate his life to the cause of the disabled and those in need. "The Society today," David went on, "with an income of nearly two million pounds each year, that supports over 50 Christian projects in the lands of the Bible, is Bob Clothier's creation." Bob was one of those men, David said, "who single-mindedly pursues a goal, dedicating himself to its achievement and inspiring others with his zeal. The success of the Society and of our partners overseas, is a memorial to a life touched by the finger of God – the life and work of Bob Clothier."

Many people in that Amersham congregation had cause to remember the life of Bob Clothier with gratitude. George Markou had come from Cyprus where the deaf workers' co-operative was flourishing and where children at the School for the Deaf were sponsored by the Society's supporters in Britain. Mher Khatchiguian, Blind Krikor's friend, came from Greece where his kindergarten for Armenian children eased some of the burden on anxious parents hoping for United Nations refugee status. And, Nadeem Shwayri had arrived with samples of the first bread baked at Al Kafaat's brand new catering school, a massive project funded by the Society in conjunction with the European Union, and the last enterprise to be conceived and implemented by Bob.

The day of peace was at hand

"The civil war in Lebanon," Nadeem told fellow guests who gathered at the Society's offices after Bob's funeral, had devastated his beautiful country and laid waste to one of the Middle East's most splendid cities. Fifteen years of internal strife had left untold numbers of innocent people dead, thousands more homeless, thousands maimed and handicapped, and enormous numbers of children with little or no education. Many of those children had never seen the inside of a school, young people had no training for employment, and adults had no jobs to go to. "But, one day," said Nadeem, "the war will surely end." And when that day of peace arrived, he said, Al Kafaat's new catering school would already have trained hundreds of young men and women to welcome the international businessmen and tourists back to the hotels and restaurants of Lebanon.

Almost as soon as Nadeem returned to Beirut after Bob's funeral, fierce battles that killed 900 people and wounded 3,000 more, broke out in the city's eastern districts. But, just as he had predicted, the day of peace was at hand. It was dawning in the hearts of the people of Lebanon, and even as battle raged around them, Christians from all over the city joined in prayers for peace. One Sunday morning, hundreds of them set out on foot, walking through shattered streets, past buildings burned out and scarred by rocket attacks, to a service at Ashrafieh, scene of some of the war's worst fighting. "All those people wanted to send a message to the men of war," said Nadeem, "that political problems can never be solved by violence and that the people of our country are longing for peace." Many of the people at the service gave personal testimony and Nadeem wrote movingly of one disabled young man, "paralysed as a result of war wounds", who had struggled to propel his wheelchair up the hill leading to the square where the service was held. The young man refused all help. "Christ carried his cross alone," he said. Among that great crowd, said Nadeem, that stood bareheaded in the winter sunshine, there were many people who had carried their own crosses alone through the bitter years of fighting. "It will be a long time, he said, "before I forget that morning at Ashrafieh and that crowd." There had been such fervency of prayer, he said, that the air itself seemed alive with it, and such a urgent desire for life that the hands of the crowd, raised collectively to heaven, seemed almost enough in themselves to ward off the rockets whose explosions continued to rock the distant streets. As the people made their way home, said Nadeem, and the rockets and explosions came closer, the bells of Ashrafieh's churches began to ring, first one, then another, until eventually, confronting the sounds of war, the message of peace sounded over Beirut.

What would life be like in a peaceful Lebanon? After so many years of war most people found it difficult to imagine weeks and months and even years when the days were not punctuated by explosions and the streets would be safe for children once more. But almost as if they sensed it was not far off, the Christian schools began to prepare for peace. "Peace, however," said John Etre, Director of the Schneller School in the Bekaa Valley, "will bring problems of its own." An armed robbery, during a month-long electricity cut, caused John to wonder what kind of young people would emerge from the war. The gang of thieves had operated in a professional way, breaking into Schneller's vocational school under cover of darkness, cutting their way through thick iron bars that shielded precious workshop machinery and stealing everything that could be carried away. "It caused us to wonder," said John, "how we could help all those whose minds had been criminalised by endless violence, and so now we plan to set up counselling centres for the thousands of young people who know nothing but war."

We pray for the peace of Jerusalem

In the Holy Land too, the population longed for peace but a generation was growing up knowing nothing but war. "We pray for the peace of Jerusalem," wrote Audeh Rantisi, "and we desire peace more than anything; peace for both Arab and Jew, for God loves us all equally." But the frustrations of over 40 years since 1948, he said, were becoming almost unbearable and as each new hope was dashed as peace talks foundered on the objections of one side or the other, despair grew greater and bitterness and hatred became permanent fixtures in many Palestinian and Israeli hearts. When the *Intifada* ended, Salwa Zananiri wrote for the *Star* about the day Rawdat el Zuhur reopened. We were full of hope, she said, "but we saw so many sad faces and heard so many tragic tales". She recalled one small girl who "related with a broken heart how her home in Bethany was demolished by the Israeli army, and her brother detained". The result of the demolition, said Salwa, was that little Rula's father suffered a heart attack and was taken to hospital, and the family of seven, fatherless, homeless and without possessions, were reduced to living in one tiny room. In Bethlehem, Salwa went on, "Nine-year-old Nora's home was raided. Tear gas was thrown into her house, the family were beaten and her father was arrested." Almost all our children have relatives who were detained during the *Intifada*, Salwa told readers, "And they themselves are exposed to regular harassment at military checkpoints and to the raiding of homes in the middle of night. The memories stay in their minds and influence how they think and behave." But, she said, "We have a dedicated staff, who attend to physical and psychological needs, and we are determined to provide our children with all the loving care necessary to enable them to struggle for liberation without fear or bitterness."

Restoration and healing

When John Etre began counselling courses for young people at Schneller School, he very quickly saw how important it was to involve the significant adults in their lives too. "Good results with the young people," he said, "have encouraged us to expand our service and expertise to their parents and families as well." A similar venture was also underway in Palestine/Israel at the Bethlehem Bible College, founded in 1979 by a group of Palestinian Christians including Audeh Rantisi. In 1992, the college named its new Counselling Centre, Al-Aman, a translation of the Arabic words meaning safety, whose aim, college principal, Bishara Awad, told readers of the *Star*, "is to help people deal with the stresses and traumas caused by political upheaval, economic catastrophe and military administration". And, a programme of regular seminars, he said, including child development, anger and conflict management, the prisoner and his family, substance abuse awareness and education, and marital relationships, would cover many issues faced by the Palestinian population of the occupied West Bank. "We aim for restoration and healing," Bishara said, "and the fruits are already being seen as our teams of professionals go through the Palestinian villages, working with families and individuals, in homes and in schools."

Other ministries sought to bring restoration and healing to the Holy Land too. In the early 1990s, the Bible Lands Society helped sponsor a conference for Arabs and Jews seeking peace, organised by the reconciliation ministry, Musalaha. Irene Arbiv was one of the conference organisers, and she told readers of the *Star* how the tragic memories of her parents, survivors of the Nazi genocide of the Jews, had left emotional scars in her own mind. "Even my name links me to the horror of the holocaust," Irene said, "since my mother named me for a woman who was exterminated in the concentration camps." Irene's mother carried the fear of persecution with her for a lifetime. "She always remained afraid," Irene said, "of what happened to you if people knew you were Jewish," and even in a safe country "mother always drew the curtains early on Friday nights to shield our Sabbath candles from the eyes of passing strangers". Irene's Musalaha colleague, Dr Vivica Hasboun, a Palestinian child psychiatrist, spoke of the damaging long-term effects on Palestinians of the negative world view that regarded them collectively as "terrorists". Palestinian children, she said, often had a poor self-image, the result of constant harassment, school closures and their perceived second class status as a conquered nation, that resulted in deeply felt anger and hostility. Parental depression and the loss of parents through divorce, imprisonment and death added to the children's unhappiness and emotional turmoil. It was hardly surprising, said Dr Vivica, that such a potent combination led to aggressive and destructive behaviour by the unhappy children of Palestine. As the conference came to an end, the Jewish and Palestinian delegates joined Pastor Suheil Ramadan as he "walked them step by painful step" through the dark days in 1948 when, like Audeh Rantisi, he fled as a refugee and nearly died. Even after he gave his whole heart to the Lord Jesus, Pastor Suheil told the delegates, it still took many years before he could be reconciled to the command to love his enemy. And he knew, he said, that the pain and anger he had carried for so long in his heart, was shared by every other Palestinian.

Peace to all Arabs

Pain and anger, the suffering of families and individuals, and reconciliation, were in evidence at the Nazareth hospital too, after it opened its palliative care ward for cancer sufferers in the 1990s. "Our aim," wrote Beris Bird, on behalf of the hospital, "is to provide holistic care for patients and their families, to alleviate physical suffering where we can, and address the emotional, social and spiritual problems that co-exist with cancer." Because the hospital was renowned for its treatment of the poor, Beris told readers of the *Star*, poor Jewish immigrants to Israel from Eastern Europe were regularly joining Palestinian patients on the King's ward, named for the King of Kings himself, "where we hear many languages each week and where our non-verbal skills are now excellent". We have learned, said Beris, that distress needs to be heard, and that when someone gives their time to hear it, then language becomes unimportant. There was one memory in particular, Beris said, that would always stay with her. It concerned four women: Lucy and Aylia, and their two daughters. Lucy, said Beris, was a Russian Jew, dying in great pain from the breast cancer that had produced secondary tumours in her brain, while Aylia, a Muslim Arab, dying in pain too had been sent away from another hospital with no follow-up care for herself or family. "We helped both those ladies," Beris told readers, "but we ourselves were helped by the care given by their daughters." Each daughter cared for her own mother, she went on, and then for the other mother. Seeham, the Muslim village girl who spoke only Arabic, often sat with Lucy, who only spoke Russian, when Aylia, her mother, was sleeping. Somehow, without verbal language, they comforted each other, said Beris, and just before Lucy died, she kissed Seeham and said, "Peace be to all Arabs." Perhaps, said Beris, "When we face life's greatest mystery, we finally see how insignificant are our differences."

Our work is on the full go

When Lebanon's civil war finally reached its end in the early 1990s, some Lebanese began wondering about their differences, that had once seemed so important but had caused so much suffering. They also looked at their surroundings with new eyes, as if the landscape was suddenly laid bare for them to see the devastation clearly for the first time. As bulldozers smashed through concrete barriers and checkpoints that had divided Beirut for 16 years, the city's inhabitants made their way to areas previously off limits to them, and were reported as standing silently for long periods, gazing as if in awe, "at the overgrown ruins of what used to be the city centre". They gazed, said a report in the *Star*, as if a dreadful realisation had overwhelmed them, of a reality they had known secretly all along, that the long bloody conflict had achieved nothing. Refugees returning to their old homes in the quarter mile wide gash of no man's land that had divided the city for so long, found nothing but shattered walls, trees growing through rooftops and a mess of rubbish-strewn floors and doors and windows thick with weeds. Thousands of families returned to find squatters in their homes, who refused to move out as their own houses were destroyed or squatted too. Other families found nowhere to live but hastily built shelters of corrugated iron and packing cases. Lebanon had become a wasteland. It had no factories, no hotels, no businesses and no shops. Schools and hospitals were in ruins. Skilled people had moved abroad and foreign investors, fearing new outbreaks of violence, refused to finance reconstruction.

Unlike most of Lebanon's schools, the Christian schools, with help from the Bible Lands Society and other overseas organisations, had struggled on from year to year and eventually survived the war. It had been an enormous effort, in the face of great difficulties and often in a piecemeal fashion, but with peace secured, they were ready to repair the remaining damage, face the future and begin work. "Gone are the days of destruction in Lebanon," wrote Nadeem joyfully in the *Star*, "our work is all on the full go." He was repairing the damage to the buildings abandoned in no man's land, he said, education and training were being offered once more to nearly 1,000 poor or disabled young people, and the trainees and graduates of Al Kafaat's catering school were eagerly waiting for the aeroplanes that would carry the visitors back to Lebanon. "I am overexhausted," said Nadeem, "but living a pleasure which I fail to describe."

Al Kafaat, like the other Christian schools, opened its doors to hundreds of extra pupils. "Never mind about over-filled classrooms, we can always push in an additional chair or a stool!" said Nadeem. The Schneller School too reported "an avalanche of applications". The war has ravaged so many families, said John Etre, "that our school has become the only hope for many who are forever scarred by the ugly angel of death and destruction". Many of those new pupils were entirely uneducated. Rather than endure the horror of children being at school when the rocket attacks began, parents simply kept them at home, and most of them had little idea how to read, how to write, or even how to hold a pencil.

Schools all over the country began to plan for the future of Lebanon. At Schneller, an enthusiastic John Etre began to build "new workshops where boys can be trained to help in the reconstruction of our country". There would be courses in plumbing, he said, and in heating, car maintenance, carpentry, and "electronics and computers, to give our children a glimpse of the modern technology the rest of the world takes for granted". And also, said John, trying to convey to readers of the *Star* the extraordinary pleasure they held for the children of Lebanon, "our children go on excursions, an activity denied them for the last sixteen years!" From Anjar, new school principal, Reverend Nerses Balabanian, wrote about outings too. "Can you imagine," he said, "that in their whole lives many of our students had never been out of their village or immediate area. They have no idea of the world beyond their own horizons." The children at Birds' Nest saw something of that world when they visited the Hungarian State Circus, making its first tour of Lebanon in nearly 20 years and pitching its tents on ground used by military helicopters only months before. "They were immeasurably excited," said the report in the *Star*, "at seeing lions, tigers and monkeys for the first time in their lives. They laughed with the clowns and lived suspense with the acrobats and had the time of their lives!" From the Centres for Armenian Handicapped, the children went to a celebration at Anjar, "the great Armenian village in the hills near to the Syrian frontier", wrote Rita Parmaksizian, "where they saw the grand spectacle of Armenian dances and songs performed by great artists from Armenia". The fledgling state of Armenia, that had been absorbed unwillingly into the Soviet Union in 1920, finally became an independent state in 1991. Other Christian schoolchildren in Beirut shared the International Day of the Children with Muslim children from West Beirut, and "presented folk dances, recitations, national songs and liturgical hymns". As the children all exchanged small symbolic gifts of friendship, Nadeem Shwayri remembered something he had written at the beginning of Lebanon's civil war to his friend Bob Clothier. How he wished, he had said, that the men of violence would make their example the Christian and Muslim children who played together in peace on the green lawns of Al Kafaat.

A glimpse of peace

In 1993, the Society's new Chief Executive, Andy Jong, visited the Holy Land, where he witnessed on television the signing of the Declaration of Principles to the Oslo Peace Agreement. "We shared this occasion with the Principal of Bethlehem Bible College, Mr Bishara Awad, and his family and friends," wrote Andy, "and spontaneous applause broke out when Palestine's leader, Yasser Arafat, shook hands with the Israeli Prime Minister, Yitzhak Rabin." Despite his own optimism, Andy remembered that later, as he made his first visits to all the Christian projects supported by the Society in the Holy Land, the expectation and excitement among the Palestinian leaders was tinged with caution and the realisation that "there was still a very long road ahead". But, he said, on the night following the historic events in Washington, nothing could dampen the jubilant spirits of the Palestinian people, who after so long had glimpsed a possibility for peace and for a Palestinian State. "The celebrations lasted into the early hours," said Andy, "in true Palestinian style, as long queues of cars, with people crammed inside and others balancing on top, drove around accompanied by the incessant blaring of horns and the extravagant waving of flags."

In the following year, Bishara Awad wrote for the *Star* about his hopes for the Bethlehem Bible College. Some of its students, he said, would become "teachers of the Word" in different schools, some would become pastors, while others would continue their theological training. "To see these young men and women being trained in the way of the Bible is very rewarding," he said, "and a sign of hope for the continuation of the church of Jesus Christ in the Holy Land." He went on to express the growing concern of Church leaders in Palestine, a concern expressed years earlier by the Arab Evangelical Church in 1949, and by many others, including Audeh Rantisi, through the decades that followed, about the number of Palestinian Christians leaving their country. But he felt reassured, he said, that 95 per cent of Bible College graduates during the previous fourteen years had stayed in the West Bank, Gaza and Israel, "where they were serving the Lord as pastors, educators, counsellors, directors in schools and hospital chaplains". Moreover, said Bishara, "We want our College to be a blessing to the entire community, a place where Christian and Muslim neighbours can come to the counselling centre and library, attend lectures on business, take an English course, or watch films together." Overseas students also visited Bethlehem to study Arabic, Bishara went on, and every year, local and foreign Christians joined together for evangelism. As much as he could, said Bishara, he and his colleagues aimed to ensure that the Bible College encouraged its graduates to work in their own land among their own people, and that both the Bible College and the land of the Bible remained a place of living Christian faith and of real Christian witness.

Living faith and witness

The Society aimed to make Helen Keller School a place of living faith and witness too and a centre of excellence. For a while, after the retirement first of Adele and then of Siranoush, the school had seemed uncertain of its direction and the Society's leadership had been concerned that it would founder. But in 1994, with a determination to continue the pioneering traditions of Mary Lovell and Bob Clothier and to reaffirm its commitment to the Christian faith, the Society set out to find a new leader for the school who had the enthusiasm and vision to take it into the twenty-first century. The successful candidate was Suad Younan, a committed Christian, a trained teacher and counsellor, and an expert in family and health education whose commitment to human rights was well known throughout Palestine.

Soon after her appointment, Suad wrote for the *Star in the East* about attitudes to blindness in the Holy Land. They had certainly changed, she said, since the days when Mary Lovell first arrived in Palestine to begin her work. It was Mary's vision, she said, and that of other Christian workers like her, that had laid the ground for the much fuller lives the Middle Eastern blind now enjoyed. And it was Bob Clothier's work, she went on, that had encouraged blind people to claim the right to independence and a share in the best education and employment opportunities the world had to offer. But despite all that good work, there were some sections of Middle Eastern society where the blind, particularly the female blind, still suffered rejection and despair. "In some communities," said Suad, "especially in those governed by strict religious and social rules, and absolute moral codes based on taboos, blind girls continue to be regarded as having no future, and certainly no eligibility for the marriage market." Little Najiyeh from Hebron, Suad told readers of the *Star*, "had once overheard her grandfather claim as a blind girl, she had no future". The remark had devastated her and when her parents later divorced and each married a new partner, leaving their daughter with the grandparents who saw so little of value in her, Najiyeh's response was to withdraw into a confused and lonely, inner world. Not surprisingly, said Suad, Najiyeh's relationships with the outer world had become difficult, and it took all the skill and patience of childcare workers to deal with the painful situation in the family home, while educational psychologists endeavoured to persuade the little girl to emerge from her inner refuge. "The days were long and exhausting," said Suad, but eventually, despite hostility from Najiyeh's family, the child became a boarder at Helen Keller and was eventually fostered. In some ways we still have a long road to travel, she said, but just as Mary Lovell and Helen Keller campaigned in the past for the rights of the blind, so we will continue to work on behalf of the current generation. "Blind children like Najiyeh deserve respect," said Suad, "they deserve secure homes, and the opportunity to fulfil their potential and take their rightful place in society."

The hand of the Lord is with us

In Egypt, Dr Mouneer was working for the blind too. Early in 1999, shortly before being ordained into the Anglican priesthood, he invited a team of international eye surgeons to Menouf and offered free treatment to the poor people of the town. Many of them suffered eye problems that were treated easily in the world's more developed countries, and as news of the campaign spread through Menouf and the surrounding area, people with hope in their hearts began crowding Dr Mouneer's waiting rooms. Among them was Labiba, an elderly woman who had been almost blind for many years. Her world had faded slowly as cataracts grew gradually over her eyes until Labiba saw nothing but the barest hint of light and the vague, shadowy shapes of her family and friends. Although previously Labiba had always been too poor to pay a doctor, when her friends told her about the forthcoming free treatment at Menouf, she became fearful that if she underwent the operation the little sight left to her would be lost for ever. She had no idea what she should do but eventually she summoned her courage and opened her heart to Dr Mouneer. There were no guarantees, he told her, but the removal of cataracts was a routine operation and there was a very good chance of success. Perhaps what convinced Labiba most of all was Dr Mouneer's assurance that the eye surgeons would pray for her as they went about their work, and eventually, with a disquieting mixture of hope and fear fluttering in her heart, Labiba underwent the operation. "It is hard to find words to describe her reaction when she saw clearly once more," the nurse who removed Labiba's dressings told readers of the *Star*, "so I will leave it to your imaginations."

"Many of our local people trust Menouf," said Dr Mouneer, "because they believe the hand of the Lord is with us." We all pray for every patient before any procedure is begun, he said, and he told readers of the *Star* about the Menouf surgeon who liked to say, "The Lord is my consultant, because he did the first operation, taking out one of Adam's ribs," and the anaesthetist who claimed "The Lord is my consultant too, because he caused Adam to fall into a deep sleep first." In the late 1990s, Dr Mouneer wrote about little Magdy, a small boy rushed into Menouf Hospital by his distraught father. "One moment he sat alone by the roadside, playing as children do," said his father later, "then a car came round the bend and lost control and crashed into my boy, leaving him lying unconscious in the road." Although we could operate on Magdy's ruptured spleen, said Dr Mouneer, we didn't have the equipment to treat his head injuries and for that reason we thought it best to send him elsewhere. Menouf's doctors sent Magdy to a hospital with computerised scanning facilities and a neuro-surgery department, but to their surprise, his family brought the boy back to them. They were unhappy with the care Magdy received at the big hospital, the family told Menouf's doctors, and even when the children's hospital in Cairo was suggested, Magdy's Coptic Orthodox parents insisted their son stay at Menouf. "God taught us a very important lesson that day," said Dr Mouneer, "about faith that defies logic and understanding." The hand of the Lord, that was so obvious at Menouf, was more important to them, said Magdy's parents, than big hospital departments and sophisticated instruments.

"Our door is ever open to you," Magdy's grateful parents said after their son made a full recovery, and they urged the hospital's Christian staff to visit their home, to pray with them and share the Gospel. "And it is a pleasure for Menouf's doctors and nurses," said Dr Mouneer, "to maintain this contact with a family who taught us that faith is not to do with intellect, but rather in trusting in our Heavenly Father who cares deeply for his children."

Towards a new Millennium

"What does it hold for us, this twentieth century?" William Essery had asked as the nineteenth century slipped away, "what wonders, mysteries, hopes and demands lie ahead?" As the twentieth century itself prepared to slip away, its people were less optimistic than their nineteenth-century predecessors. After the most brutal hundred years in history, a century that had witnessed bloodletting and barbarities far in excess in every way of the Bulgarian Atrocities in 1876 or the Armenian Massacres of 1895, the people of the twentieth century were wary of what the future might hold.

But despite its fears and apprehensions, and the violence that continued to rock the Middle East and the Balkans, as the Millennium approached, the world prepared to honour the 20 Christian centuries since the birth of Jesus. Bethlehem planned big celebrations and for several years the Bible College had been training young men and women as tour guides for the thousands of visitors expected to descend on the Holy Land. Candidates for the jobs faced rigorous requirements, four years of college education and fluency in three languages and an arduous course in Bible study, Biblical history and Biblical archaeology as well as field trips to historical sites and archaeological digs. "These students," said Bishara Awad, "will all be licensed guides with official recognition from the Ministry of Tourism and they will be a mirror for our community and for our country as they direct tourists to the holy sites." But perhaps more importantly, he said, as well as the ruins of past ages, the young guides would also introduce the pilgrims to some of the "living stones in the land", those Christians who maintained their faith in the face of mounting hardship.

For most of its history, Bishara reminded readers of the *Star*, from the time of Jesus to the present day, the church in the Holy Land had been a suffering church. Yet it was from this small suffering church, he said, that the Good News of the Kingdom was spread and the world was blessed. We are still a suffering, struggling church, said Bishara, and for this reason we cherish the love and support of our Christian brothers and sisters outside Palestine. Christians here face physical and spiritual challenges on a daily basis, he said, and their very existence as a people and a church is being threatened. As we prepare to mark 2,000 years of history that we share with the world, remember us in your prayers.

Chapter 17

Proclaiming the Year of the Lord
The Future

The Millennium raised huge hopes. After a decade that had witnessed violence in many parts of the world, but particularly in the Middle East and the Balkans, millions of people were anxious that the year 2000 should mark a new beginning for the human race. Prayers were published in newspapers, Christian leaders called for reconciliation between the nations, and all around the globe, people of many faiths, with hope in their hearts, prayed that humanity would overcome its divisions and move forward together towards a future based on peace and justice for all. Christians prayed that at last the whole world would listen to Jesus, the man born in Bethlehem 2000 years earlier, whose message speaks of God's desire for a loving relationship with humanity, and of forgiveness, true freedom, and life in all its fullness.

But as the Millennium came and went, despite the hopes and prayers, the violence, the injustice and the hatred continued, and in the Middle East, the lands of the Bible remained a battleground. Fear of violence kept away most of the visitors the Bethlehem Bible College students had planned to welcome, and as the new Millennium opened, the words of Henry Labouisse that had appeared in the *Star* in 1959, the United Nations Year of the Refugee, remained a grimly accurate prediction. The issue of the Palestinian refugees, Henry had said, was a bar to future peace in the Middle East and the air of the region was so charged with tensions and hatreds, claims and counterclaims, that deadlock had been reached. But, someday, somehow, he had continued, the deadlock must be broken. Not just for the refugees, but for the sake of peace in the Middle East and peace in the whole world. In the year 2000, the tensions and hatreds remained, claims and counterclaims continued to be traded by all sides in the conflict, and the deadlock remained unbroken.

Despite a level of autonomy granted to Palestinians in the West Bank and Gaza during the 1990s, the peace process that had begun with the Oslo Agreement broke down time and again. Issues concerning the transfer of land to Palestinian sovereignty, Jewish settlements on Arab land, the withdrawal of Israeli troops from land occupied after the war of 1967, the return of more than two million refugees, and the final status of Jerusalem, all proved too contentious for a solution to be found. Forty years after the *Star* had published Henry Labouisse's article, peace seemed as far away as ever.

Projects under fire

In May 2000, with another round of peace negotiations underway, Palestine's leader, Yasser Arafat, said the Palestinian people had already waited too long for a land of their own. In July, despite the efforts of the American President, Bill Clinton, to keep the faltering process alive, the talks broke down once more. "If the gaps can't be bridged," Clinton reputedly told Yasser Arafat and Ehud Barak, the Israeli Prime Minister, "the alternative is unthinkable." Late in September, in an atmosphere already charged with frustration and tension, riots broke out in Jerusalem after Ariel Sharon, then the leader of Israel's right-wing opposition party, entered the *al-Haram al-Sharif*, Islam's second most holy site that is also the historic site of the Jewish Holy Temple.

Sharon's act was seen by many Palestinians as a statement of intent, that Israel intended to claim all of Jerusalem and its sacred sites for itself, and that despite years of negotiations, there was no intention that a Palestinian state should ever exist. The *Al-Aqsa Intifada* that followed Sharon's visit spread through the occupied territories as hundreds of stone throwing Palestinian youths confronted the Israeli Army and riot police who retaliated with rubber bullets, live ammunition and tear gas. It was the worst violence in the region since the war of 1967 and images of the conflict appeared constantly in the world's media. When the death of twelve-year-old Mohammed Jamal al-Durah, killed in the crossfire despite his father's attempts to shield him from the flying bullets, appeared in newspapers and was shown repeatedly on television, sympathy for the Palestinian people, long absent from much of the Western world, began to grow. In December, as it attempted to contain the violence and also prevent access to the world's media, Israel began to close off the Palestinian cities of the West Bank. An earlier age would have called such actions a siege.

"We're running out of blood and bandages," said the headline on the Society's Holy Land Emergency Appeal, "they're bringing wounded children into hospitals starved of medical supplies." As desperate requests from its project partners in the Holy Land reached it in Britain, once again, the Society appealed to its supporters. Our Christian partners report that thousands of people are wounded, said Andy Jong, the Society's Chief Executive, and that among them, one in three are children, often carried bleeding into the hospitals we support throughout the Holy Land. "They've been hit by live or rubber coated bullets shot by ground troops or from helicopters," Andy continued, "as well as by missile shrapnel, and most wounds are to the head, the eyes or the chest." Reports from the Holy Land described how blood donors were turned away from hospitals by soldiers, how medical staff, desperate to reach their patients, were forced to defy roadblocks and curfews and how medical supplies were exhausted as fast as hospitals could secure them. "We have sent £39,000 already," Andy assured supporters, "but at least £150,000 more is needed if children's lives, limbs and eyesight are to be saved." In the end, BibleLands, the name by which the Society had been known since 1996, raised £552,439 for the Holy Land Emergency Appeal that followed the outbreak of the Al-Aqsa Intifada.

In June the following year, as violence in the Holy Land escalated, BibleLands opened another appeal. Projects Under Fire, said the headline on the appeal literature, and beneath it ran the caption, Keeping hope alive: putting healing before hatred. Urgent help from BibleLands is reaching the Christian projects we support, the Society told its supporters, "and their leaders send thanks together with news of fresh violence as people's homes are being bombed by night and their roads blocked by day".

Bethlehem Bible College reported that its communications systems and water supplies had been wrecked by artillery fire and that a teacher had been wounded. The St John Ophthalmic

Hospital in Jerusalem reported children with wounds to their eyes being admitted with distressing regularity. Disturbing messages from the Star Mountain Centre at Ramallah described how children with disabilities were cut off by curfews and roadblocks from the essential therapies they needed, while from Bethany, Henrietta Farradj at the Four Homes of Mercy recounted the struggles of her staff to maintain their services to the disabled and deprived Palestinians of Jerusalem in the face of a rapidly deteriorating situation. "Our Christian partners in the Holy Land are being driven to the brink," said Andy Jong, "and although they'll never run out of commitment, without our help, they cannot survive."

In September 2001, BibleLands' new newsletter, LifeLines, appeared with the headline Children Under Siege. A front-page article described Israeli Army roadblocks and checkpoints that made it almost impossible for Palestinians to move between their towns and villages, to take children to school or to hospital appointments, and for adults to travel to and from work. In the previous ten months 500 Palestinians had been killed and another 15,000 injured, said the article, and it went on to describe how the huge escalation of military violence, virtual imprisonment and extreme deprivation, was causing a major humanitarian crisis for the Palestinian people. LifeLines also contained the Society's condemnation of a series of suicide bombings by Palestinian militants aimed at Israeli civilians. But, just as LifeLines was about to be mailed, something happened. On 11 September, four passenger jets filled with innocent people were hijacked by the Islamic terrorist group, Al Qaeda. One aircraft was aimed at the Pentagon in Washington, another crashed in a deserted field, while two others were flown deliberately into the World Trade Centre in New York. Thousands of innocent people died. "Suddenly," said the special letter that was eventually sent with LifeLines, "the world has become more unsafe and we need to help each other come to terms with the madness."

A harvest of deportation and massacre

In the months after 11 September hijackings, as fear of further attacks followed and the hunt for the terrorists began, it seemed to many in the Western world that the "madness" had come to stay. In other parts of the world, in the Middle East, in the Balkans and in Africa, people could say, with justification, that the "madness" had been part of their lives for centuries. To some of them, the attention devoted to the tragedy in New York seemed to echo the article in the *Star in the East* by Herbert Adams Gibbons that followed the massacres of Armenians in 1909. Remember the San Francisco earthquake of 1906, Herbert had asked, remember the endless newspaper reports, the funds, the prayers and the sermons? But, he had continued, although we grieve for the victims in America, "they at least are in the midst of a friendly country where every hand is stretched out to help them". How much more, he said, "our sympathy and our prayers and our money are needed by the Armenians, a whole nation whose sufferings have been intensely horrible, whose present is unspeakably sad, and whose future seems dark and hopeless". We must not forget the Armenians, Herbert had added. In the March 1924 edition of the *Star*, under the heading, The Scattering of a Nation, Samuel Gentle-Cackett wrote, "The twentieth century is an epoch making time. When its history comes to be written, there will be no more extraordinary story than the exodus of the Armenians." By the end of the twentieth century, the exodus of the Armenians had been virtually forgotten. The massacres of 1895, the Genocide of 1915, and the events of 1921 in Cilicia, were rarely mentioned in history books. Few people knew anything about the catastrophe at Smyrna. Political and economic considerations had ensured that the deportation of the Armenian nation from its homeland and the murder of so many of its innocent people was almost erased from the history of the world. More than 80 years after 1915, most of the world's Armenians remained as exiles. Despite help from their wealthier countrymen, and from Christian organisations like Bible*Lands*, the Armenian communities, especially in the Middle East, continued to reap the harvest of deportation and massacre as they suffered high levels of poverty, unemployment and family breakdown. In 1999, Bible*Lands'* Easter Appeal had raised approximately £150,000 to help ensure the continuing survival of Armenian Evangelical schools in Lebanon. The funds not only enabled the schools to implement the modern curriculum requirements of the Lebanese Ministry of Education but they also ensured, almost 150 years after the Society made its first grants to students at

Armenian Protestant schools, that Christian education survived among their descendants.

Since its independence from Britain and Egypt in 1954, Sudan has been almost continually in the grip of civil war. Its most recent outbreak began in 1983 and thousands of Sudanese people, fleeing the conflict, make up an enormous Diaspora around the world. By 2001, around 12,000 Sudanese refugees were making their way to Egypt each year to join the three million already sheltering there. Most arrived with nothing, and many continue to suffer unemployment, sickness and depression. Suicide among the refugees is common. The Christian projects in Egypt, including the Joint Relief Ministries in Cairo, supported by Bible*Lands* and other Christian charities' struggle to provide friendship in an environment often hostile to refugees, as well as medical and psychological care, training for jobs, and education for children and young people. They also provide help in the long and often discouraging process of gaining the official United Nations Refugee Status that will ensure eventual resettlement in other lands.

The Balkans, where so much of the early work of Bible*Lands* took place, was torn apart once more by ethnic strife in the 1990s. Reports similar to those that had shocked William Essery and Samuel Gentle-Cackett in earlier years, of massacre, of rape and of innocent victims buried hastily in mass graves, also shocked the people of the late twentieth century. Columns of refugees, mostly made up of women and children and old men, struggling along treacherous mountain tracks, were shown on worldwide television. The stories the refugees told differed little from those of earlier Balkan victims, when Mrs Marriage-Allen had said of the Macedonian refugees in 1903, "they tell of fearful things".

Standing steadfast and true

Conflict in the Balkans had been partly the result of the collapse of the Soviet Union in 1989 that had set free tensions and aspirations held in check since the end of the Second World War. Among those aspirations was a profound desire for a spiritual dimension to life and in Bulgaria the end of Communism led to a resurgence of the Christian faith. As this book was being written, the Reverend Dony Donev, of the Bulgarian Evangelical Alliance, told the author, that "At this present time, the Protestant Church in Bulgaria is entering a new era in its history, but after such a long period under atheist dictatorship, it badly needs reformation in doctrines and practice as well as real dynamic leadership that will guarantee the religious freedom of our young, democratic society." Such a spiritual strategy is not new to Bulgaria, Dony said, "Years ago a missionary school in the town of Samokov served as a training centre for Christian leaders who received there the theological education that enabled them to carry their faith to the Bulgarian nation." Samokov today, said Dony, is a great centre of revival that just recently has witnessed the largest revival among gypsies that has ever taken place in Europe. Miracles occur, thousands are saved, the church is growing, and most importantly, religious education and ministerial training is once more being provided to a new generation of ministers whose prophetic impact on Bulgaria will be profound. "All across Bulgaria," said Dony, "people are coming out for Christ and are standing steadfast and true!"

The Christians of the Holy Land also continued to stand steadfast and true. By Christmas 2001, some 5,000 Palestinian children had been killed or injured in continuing violence, and BibleLands issued another Holy Land appeal designed to keep the besieged Palestinian Christian schools open. "Christmas is just weeks away," said the appeal, "a time for peace and goodwill for all people. But sadly, once more we are asking for your help." The appeal highlighted the concerns of Christian leaders in the Holy Land where half the Palestinian population were under 18, growing up in a frightening world where every day another child, "someone's best friend, brother, or sister is injured or killed or arrested, and another classroom seat becomes empty". The people of the Holy Land, said the appeal, were surrounded by anger, hatred and fear, and school was one of the few places where children of all faiths could find a semblance of normality. It was essential, the Christian leaders had said, that the schools stayed open, and that their teachers, working under intense physical and emotional pressure, were supported. "We are surrounded by tanks," said a teacher at one school, "please keep praying for us!" "Help us ease the burden of all the children suffering here both economically and in spirit," said another. "As a Christian school," said a third, "we do our very best to impart to those around us a sense of hope and love, not despair and hate."

One of those schools struggling to stay open in the face of conflict was the Helen Keller School in Jerusalem. In early April 2002, a series of e-mails arrived in Britain from the school describing events that had taken place in the streets outside. "The last couple of days have been a terrible time for the Helen Keller School," read one message, "there has been a military checkpoint outside for some time and now the inevitable has happened." The messages went on to describe how an Israeli peace demonstration, made up of left-wing members of the Israeli parliament, peace activists and Israeli education and healthcare professionals, all protesting against the harassment of Helen Keller's staff and the parents of its blind children, had been broken up with teargas by the Israeli Army. As the gas drifted across the school compound, the message said, and protestors ran to escape pursuing soldiers, the blind children, many of them already virtual prisoners on the premises due to the siege of their home towns, became even more terrified. "These children," said another e-mail, "who are already traumatised by their lack of sight and who are only aware of the events going on around them by the sounds they hear are further distressed by the fact that they are unable to go home and be with their families in Palestine's besieged communities, many of whom now have no water, food or electricity."

Several days later, Suad Younan, the Helen Keller School Principal, telephoned Bible*Lands*' office in Britain to say that a curfew had been extended to the whole of East Jerusalem. Many of the staff had decided to remain overnight in the school in order to care for the children, she said, and she went on to express her fear that if the army entered the school to search it there would be damage to property and trauma for staff and children. Several staff, said Suad, had already suffered similar violations at home. In Bethlehem, home to the school cook and under curfew for weeks, food and medical supplies had virtually run out, while piles of uncollected rotting garbage were causing a health hazard. A science teacher was also under strict curfew in Ramallah, said Suad, although she was at least relieved that her husband and son had returned home after being arrested, detained and interrogated. The conditions of detention for the men rounded up are pretty horrific, Suad added.

In an occupied land

Among Bible*Lands*' staff visiting the Holy Land during those critical months was Nigel Edward-Few, the Society's newly appointed Director of Communications. It was Nigel's first visit to the country and at first, everything looked normal. "It was only when I reached Bethany," he said, "and saw the run-down buildings, the potholes in the roads and the poverty of the people, and contrasted it with what I'd seen in Israel earlier, that I began to realise what it meant to be a Palestinian in an occupied land." Something else that told Nigel what it meant happened next day. "It really pulled me up!" he said. When a pretty, articulate girl of fourteen told him that her father had planned to be a suicide bomber and that she wanted to follow in his footsteps, Nigel began thinking about the levels of anger and frustration that led to such actions and also about ideologies that made them seem acceptable. When he was woken up in the early hours of the next morning, "by the most terrible noise I'd ever heard", Nigel had another insight into life in occupied Palestine. The noise came from F16 fighter jets and helicopter gunships over the little town of Bethlehem that was also being pounded by artillery.

Everywhere I went in the Holy Land, said Nigel, I saw a society breaking down under pressure, a society where what little hope is left is rapidly draining away. He went on to describe broken and damaged families where unemployed fathers suffered depression, where wives and children were abandoned and children were abused. He described adults desperate for jobs, school children and students desperate for education, hospital patients desperate for security of treatment, and disabled young people desperate for love and affection. But he also described Christian centres that are oases of calm in the middle of a bewildering and frightening situation and Christian workers who take extraordinary risks to be with the pupils and patients they love and care for. "As our Christian partners in the Holy Land take these risks," said Nigel, "braving gunfire and teargas, abuse and humiliation at military checkpoints, and insecurity and financial hardship for themselves and their families, they are continuing a long and honourable tradition." That tradition is the story of Bible*Lands*, he said, "where Christian men and women have shared the compassionate ministry of Christ to those who have suffered pain of the most unbelievable kind – who have suffered as races, as ethnic groups, as faith communities, as families and as individuals – through war, persecution, prejudice, injustice, cruelty, disablement or devastating physical poverty and need".

The heart of Bible*Lands*

In October 2002, Nigel Edward-Few succeeded Andy Jong as Director of Bible*Lands*. "It is the Gospel of Service," he said, "that is at the very heart of Bible*Lands* and at the very heart of all those men and women down the years who have devoted their lives to the people who live in the lands of the Bible." There are too many of them to name, he continued, from Cuthbert Young onwards, but I believe that when they set out in life most of them would not have been described by the world as being exceptionally capable or marked out for greatness. But, because they listened for God's call, and followed where it led them, God gave to them courage and purpose, and through their obedience and sacrifice, he has done great things. The continuing story of Bible*Lands* is a *living* epitaph, said Nigel, both to the power of the Christian message itself – the complete love of God incarnate in Christ – and to our response, as exemplified by the loving service of those who have worked for the Society and with the Society, under God's banner, over the last 150 years.

Throughout those 150 years the Society has maintained some of its very first commitments. One of them is the decision taken at Exeter Hall in July 1854, to give special emphasis to local Christians in the lands of the Bible and to work in partnership with them. In more recent years the Society has been able to extend its commitment to partnership by ensuring that its pilgrimage groups of Western Christians visit the projects they support in Israel/Palestine, in Lebanon and in Egypt. Many of the Christians who meet during such encounters, not only develop a greater understanding and sympathy for each other, but also reflect, just as William Essery reflected in 1901, on the wonderful diversity of the body of Christ and how Christians of all lands are joined together in holy unity. In some other respects, the Society has changed. Whereas in 1854 its aim was to highlight "Evangelical truth" and to work primarily with Evangelical churches, over the long years it has broadened its area of service and now works in partnership with Christians of many denominations. And, although its commitment is to the Christian faith and to living the Gospel in action, it no longer regards the followers of other faiths as enemies. Instead it welcomes them as friends and prays that they may hear the message of Jesus and receive the grace that comes through knowledge of him.

The Society has also witnessed many changes in the world. Old empires have passed away. New empires have come into being and some of them have passed away in their turn. Old enemies have become friends and old friends have become enemies. Borders have been swept away and new boundaries imposed. Nations have been driven from their homes while other nations have sought to find new homes. The world has made promises it later chose to forget. But, some things have remained constant. One of them is that the regions where the Society has worked have too often been bloody battlegrounds.

As this book neared completion in the last days of 2002, the Powers were planning for war. They were no longer the Great Powers of 1854, who were at war in the Crimea when Cuthbert Young founded the Turkish Missions Aid Society. Late in 2002, the United States of America, the most powerful military and economic power on Earth, and its British ally, made clear to the world that they intended to ensure, by force if necessary, that the Iraqi dictator, Saddam Hussein, complied with United Nations resolutions to remove from Iraq weapons of mass destruction. Failure to comply could result in invasion and a forcible change of the Iraqi regime. Many voices around the world, particularly in Islamic nations, questioned the morality of demanding of Iraq what is not demanded of Israel who has failed since its birth to comply with United Nations resolutions regarding Palestinian land and Palestinian refugees.

In November 2002, after an absence of four years, United Nations weapons inspectors returned to Iraq to search for evidence of nuclear, biological and chemical weapons research and manufacture. An apprehensive world followed their movements and their statements. As Christmas approached and an Iraqi Government dossier claiming to list all activities in Iraq relating to weapons research and production met with rejection by the Western powers, Western munitions, armour and equipment continued to make their way to the Middle East, to join huge stocks already in place there. Troops were on alert, awaiting orders. In another part of the Middle East, violence continued to beset Israel/Palestine, where militants on both sides grow more aggressive, where increasing numbers of young Palestinians regard suicide bombing as an honourable way of death, and where Israel continues to maintain a stranglehold on the occupied territories. After the Al Qaeda attack on New York in 2001, the terrorist bomb that targeted civilians on the Indonesian island of Bali in October 2002, and the siege of a Moscow theatre by Chechen separatists that followed shortly afterwards, nations that once felt safe, now feel themselves exposed. Many people, West and East, fear that war on Iraq will lead to an increase in conflict in Israel/Palestine, that will in turn cause havoc throughout the whole Middle East and will also have violent repercussions in the West.

By the time this book is launched in May 2003, the Middle East and the world will have changed. But, whatever is the outcome of events now taking place, there is another thing constant in the long history of BibleLands that will continue to be an important factor in the lives of the people who live in the ancient lands of the Bible. As much as the area of its work has often been bloody battlegrounds, it is equally true that the Christian workers the Society has supported and partnered in those battlegrounds through 150 years and continues to partner there today, will always be found in the thick of the battle. There they will continually seek to make evident, each in their own way, the great passion that led Cuthbert Young to found the Society in 1854, "the truth as it is in Jesus". And in making that truth evident, Cuthbert Young's successors today, just as in earlier years, will always be working where the need is greatest, following in the footsteps of Jesus, the master himself, who came to give sight to the blind, to release the oppressed and to proclaim the year of the Lord's favour.

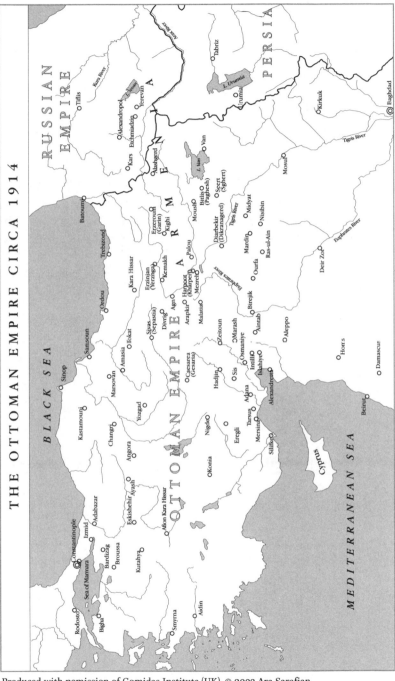

THE OTTOMAN EMPIRE CIRCA 1914

RUSSIAN EMPIRE

PERSIA

ARMENIA

OTTOMAN EMPIRE

BLACK SEA

MEDITERRANEAN SEA

Tiflis

Alexandropol
Etchmiadzin
Erevan

Kars

Batoum

Trebizond

Ordou

Samsoun

Sinop

Kastamouni

Changri

Angora

Eskishehir
Ayash

Afion Kara Hissar

Adabazar
Izmid
Constantinople
Bardizag
Broussa
Kutahya

Rodosto
Bigha
Sea of Marmara

Smyrna

Aidin

Kara Hissar

Erzinjan
(Yerznga)

Kemakh

Sivas
(Sepastia)

Tokat

Amasia

Marsovan

Yozgad

Kangri

Konia

Nigde

Eregli

Mersin

Tarsus

Silifke

Cyprus

Erzeroum
(Garin)
Kighi

Moush

Bitlis
(Paghesh)

Seert
(Sghert)

Diarbekir
(Dikranagerd)

Mardin

Nisibin

Midyat

Ras-ul-Ain

Ourfa

Birejik

Aintab

Marash

Osmaniye

Sis

Intili

Isahiye

Adana

Alexandrette

Aleppo

Homs

Beirut

Damascus

Deir Zor

Mosul

Kirkuk

Baghdad

Tabriz

L. Urmia

Urmia

Bashgerd

Van

L. Van

Palou

Kighi

Harpoot
(Kharpert)
Mezreh

Agn

Arapkir

Malatia

Divrig

Caesarea
(Gesaria)

Hadjin

Zeitoun

Kara River

Aras River

Tigris River

Euphrates River

Tigris River

Euphrates River

Produced with pemission of Gomidas Institute (UK). © 2003 Ara Sarafian

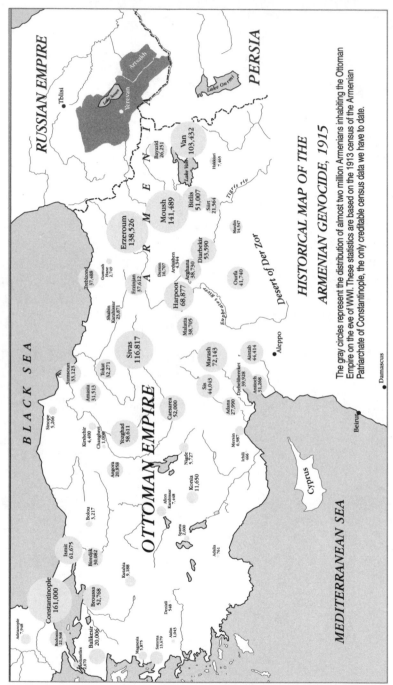

RUSSIAN EMPIRE

Tblisi

Lake Sevan

Yerevan

Artsakh

PERSIA

Lake Ourmia

A R M E N I A

Bayazid
26,251

Van
103,432

Moush
141,489

Bitlis
51,007

Hakkari
7,465

Lake Vahn

Tigris riu

Siirt
21,564

Mardin
14,547

Erzeroum
138,526

Diarbekir
53,590

Arghana
58,750

Desert of Der Zor

Trebizond
37,488

Gumush Hane
2,749

Dersim
16,707

Ardahen
4,344

Erzinjan
37,612

Harpoot
68,877

Euphrates River

Ourfa
41,740

Shabin Karahisar
23,871

BLACK SEA

Malatia
38,705

Aleppo

Sivas
116,817

Marash
72,143

Damascus

Samsoun
33,125

Tokat
32,271

Amasia
31,513

Caesarea
52,000

Sis
44,043

Aintab
44,414

Antioch
31,266

Djebelberekel
39,928

Sinope
5,266

Kirsehir
4,400

Yozghad
58,611

Changheri
1,009

Adana
27,990

Mersin
6,987

Ichili
466

Angora
20,858

Nigde
5,727

OTTOMAN EMPIRE

Konia
11,650

Bolou
3,217

Afeon Karahisar
7,448

Ismit
61,675

Spata
2,600

Cyprus

Kutahia
9,188

Biredjik
30,082

Constantinople
161,000

Brousssa
52,768

Denizli
548

Adrianople
7,948

Rodosto
22,568

Balikesir
20,006

Aidin
1,043

MEDITERRANEAN SEA

Dardanelles
6,070

Magnesia
5,875

Smyrna
13,679

Beirut

HISTORICAL MAP OF THE
ARMENIAN GENOCIDE, 1915

The gray circles represent the distribution of almost two million Armenians inhabiting the Ottoman Empire on the eve of WWI. These statistics are based on the 1913 census of the Armenian Patriarchate of Constantinople, the only creditable census data we have to date.

The Balkan Wars

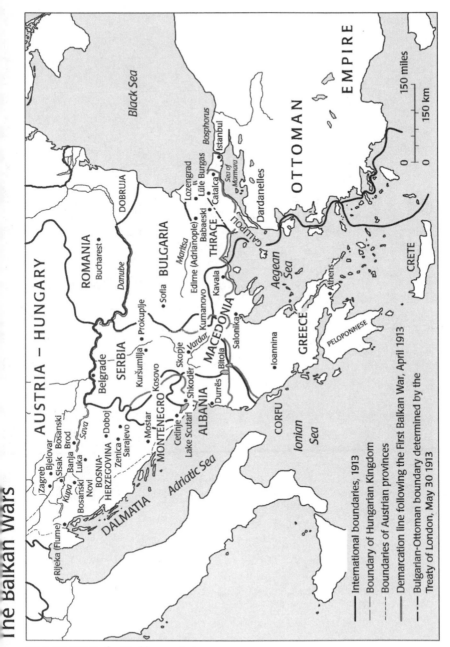

Maps © Granta Books. Used by permission.

World War I

Maps © Granta Books. Used by permission.

Palestinian loss of land, 1946-1999

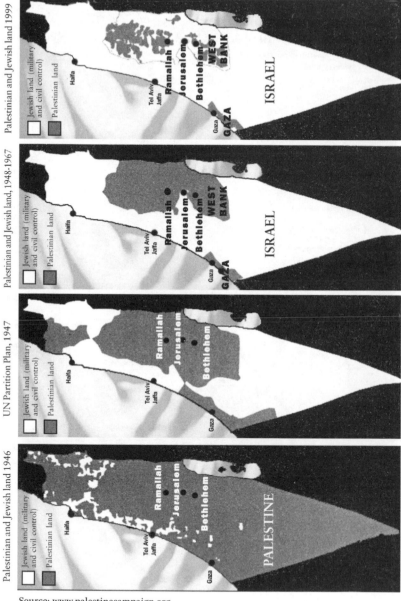

Source: www.palestinecampaign.org
Used by permission.

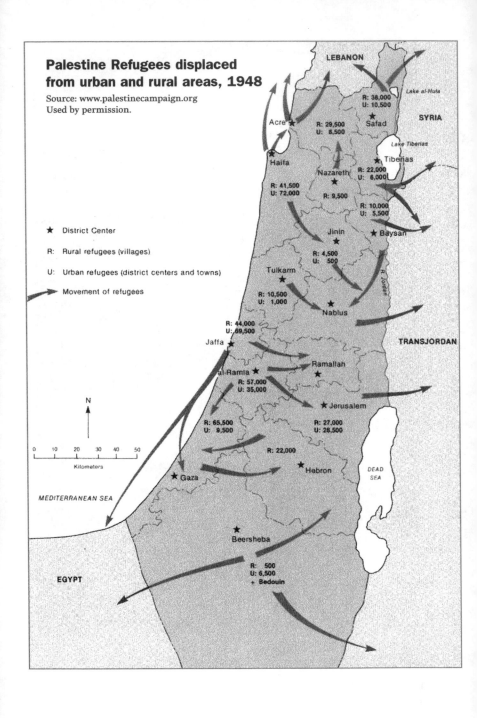

Palestine Refugees displaced from urban and rural areas, 1948

Source: www.palestinecampaign.org
Used by permission.

★ District Center

R: Rural refugees (villages)

U: Urban refugees (district centers and towns)

➡ Movement of refugees

LEBANON

Lake al-Hula

SYRIA

R: 38,000
U: 10,500

★ Safad

R: 29,500
U: 8,500

Acre ★

★ Haifa

Lake Tiberias

★ Tiberias

Nazareth ★

R: 22,000
U: 6,000

R: 41,500
U: 72,000

R: 9,500

R: 10,000
U: 5,500

★ Baysan

Jinin ★

R: 4,500
U: 500

Tulkarm ★

R: 10,500
U: 1,000

Nablus ★

TRANSJORDAN

R: Jordan

R: 44,000
U: 69,500

Jaffa ★

al-Ramla ★

Ramallah ★

R: 57,000
U: 35,000

★ Jerusalem

R: 65,500
U: 9,500

R: 27,000
U: 28,500

R: 22,000

Hebron ★

DEAD SEA

N

0 10 20 30 40 50

Kilometers

★ Gaza

MEDITERRANEAN SEA

★ Beersheba

R: 500
U: 6,500
+ Bedouin

EGYPT

Bibliography

Annual Reports, Turkish Missions Aid Society / Bible Lands Missions Aid Society: 1854–2002.

Minutes, Turkish Missions Aid Society / Bible Lands Missions Aid Society: 1854–2002.

Aitken, Eleanor, *Ariadne's Thread: Through the labyrinth to Palestine and Israel*, Cambridge: Cornelian Press, 1999.

Antreassian, The Reverend Dikran, *Musa Dagh: The banishment of Zeitoun and Suedia's revolt*, Armenian Missionary Association of America, 1993.

Armenians, The, London: The Minority Rights Group, 1976.

Bryce, James and Toynbee, Arnold, *The Treatment of Armenians in the Ottoman Empire, 1915–1916*, Ed. Sarafian, Ara, Reading: Taderon Press, 2000.

Essery, The Reverend William, *The Ascending Cross*, London: The Religious Tract Society, 1904.

Gentle-Cackett, Samuel, *Does God...?* Unpublished manuscript.

Glenny, Misha, *The Balkans 1804–1999*, London: Granta Books, 1999.

Hamlin, Cyrus, *My Life and Times*, Boston: Congregational Sunday-School and Publishing Society, 1893.

Hirst, David, *The Gun and the Olive Branch*, London: Faber & Faber, 1977.

Horton, George, *The Blight of Asia*, Indianapolis: The Bobbs-Merrill Company, 1926.

Houseplan, Marjorie, *The Smyrna Affair*, New York: Harcourt Brace Jovanovich Inc., 1966.

Khalidi, Walid, Ed., *All That Remains*, Washington DC: Institute for Palestinian Studies, 1992.

Rantisi, Audeh, *Blessed are the Peacemakers*, Grand Rapids: Zondervan Books, 1990.

Safieh, Afif, *Children of a Lesser God*, London: Palestinian General Delegation to the UK, 1997.

Star in the East, pub. Turkish Missions Aid Society / Bible Lands Missions Aid Society: 1883–2002.

Glossary

Chapter 1

Evangelical: is used in this book, especially in chapters relating to the nineteenth century, to refer to the popular Protestant movement that originated in the 1730s. It does not refer to any particular denomination.

Helpmeet for Man: an idea that gained prominence among Victorian Evangelical Christians that women were created to be an helpmeet to their husbands, that is a friend, companion and fellow worker and a person in her own right worthy of respect. John Angell James wrote about the proper role of an helpmeet in Woman's Mission, (in Female Piety or the Young Woman's Friend and Guide through Life to Immortality, 1852). Also Genesis 2: 18 (King James) "I will make him an help meet for him."

Millet: independent religious grouping within the Ottoman Empire e.g. the Protestant millet.

Tanzimat-i Hayriye: The Auspicious Re-orderings: a series of attempts to modernise the structure of Ottoman government, beginning in 1839, that were also a source of contention between established interests of landowners and administrators and those who sought a greater degree of freedom.

Hatt-i Hümayun: elements of the Tanzimat that followed the Crimean War.

Druze: religion and group of people originating in the Middle East with members based in Lebanon, Syria, Israel and Jordan. Currently there are also important Druze communities abroad, living in Europe and USA. Although not regarded as Muslims by other Muslims, the Druze regard themselves as Muslims and also as carriers of the core of the religion.

Maronite: largest indigenous Uniate or Eastern church in Lebanon. Communion with the Roman Catholic Church that was established in 1182, was subsequently broken before being formally re-established in the sixteenth century. Directed and administered by the Patriarch of Antioch and the East with bishops generally nominated by a church synod from among the graduates of the Maronite College in Rome. In 1857 and 1858 a Maronite peasant revolt against large landowning families in Lebanon was followed by a struggle in 1860 between the Druzes and Maronites over land ownership, political power, and safe passage in the territory of the other.

Orphan: orphan in the nineteenth century referred to children who had lost a father, as well as to children who had lost both parents.

Chapter 2

Moon Type: The Moon system of embossed reading was invented by Dr William Moon in 1845. A simple method based upon the standard alphabet with 14 characters used at various angles, each with a clear bold outline. For many elderly blind people especially, Moon is easier than the more complex Braille system.

Anxious Inquirers and Saints' Rests: popular Victorian texts written for Christians seeking assurance of salvation. "The Anxious Inquirer After Salvation Directed and Encouraged" by John Angell James, for example, was first published in 1834 and remained almost constantly in print throughout the Victorian period. James was among the 63 men who attended the breakfast meeting at Adelphi in May 1854 that preceded the formation of the Turkish Missions Aid Society.

Chapter 3

Ira Sankey: American evangelist and songwriter. Author of *Sacred Songs & Solos*, probably the most popular hymn book among late Victorian Evangelical Christians. Often worked with evangelist and preacher, Dwight Moody, and together they made three successful trips to Britain in the late nineteenth century.

Chapter 6

Pan-Islamic Movement: Muslim Revival Movement that began in the mid-nineteenth century as an attempt to maintain cultural, educational, religious and political identity in the face of increased western influence and secularisation. Thought and doctrine on which the movement was based came especially from Russia, Turkey and Persia.

Chapter 8

Near East Relief: Successor to American Committee for Armenian and Syrian Relief and now The Near East Foundation. Began life in 1915 at the instigation of American Ambassador to Turkey (1913–1916), Henry Morganthau, as thousands of Armenians, Greeks and other minorities in the Near East were forced from their homes and were dying from hunger, disease, and exposure. The American Board of Commissioners for Foreign Missions was represented on Near East Relief.

Chapter 9

American Women's Hospitals: organisation of women physicians and surgeons of the United States under the auspices of the War Service Committee of the Medical Woman's National Association. Work divided into Hospitals for Civilian Relief, with associated dispensaries, in Serbia, France, Russia and Rumania. Other sections focused on Service in US Army Units in Europe; Army Hospitals for Acute Convalescent Cases in the US, a medical substitution service in US based hospitals and in private practice for doctors who went to the fighting areas of Europe. Its headquarters were based in New York City.

Chapter 12

UNRWA: United Nations Relief and Works Agency for Palestine Refugees in the Near East was established by United Nations General Assembly resolution 302 (IV) of 8 December 1949 to carry out direct relief and works programmes for Palestine refugees. The Agency began operations on 1 May 1950. In the absence of a solution to the Palestine refugee problem, the General Assembly has repeatedly renewed UNRWA's mandate, most recently extending it until 30 June 2005.

Chapter 14

Phalange Party: Formed in 1936 as a Maronite paramilitary youth organisation by Pierre Jumayyil. Ideology on the right of the political spectrum and doctrines that emphasise a free economy and private initiative. Phalangist ideology focuses on the primacy of preserving the Lebanese nation, but with a "Phoenician" identity, distinct from its Arab, Muslim neighbours. Party policies have been uniformly anti-communist and anti-Palestinian and have allowed no place for pan-Arab ideals. Throughout the 1975 Civil War, the Phalange Party was the most formidable force within the Christian camp, and its militia shouldered the brunt of the fighting.

Lebanese Front: a mostly right-wing Christian coalition that included the Phalange.

Index

Adana: 106, 107, 133, 134, 135, 136, 153, 166, 167
Adrianople: 110, 174
Aintab: 63, 67, 69, 78, 132, 133, 134, 143, 211
Al-Kafaat, Beirut: 214, 217, 218, 219, 227, 231, 232, 238, 239, 246, 248, 254, 255
Albania, also Albanian: 58, 59, 173, 183
Aleppo: 129, 130, 133, 143, 144, 149, 150, 151, 166, 168, 181, 198
Alexandretta, Sanjak of: 169, 174, 182, 231
Allenby, General: 127, 129, 134, 177, 187
American Board of Commissioners for Foreign Missions (American Board): 27, 28, 29, 30, 33, 34, 35, 36, 39, 41, 44, 59, 63, 114, 120, 134, 144, 154, 155, 157, 198
Anatolia College: 123, 144, 145, 181, 198
Andeweg, Father Andy: 213, 214, 218, 219, 220, 221, 229
Anix, Dr Mouneer: 244, 258, 259
Anjar Colony, Lebanon: 174, 231, 254, 255
Antioch: 46, 106
Antoura Orphanage: 129, 130
Armenian, also Armenian: 25, 26, 27, 28, 29, 30, 31, 32, 35, 39, 40, 41, 44, 47, 48, 49, 50, 56, 57, 61, 63, 64, 65, 67, 68, 69, 70, 71, 72,

73, 75, 76, 78, 79, 81, 88, 90, 99, 100, 101, 102, 103, 104, 105, 106, 107, 109, 110, 114, 115, 119, 120, 121, 122, 123, 124, 125, 127, 128, 129, 130, 131, 132, 133, 135, 136, 137, 138, 139, 140, 142, 143, 144, 148, 149, 150, 151, 153, 158, 162, 164, 165, 166, 168, 169, 170, 173, 174, 175, 177, 181, 182, 183, 184, 185, 186, 190, 194, 195, 196, 199, 200, 210, 211, 231, 236, 237, 240, 245, 248, 255, 260, 265, 266
Armenian Evangelical Church, also Union: 29, 63, 70, 73, 78, 143, 165, 182, 214, 215
Arnott, Jane: 43, 87
Assiout: 54, 85, 88, 98, 161, 181
Awad, Bishara: 251, 255, 256, 260

Baghdassarian, Gregory and Emma: 47, 48, 49, 50, 51, 52, 53, 61, 75, 79, 196, 207, 212
Bedfont: 99, 102, 108, 130, 131, 132, 134, 141, 153, 154, 170, 175, 181, 208
Bethany Home, Bedfont: 131, 132, 208
Bethlehem Carol Sheet: 197
Bible, translations, also Braille: 42, 58, 85, 90, 167, 176, 177, 178, 240
Bible College, Bethlehem: 251, 255, 256, 260, 261, 263

BibleLands

After 150 years of service, BibleLands is still bringing Christ's compassion to the needy in the lands of the Bible.
As you will have read in this book, BibleLands has been at the very heart of Christian, compassionate ministry for 150 years, since its conception in 1854 at the height of the Crimean War. Throughout the 20th Century and now into the 21st, BibleLands has maintained its crucial focus – **tending, treating and teaching the young, the sick and the needy in this strategic but unsettled region – regardless of their faith or nationality.**
As a non-governmental, non-denominational Christian charity, BibleLands currently works in partnership with more than 60 Christian-led Projects in Israel/Palestine, Lebanon and Egypt. Our Partners bring the compassion of Jesus as they continue to bring healing and the peaceful things of God to those most in need in the lands of the Bible.

• **In Israel/Palestine**, our Partners in the Projects and communities in which they live, work under the most difficult conditions. In many cases, they face and endure the consequences of daily acts of terrorism, military action, curfews and travel restrictions. Added to this, they suffer very high levels of unemployment, continual interruptions to education at all levels, below-the-breadline poverty, shortages of basic necessities, and economic uncertainty. Despite all of this, our Partners strive to maintain continuity and stability in their communities, particularly for the sake of the children in their care.

- **In Lebanon**, many years of civil war have devastated the country and, as the infrastructure is rebuilt, our Partners seek to provide many of the key services that impoverished people could otherwise not afford.

- **In Egypt**, our Project Partners provide urgent medical and social care both to desperately poor Egyptians and to the many refugees who have fled into Egypt from Sudan, Somalia and Ethiopia in recent years. This overwhelming demand has placed a heavy burden on the available resources where they congregate, which cannot be met without the help of partnerships such as that between Bible*Lands* and its Partner agencies.

Bible*Lands*' sixty Projects Partners in these three countries, work in six Key Areas of Service:

- **EDUCATION:**
  Bible*Lands* supports schools and colleges that offer good quality Christian-based education for children whose families could not otherwise afford it.

- **SOCIAL CARE:**
  Bible*Lands* works in partnership with those caring for the orphaned and others living in particularly deprived circumstances across the region.

- **MEDICAL CARE:**
  Bible*Lands* funds specialist surgery facilities, clinics and general hospitals, as well as local primary and secondary health care programmes, in circumstances where travel to such specialised medical centres further afield is difficult.

- **SPECIAL NEEDS:**
  Bible*Lands* and its Project Partners seek to provide education and specialist training to children and young people who are blind, deaf or who have other major physical or intellectual disabilities.

- **VOCATIONAL AND ADULT TRAINING:**
  Bible*Lands* supports Project Partners providing degree-level nursing training, as well as vocational training and rehabilitation facilities for young people.

- **SUPPORT AND CARE OF REFUGEES:**
  Bible*Lands* works with Project Partners who provide urgent medical and social care, both to desperately poor Egyptians and to the many refugees who have fled into Egypt from Sudan, Somalia and Ethiopia.

Bible*Lands* and its Project Partners are entirely dependent upon the generous donations of its supporters, grants from trusts, its child/project sponsorship schemes, appeals and legacies, and through the sale of gifts, cards and other materials to support the work of the Charity.

Without the prayerful and financial ministry and encouragement of its supporters and donors, the valuable work of helping so many in need, especially the children, could not continue. People in this strategic but unsettled region need our help as much as ever.

We hope that this book and this brief resumé of Bible*Lands'* current priorities will give you a broad insight into our work and will encourage you to contact us for further information about how our Partners address those desperate needs.

We look forward to hearing from you and hope to welcome you into the Bible*Lands* supporting family in the very near future.

For further information on the work of Bible*Lands* and its
Project Partners in the lands of the Bible, please contact us at:

**Communications Team, Bible*Lands*, PO Box 50,
High Wycombe, Buckinghamshire HP15 7QU.
Tel: 01494 897950   Fax: 01494 897951
E-mail: info@biblelands.org.uk
Website: www.biblelands.org.uk**

**Registered Charity Number: 1076329
A Company Limited by Guarantee No. 3706037
Registered in England & Wales**

BibleLands and its Project Partners
as at March 2003

(Please note that although BibleLands supports a core base of long-term Project Partners, others may change)

ISRAEL/PALESTINE

Project	Town	Type of Work	BibleLands' Area of Focus
Bethany Girls' School	Bethany	School for girls	Education
Hope Secondary School	Bethlehem	Secondary school	Education
Rawdat El Zuhur	Jerusalem	Junior school	Education
Talitha Kumi Evangelical School	Bethlehem	School for all ages	Education
Arab Evangelical Home and School	Hebron	Home and school, mainly for boys	Education / Social Care
Jeel Al Amal	Bethany	Home for boys of all ages	Education / Social Care
Al Ahli Hospital	Gaza	General hospital	Medical
Spafford Children's Centre	Jerusalem	Social centre	Medical
St. John's Ophthalmic Hospital	Jerusalem	Ophthalmic hospital	Medical
St. Luke's Hospital	West Bank	General hospital	Medical
Bethlehem Arab Society for Rehabilitation	Bethlehem	Centre for physically disabled children	Medical / Special Needs
Annahda Women's Association	Ramallah	Centre for mentally disabled children	Special Needs
Four Homes of Mercy	Jerusalem	Home for children / disabled / elderly	Special Needs
House of Hope	Bethlehem	Home for disabled children and adults	Special Needs
Princess Basma Centre for Disabled Children	Jerusalem	School for disabled children	Special Needs
Sheepfold	Bethlehem	Home for children with special needs	Special Needs
Star Mountain	Ramallah	Centre for mentally disabled children	Special Needs
Helen Keller Centre for the Visually Impaired	Jerusalem	Centre for blind children	Special Needs / Education
Bethlehem Bible College	Bethlehem	Bible college	Vocational and Adult Training
Nazareth School of Nursing	Nazareth	Nursing school	Vocational and Adult Training

Project	Town	Type of Work	Bible*Lands'* Area of Focus
Anjar Armenian Evangelical School	Anjar	School	Education
Armenian Evangelical Central High School	Beirut	Secondary school	Education
Armenian Evangelical College	West Beirut	School for all ages	Education
Armenian Evangelical Guertmenian School	Beirut	Primary school	Education
Armenian Evangelical (Shamlian Tatikian) School	Beirut	School for all ages	Education
Armenian Evangelical Social Centre	Beirut	School and social centre	Education
Armenian Evangelical Torossian School	Beirut	Primary school	Education
Love School for Bedouin	Zahle	School for Bedouin children of all ages	Education
Swiss Evangelical School	Mejdelanjar	School	Education
Johann Ludwig Schneller School	Bekaa Valley	School for all ages	Education / Vocational and Adult Training
Cedar Home Orphanage	Beirut	Home for orphaned girls	Social Care
Birds Nest	Jbeil (Byblos)	Home and school	Social Care / Education
Centre for Armenian Handicapped	East Beirut	Centre for deaf and mentally disabled children	
St. Luke's Centre	Beirut	Centre for mentally disabled children	Special Needs
Zvartnotz Centre	East Beirut	Centre for mentally disabled children	Special Needs
Al Kafaat – Cedars Capabilities Centre	Beirut	Centre for deaf children	Special Needs / Education
Al Kafaat – Cedars Capabilities Centre	Beirut	Centre for mentally disabled children	Special Needs / Education
Al Kafaat – Cedars Capabilities Centre	Beirut	Centre for physically disabled children	Special Needs / Education
Blessed (Leb. Evan. School for Blind)	Beirut	School for blind children	Special Needs / Education
Al Kafaat – Cedars Capabilities Centre	Beirut	Centre for vocational training	Vocational and Adult Training

EGYPT

Project	Town	Type of Work	Bible*Lands*' Area of Focus
Hadana Kindergarten	Cairo	Kindergarten (linked to Boulac)	Education / Social Care
Boulac Social Centre	Cairo	Social centre	Social Care
Diocese of Egypt Social Work Board	Cairo	Social work board	Social Care
Harpur Memorial Hospital	Menouf	Hospital	Medical
El Saray Church	Alexandria	Eye clinic and special needs unit	Medical / Special Needs
Deaf School	Cairo	School for deaf children	Special Needs / Education
Shams El Birr	Giza	Hostel for blind girls and women	Special Needs / Vocational and Adult Training
All Saints Joint Relief Ministries	Cairo	Refugee centre – medical / pastoral	Support and Care of Refugees
Sonshine School / St. Mark's Church	Alexandria	School for Sudanese refugees	Support and Care of Refugees
St. Andrew's JRM	Cairo	Centre for refugees – training / education	Support and Care of Refugees

SUDAN

Project	Town	Type of Work	Bible*Lands*' Area of Focus
Bishop Gwynne College	Juba	Theological college	Education
Diocese of Lui	Lui	Social / Relief work	Social Care
Diocese of Mundri	Mundri	Social / Relief work	Social Care